Allen Tate

A LITERARY BIOGRAPHY

RADCLIFFE SQUIRES

Allen Tate

A LITERARY BIOGRAPHY

PEGASUS · NEW YORK

A DIVISION OF THE BOBBS-MERRILL COMPANY, INC., PUBLISHERS

Allen Tate is part of a series,
Pegasus American Authors,
prepared under the General Editorship of Richard M. Ludwig,
Princeton University.

*Library of Congress Catalog Card Number: 75-128673
First printing*

For
Peter Taylor

Contents

The author wishes to express his grateful acknowledgments to the following magazines in whose pages portions of this book first appeared: *The Michigan Quarterly Review*, *The Sewanee Review*, and *The Virginia Quarterly Review*.

Author and publisher are grateful to the following for permission to quote from published works:

Allen Tate, *Poems 1960*; Charles Scribner's Sons, New York

Allen Tate, from *Essays of Four Decades*; Swallow Press, Chicago: © 1968

R. K. Meiners, from *The Last Alternative*; Swallow Press, Chicago: © 1963

Louise Cowan, *The Fugitive Group: A Literary History*; Louisiana State University Press

M. E. Bradford, *Rumors of Mortality*; Argus Academic Press, Inc., Dallas, Texas

Malcolm Cowley, *The Flower and the Leaf*; Mr. Cowley and the Viking Press, New York

Allen Tate, *The Fathers*; Mr. Tate and G. P. Putnam's Sons, New York

Excerpt from *The Letters of Hart Crane, 1916-1932*, ed. Brom Weber, © 1952 by Brom Weber, by permission of Mr. Weber

To the following for permission to quote from unpublished letters and works:

Mr. John Crowe Ransom

Mr. Robert Penn Warren

Mr. Andrew Lytle

Mrs. Donald Davidson for permission to quote from unpublished letters of Donald Davidson

Mr. Allen Tate

❧ Preface ❧

WRITING ABOUT A LIVING CONTEMPORARY, HIMSELF A WRITER, IS A delicate matter. It requires a gentlemanly contract whose stipulations are all the more strict for being unstated. The writer may not, for example, ask the subject how to "interpret" a given poem. The subject may not press insights upon the writer. Allen Tate and I lived by the letter of the contract. But that is not to say that I am not deeply indebted to Mr. Tate. He made his papers and letters in various libraries available to me and provided copies of items that are hard to come by. Even more, he gave me his precious time and the hospitality of his home.

I am grateful also for courtesy and help from the staffs of the libraries at Columbia University, Princeton University, and the University of Victoria. Finally, I wish to thank a number of persons whose love of truth and scholarship is such that they will not wish to be thanked. They are: Mr. Alexander P. Clark, Mr. Louis Coxe, Mr. Joe Lee Davis, Mr. Hubert English, Mrs. Lincoln Fitzell, Mr. Brewster Ghiselin, Mr. Warren Kliewer, Miss Carol Anne Middleton, Mr. Robin Skelton, Mrs. Caroline Gordon Tate, Mr. Ben C. Toledano, Mrs. Yvor Winters. And, as always, my wife Eileen.

R. S.

Allen Tate

A LITERARY BIOGRAPHY

CHAPTER ONE

❧ The Early Years ❧

IN JULY 1911 A SLENDER BOY OF ELEVEN STOOD IN THE TOWN square in Mount Sterling, Kentucky, watching as the sheriff dragged behind his horse the body of a Negro who had been lynched. The boy was blond, blue-eyed, with very fair skin and a prominent forehead. He watched without change of expression, but forty years later he remembered what he had seen and wrote a poem about the incident, a poem which marks one of the summits in the career of a master of twentieth-century letters. His name: Allen Tate.

It is a commonplace of biography to begin with a resumé of antecedents, often with the implication that the subject inherited certain traits from his ancestors. The temptation to claim that he derived, shall we say, "practicality" from his paternal grandfather and "sensitivity" from his mother is overpowering. Any such claim is, of course, barbarous genetics. Nevertheless, the study of Allen Tate must begin with genealogy. It must begin there, however, not because the genealogy establishes the origins of personal traits but because Tate has been profoundly concerned with the past in his art. If one term applies most directly and pervasively to Allen Tate's work it is "tradition." Through tradition we understand the most intimate and personal moments of Tate's poetry. Tradition nourishes both his poetry and prose. In a nearly paradoxical way it is also a cruel revenant, even at times a spectral menace. That need not astound. What feeds an art can also take from it. Yet Tate escapes a complete tyranny of the past, for his yielding to the past becomes a contemplation whose intensity in turn becomes a triumph, if not an emancipation.

The genealogical strands of both his maternal and paternal sides extend back to the colonial waves from England in the seventeenth and eighteenth centuries. On the side of his mother, Eleanor Parke Custis Varnell (1865–1929), the Varnell family arrived in Saint Mary's County, Maryland in the late seventeenth century and settled afterward in Charles' County. Tate's maternal grandfather, George Henry Varnell (1833–1889), graduated in law from Georgetown University, but never practiced his vocation, perhaps because his talents as a land speculator and lumberman met with remarkable success. By 1860 he owned about 200,000 acres of Western timber land in five states and kept eighty-one slaves. In 1852 he married Susan Armistead Bogan (1834–1909) of Fairfax County, Virginia. Tate's mother was born in Fairfax County at "Chestnut Grove," an old farm house built on the land of "Pleasant Hill," a mansion burned in the Civil War, and used as the setting of Tate's novel *The Fathers*. She spent part of her girlhood in Washington, D. C., part of it in St. Louis, and part in Mount Vernon, Illinois with the family of her uncle, John Stewart Bogan. This uncle was the son of Major Benjamin Lewis Bogan (1795–1870), a grandson of Colonel Fielding Lewis of "Kenmore," Fredericksburg, Virginia; he was the prototype of Major Lewis Buchan in *The Fathers*.

The paternal lineage begins in 1690 when sixteen-year-old Robert Allen arrived at Port Tobacco, Maryland, where he was for six years the indentured servant of a cabinet maker. His grandson, Rhodam Allen (1742–1820) who was born in Stafford County, Virginia, migrated to Tennessee in 1794, and moved the next year to Shelby County, Kentucky, leaving his son Rhodam (1785–1850) in Tennessee. On the death of Rhodam, Tate's great-grandfather, John Robert Allen (1808–1866) inherited the family farm "Oak Grove" in Shelby County. The house— in the "West Indies" style of architecture—dated from 1795 and stood until it burned in 1890. His daughter, Josephine

Allen (1840–1867), married James Johnston Tate (1819–1872).

The Tates originally came to America from County Antrim, Ireland and were likely of both lowland Scottish and Irish ancestry. Four brothers, the eldest, Samuel, came to America in their own ship in the mid-eighteenth century. They migrated down through Virginia to North Carolina and pioneered later into Tennessee. James Tate, Allen's grandfather, was originally of "Fishing Creek Plantation," Chester County, South Carolina. A schoolmaster who carried both a Bible and a Latin grammar with him, he came to Kentucky in about 1840. He tutored members of the Allen family and eventually married his own pupil. Allen's father, John Orley Tate (1861–1933), was born of this union.

John Orley Tate, an orphan from the age of eleven at "Oak Grove," lived on the patrimony from his grandfather, John Robert Allen. He had no occupation at all, but when he fell in love with Eleanor Varnell, her father insisted, as a condition of the marriage, that the young man supervise the Varnell lumber business in Illinois. Thus the young couple, who were married in 1887, spent the years from 1889 to 1894 in Mount Vernon, Illinois. Eleanor Tate had, to be sure, lived in Mount Vernon as a child, and several of her first cousins still lived there. Allen's older brother, Benjamin Ethan Tate (1890–1968), was born in Mount Vernon; his eldest brother, James Varnell Tate (1888–1957) was born in Washington, D. C. (John Orley) Allen Tate, almost ten years younger than his nearest brother, was born in Winchester, Kentucky on November 19, 1899.

There was nothing very definite about Allen's religious training. Although the Varnell side of Tate's family in the seventeenth century had been Roman Catholic, Tate's grandfather, George Henry Varnell, left that church upon marrying into the Presbyterian Bogan family. Some of the early Allens had been Methodists. When they became wealthy land owners, however, they tended toward the Episcopal Church, and Tate's father had been baptized into that denomination. But his father later became a Robert G. Ingersoll Free Thinker and never attended church. His mother was an infrequent churchgoer, but was nevertheless quite puritanical. She forbade dancing or playing cards on Sundays. Young Allen went to Presbyterian Sunday

School intermittently until he was about sixteen; then not at all.

As a child Allen got the rich feel of the border South, its almost melancholy verdure, its cottonmouth threat, its sensuality. He learned the usual sports of boys. In the overpowering summers he fished and swam. He knew the marvelous springs of Kentucky, when the mountains suddenly show a nearly transparent skin of pale green, and dogwoods bloom along their parallel boughs, and silver bell trees flower against the evergreens. In the hush of the vernal balance he found the first trilliums; the red ones, smelling like carrion; the yellow ones, smelling of lemon above their pendant leaves mottled like the thighs of frogs.

He learned about people, too. He knew the closely-knit life of the Kentucky towns as well as the tight-lipped life of the hill people. He listened to the bluff talk of horse breeders in the blue grass country. He heard elders talking of where their people had come from; in the talk of the country people he felt the exciting undertow of fundamentalist fanaticism. He knew, thus, the polarities of life, the disintegrations and unities, those extremes which southern life somehow has always rendered more extreme. They would worry him throughout his career. But if he knew at first hand life's dark potentials, he also knew the opposite, its potential for balance, virtue, and unity. He tells us:

> As a small boy I knew a man who lived on a farm a few miles from a Kentucky county-seat, the population of which was about five hundred. . . . He was a lawyer whose office was up a dingy flight of stairs above the feed store on the courthouse square. He had "read" law after the war in the office of an older lawyer; but before the war he had been graduated from a small sectarian college, a day's buggy-ride from the family farm; and while he was reading law for the state bar examinations he taught mathematics at his *alma mater*. (I once had his books on Conic Sections and the Integral Calculus.) I think I must have seen him last when I was about twelve or thirteen. It was summertime. He wore a shapeless, sweat-stained panama, black alpaca coat, unpressed broadcloth trousers, and string tie; he was very tall and very fat, with a smooth round face and unkempt white hair. I could not then have understood that there was no difference between his vocation and his avocation, or that he did not know which was which. From early spring to

early fall he spent most of his time on his farm. He sat under a tree in a far corner of the yard—which in England
would have been called a park—reading Mommsen's *History of Rome*, or perhaps Lord Clarendon's *History of the
Rebellion;* for he fancied himself a Jacobite. Back of his
house stood an abandoned ice-house, down in the depths of
which, on the sawdust floor, he had his laboratory appara-
tus with which he performed his chemical experiments—for
what purpose and to what conclusions I do not know; and I
doubt that he knew: he was only increasing his knowledge.
He might have answered questions with obvious appeal to
authority—"As Plato *says* in the *Phaidros*" putting the verb
in the present tense because Plato had lived only recently;
or he might quote the *Georgics* and look hurt if the company kept an uncomprehending silence. . . .

He was not a scholar; that is to say, he was not a professional scholar. He knew a little about many things—
mathematics, science, the ancient classics, agronomy,
the law; yet all of the little that he knew was alive in
his daily life and was constantly brought to bear upon the
human condition as he could know it in his place and time.
Without being conscious of representing anything at all, he
was an exemplar of the classical apothegm: Nothing too
much. One would know that he would be as considerate of
the plain people of his community as of Senator James or
Justice McReynolds. He was, in short, an educated man.[1]

By present day standards, Allen's early schooling was scattered and casual. He was taught to read at the age of five by his
mother. Mrs. Tate, herself an avid reader, indiscriminately de-
voured a novel a day. Allen himself in his early years probably
read some Dickens, perhaps some Scott; undoubtedly some popular history. Certainly by the time he was thirteen he had read
much of Edgar Allan Poe. The home library contained some
books of his great-grandfather, Major Benjamin Lewis Bogan,
including "the 1800 edition of 'Lyrical Ballads' with corrections
of Wordsworth's grammar in his great-grandfather's hand."
Though in later life Tate came to prize the book as a possession,
he does not remember having read it as a boy.[2]
Most of his summers were spent with his mother in Washington and in Fairfax County, Virginia, or at various "springs" in

the mountains of Virginia and Tennessee. His mother preferred to think of Virginia as the family's true home. "One of his earliest recollections was a walk to the stone foundations and ruined chimneys of 'Pleasant Hill,' the family 'place' that had been burnt" on July 17, 1861 "by General Blenker's New York 'Dutch' Brigades in the Union advance to First Manassas."[3] Not only were Tate's summers spent away from the Kentucky farm. The father's business interests, often moribund, shunted the family about a good deal. Furthermore, Mrs. Tate moved to Nashville, taking Allen with her, in 1906 when the two elder brothers entered Vanderbilt University. Tate's winters from 1906 to 1909 were spent here, and his first formal schooling was at the Tarbox School in Nashville in the fall of 1908. But he was enrolled for only three months and was not in school again until the following fall when he entered The Cross School, a private academy in Louisville, Kentucky. Here the little boy astounded his teacher by reciting "The Chambered Nautilus" and Poe's "To Helen" from memory. The Cross School, which gave Allen a consistent schooling until the spring of 1912, emphasized classical studies. Allen learned the Latin paradigms and read in Cornelius Nepos' *Lives.*

From 1912 to 1914 he attended a public high school in Ashland, Kentucky. A temporary business interest moved the family once again, and Allen spent a half year in 1915 in high school in Evansville, Indiana. Then in 1916 his father moved them all to Cincinnati where he was engaged in a failing business. Here Allen got in another half year of education at the Walnut Hills High School. The last year had been rather aimless; then his education took a different turn.

Rather early in childhood, Allen had become aware that what contented others often bored him. He had wondered sometimes if there were a place in the world for him at all. He recalls this knowledge of his "difference" comically:

> When I was about twelve my mother said to me one day, "Put that book down and go out and play. You mustn't strain your mind; it isn't very strong." (As a boy of four or five I had a big bulging head; my elders, who discussed children in those days as if they were inanimate objects, used to say, "Do you think he has water on the brain?")

The family belief that I was an imbecile redoubled my secret efforts to prove them wrong: secret efforts, because
outwardly until I was through college I was trying to appear to be just like other boys—a rôle in which I was not
successful.[4]

Among his secret efforts were a few poems he wrote when he
was fourteen, yet he thought little of them. Later, he hoped to
distinguish himself, as a musician. His opportunity came after
his six months at Walnut Hill High School, for he was sent from
October 1916 to April 1917 to the Cincinnati Conservatory of
Music. He had excellent teachers, studying violin under the Bel-
gian violinist Jean Ten Have and the master Eugen Ysaÿe. His
interest in violin remained with him into his later years, and one
memory from the Cincinnati Conservatory enters importantly
into his late poem "The Buried Lake." Even though many years
later Paul Rosenfeld remarked on Tate's ability to play Mozart,
the boy was not gifted. When Ysaÿe remarked that Allen was
not creating music, it was a bitter blow. He gave up his musical
ambitions and decided to return to academic studies. According-
ly, after a summer spent partly with his mother in Washington,
D. C., partly with his cousins in Virginia, he entered Georgetown University Preparatory School with a view to following in
the steps of his older brothers at Vanderbilt. Considering the
hodgepodge of his earlier schooling, one is not exactly astounded
that there were gaps in his preparation. He had proved himself
an apt student of Latin, but his knowledge of mathematics was
meager. In Nashville, in the summer of 1918, the future medieval scholar, Dorothy Bethurum, tutored him in mathematics,
and he successfully passed the examination in that discipline.
However, as a result of his having moved about so much, his
transcript was muddled and showed him deficient in other required units. He was accepted at Vanderbilt, but with the pro-
viso that he pass an examination in third-year Latin. That gave
him no trouble. The examination was not on Cicero, as it should
have been, but on a passage from the second book of the
Aeneid. Allen knew Book II by heart.

The young man who entered Vanderbilt in September 1918
did so with no special interest in literature. When he left Vanderbilt he was a published poet with a rising reputation and he

was completely dedicated to letters. At this point it is well to
pause and ask what the early life "means." The answer must be
"everything" and "nothing." The causations in life are often secret, dimly recalled and ill understood. Inevitably they are intricate; many pressures bend together to bend a life. No one can
untangle them and set them all forth clearly. Yet, with our passion for assigning causes—it is a fault but not a wicked
passion—we can say that certain elements form the ambience in
which the mystery of life subsists. In Tate's early life two elements seem worth noting.

In the first place one sees that Tate grew up inheriting a
background which has come to be called the "Southern Myth."
The phrase may be misleading if only for the reason that it is
not a myth competent to explain reality, but indeed is in itself
historical reality. But we call it a myth and what we mean by it
is a background which we find again and again behind southern
literature in this century. By its very nature this myth is
entropic; it deals in diminuendo intervals. It begins with heroic
westerings from Virginia or the deeper South, from the
Tidewater society into the wilderness of Georgia, Mississippi,
Tennessee, Kentucky. Here, the myth tells us, empires in land
were set up by the heroes, empires sustained briefly by courage
and faith in man as God's own creature whose society will be
God's society, rather than faith in man as man's creature whose
society will be solely man's. Then decay ensues as a result of
believing that one "possesses" the wilderness and may therefore
exploit it. And then the heroic quality of life disappears. (The
vast timberland is being lumbered at the end of Faulkner's
"The Bear," one remembers.) Finally, the "new man" arises who
"adjusts" to the entrepreneurism of the fallen world, or prospers
by evil wits. The lesser southern writing of this century has
tended to dwell on the heroic past or the decadent present. The
finest southern writing has tended to touch the myth only where
it is mobile—that is, at the point of change from hero to modern
man, where we see the falling action of tragedy.

A second element, hardly separable from the first, is the aura
of disorder that surrounds Tate's early life: the spasmodic tempo
of his education and the family's continual peregrinations neces-
sitated by John Tate's deteriorating economic situation. To

be frank, Tate's father, the rather dreamy orphan, untrained for any practical pursuit and probably ill-suited by temperament as well, could not make a go of his business ventures. The disasters were slow and insidious, but the family was living on capital after about 1912, selling off land and real estate. After 1920 the parents were supported by Ben, who also saw Allen through his last two years of college.

A further complication enters the picture. After 1907 Tate saw very little of his father. Years later Ben told him that their father had been involved in some kind of scandal—not a financial one—and had been asked to resign from a men's club. He resigned not only from the club but from society in general and seemed to behave almost as if he had lost his will. Caroline Gordon remembers him as a "delightful" person but ineffectual, unable, for example, to get out of his dressing gown and into street clothes until mid afternoon. Mr. Tate withdrew, and Mrs. Tate herself chose to remove the children and herself from him as much as possible: hence, the summers in Virginia, the sojourns with her sons in Nashville when they went to college. In later years, as he looked back, Tate observed to Mark Van Doren that there had been an indifference between himself and his father, perhaps even a contempt.[5] That is not, of course, the whole story, for Mr. Tate was a "gentleman," he believed in "learning," and, despite all his financial difficulties and his withdrawal, he was not lacking in essential virility.

There would appear to have been two results from the father's abdication. One, Mrs. Tate was forced to assume a determinant role in the family's affairs. Not that she was by temperament a domineering woman. But there was a vacuum, and she felt compelled to fill it, at least until her son Benjamin was able to act as paterfamilias. A second and far more significant result may be seen in the effect of all this disorder on Tate and his brothers. To be sure, one must hew his way through the facile interpretations which spring up like jungle undergrowth: through the sociological view that would hold that such a family situation would paralyze the sons so that they would do nothing; through the psychological view that would hold that the sons would develop an Oedipal trauma. The truth is merely human, simple, and predictable. The boys were aware of what failure meant, they feared it, and they determined not to fail. For two of them, Ben and Allen, their determination knew ample fulfillment.

Benjamin Tate became rich. After several minor jobs in the coal business he formed two coal companies in Cincinnati and served as president of both of them from 1920 to 1954. In time his financial interests spread in many directions and he became a member of the board of directors of a number of large companies, including the Union Central Life Insurance Company and Western Union Telegraph Company. In 1944 he served as Chairman of the Robert Taft for Senator Committee and in 1948 the Robert Taft for President Committee. He was also a trustee of Vanderbilt University. If his interests were for the most part very different from those of his literary brother, the two were nevertheless close. They kept up a lifelong correspondence, and Ben was immensely proud of Allen. He could not read his poetry with comprehension, but it delighted him to send Allen crossword puzzles wherein the name "Tate" fit for "American poet." He did read Tate's novel *The Fathers* with interest—even though it is doubtful that he recognized that his own success had provided the model for George Posey. Their older brother, Varnell, was for a time associated with Ben in business, but he was of a milder, less aggressive temperament and never advanced as far.

As for Allen—quite beyond his success as a man of letters—it is fairly obvious that his concern with order in life and literature, his passion for form in his own work, owe much to a reaction against the disorders surrounding his early life. There are doubtless other reasons, and among them is the simple fact that he entered Vanderbilt at a particular time and encountered there a particular quality of mind, a particular custom and demeanor.

When Allen entered Vanderbilt his family was virtually penniless. He did not know this; he did know that he brought with him a family name which "counted for something." The year itself was significant. The Great War was over, and the South was beginning to abandon its isolation from the North. Moreover, in 1918 the old classical concentration which the University had maintained since its inception was melting away.

When John Crowe Ransom, for example, graduated from Vanderbilt in 1909 it was presupposed that an entering student would bring to the University a preparation of four years of Latin and three of Greek. For a major in English literature, an additional two years of Latin and Greek were required as well as two years of French and German, "two and a half years of Biblical literature and one of Anglo-Saxon."[6] But after the War the University yielded to the "utilitarian" view of education which swept the country. Even so, undergraduates at Vanderbilt tended to take Latin and Greek, and Tate recalled later that T. S. Eliot had said to him in 1956, "You may not have had a very large curriculum in the Southern colleges, but it was sound, because you had the Latin, Greek, and mathematics. . . . At Harvard, . . . the curriculum had been ruined by my eminent cousin, Charles W. Eliot. . . . I never got any education until I graduated from Harvard, because it was sort of like a cafeteria: you just took one little thing after another."[6]

Though Tate and most of his friends did take Greek and Latin, they were aware of the change of emphasis, a change which split the University and its departments. Everyone took sides. The side that Tate took centered its wrath in the person of the Chairman of the English Department, Professor Edwin Mims. For Mims represented to them the "new South" which began to emerge after World War I—more utilitarian, more positivistic, more, in short, like the North. But even had Mims been on the side of the classicists, his rhetorical style, his uncritical approach to literature, would have alienated Tate. There were other teachers, however, who commanded his respect. One of these, Walter Clyde Curry, a brilliant though somewhat perverse scholar of medieval and renaissance literature, lent Tate books, gave him literary conversation, and welcomed him in his bachelor quarters at Kissam Hall. Curry also encouraged Tate to write poetry. He himself was writing poems at the time, almost all of them sonnets. He published frequently in the *American Poetry Magazine* put out in Milwaukee. In this magazine appeared Tate's first poem to be published. It was called "Impossible." A second poem—quite overlooked by Tate's bibliographers—also appeared there. As if in deference to Curry, it was a sonnet, but its significance lies in

the clear indication that Tate had already begun to shape his
style before the Fugitive group came into existence. This
particular issue (Autumn 1921) is as fascinating as a museum. It
contains poems by Lucius M. Beebe and Joseph Auslander. It
features an advertisement wherein Vice President Coolidge is
quoted in an endorsement of another little magazine whose
"genuine inspiration for courageous living" he approved. As if
to make the Vice President happy all the poems in the issue
deal in ready-made pieties—except Tate's "Red Stain." However, he maintained the magazine's convention of poets with
three names by signing himself "Orley Allen Tate." Here is the
poem:

> In a pyloned desert where the scorpion reigns
> My love and I plucked poppies breathing tales
> Of crimes now long asleep, whose once-red stains
> Dyed stabbing men, at sea with bloody sails.
>
> The golden sand drowsed. There a dog yelped loud;
> And in his cry rattled a hollow note
> Of deep uncanny knowledge of that Crowd
> That loved and bled in winy times remote.
>
> The poppies fainted when the moon came wide;
> The cur lay still. Our passionate review
> Of red wise folly dreamed on. . . . She by my side
> Stared at the Moon; and then I knew he knew.
>
> And then he smiled at *her;* to him 'twas funny . .
> Her calm steel eyes, her earth-old throat of honey!

Nothing would be served by dwelling on the youth, the nineteenth-century echoes, the occasional hokum of this piece.
Beyond these elements stands the prophecy of Tate's later
poetry—in the wry fever of the last two lines, and the gaunt
authority of the vocabulary in the first line. The young Mr. Tate
was not so graceful a sonneteer as Professor Curry but he was
already a better poet.

In Curry's rooms Allen first met John Crowe Ransom. He has
preserved the memory of that meeting:

I remember the bright autumn day when I first saw John Crowe Ransom, almost forty-nine years ago, in the suite of Walter Clyde Curry at Vanderbilt. At that time both Mr. Ransom and Dr. Curry were young bachelor professors. Mr. Ransom, having reached the ripe age of thirty-one, had just returned from the A.E.F. in France to resume his teaching at his *alma mater.* He came into Dr. Curry's study accompanied by a professor of mathematics, whom to my sorrow I already knew. I was introduced. Mr. Ransom took a step forward, bowed slightly, and shook my hand in the European style: the fingers only, not the full grasp. He backed away and sat down while the random conversation continued. I am sure that he did not speak until a few minutes later, when he rose, went to the bathroom door, and smiling said: "Back in a minute!" I did not hear him speak again until a few months later I looked up to him from the back row of his classroom.[8]

From the back row of that classroom Tate watched a teacher who in all ways contrasted with Edwin Mims. Ransom proffered no hortatory inspiration, no grandstanding, no stunting. He did offer reserved analysis, teasing understatement. "The civility of his demeanor was a gentle but severe reminder that we must try to behave as gentlemen, even when we were not. His role was that of *par inter pares,* a character to emulate but not to imitate; for nothing would have disturbed John Ransom so much as to turn out diminutive copies of himself. His courtesy relieved us of the necessity to commit regicide in order to be ourselves."[9]

Tate also felt the greatest respect for Herbert Charles Sanborn who taught him philosophy and Herbert Cushing Tolman who taught him Greek. From Ransom he obtained respect for intellectual honesty. From Sanborn he learned a philosophic custom of mind, which was to remain with him throughout his life. And with warm affection he has commemorated Tolman:

In his Greek classes he usually gave, towards the end of the period, a "prelection" of the assignment for the next day. On one occasion he recited a free translation of a Pindaric ode. When he had finished I raised my hand and asked:

"Dr. Tolman, could we have read that translation somewhere?" "No, sir," he replied, "my reading is the way John
Dryden might have rendered it into English prose."[10]

Allen had joined Phi Alpha Delta fraternity when a freshman,
but a more important association was the Calumet Club. This
club, of which Tate became president, was a literary society
composed of both students and faculty members. Ransom, Curry, Donald Davidson, and Alec Stevenson were members. It
sponsored a humor magazine in which Tate published a poem
modeled after Villon, "A Ballade of the Lugubrious Wench,"
which gave, according to Louise Cowan, "some small portent of
the author's later poetic ability."[11] Despite his interest, however, in the Calumet Club and the poems he was writing, he still
felt no strong commitment to becoming a writer. But that was
to change. For Donald Davidson, a young instructor in English,
asked him to come to a "discussion group." The group turned
out to be the nucleus of the Fugitives, one of the most remarkable literary associations this country has produced.

CHAPTER TWO

❧ The Fugitives ❧

THE INFORMAL GROUP TO WHICH ALLEN TATE WAS INVITED OWED its existence partly to the community of literary interests between John Crowe Ransom and Donald Davidson, partly to the spirit of a rather strange mystagogue, Sidney Mttron (pronounced Metatron) Hirsch, and partly to the impetus which the intimations of cultural change after the First World War gave to literary movements everywhere in the western world. Literary movements thrive on disaster.

John Crowe Ransom, a native of Pulaski, Tennessee, graduated from Vanderbilt in 1909, received a B.A. from Oxford in 1913, where he was a Rhodes Scholar. In 1914 he returned to Vanderbilt as an instructor in English. Donald Davidson had entered Vanderbilt in the year Ransom left, but after his freshman year he was for financial reasons unable to continue and spent the next four years as a teacher in small towns. He was able to return to Vanderbilt in 1914 and took a course in Shakespeare from Ransom. The two soon became good friends. At the same time Davidson had found his way into another circle of friends. These included Stanley Phillips Johnson, Alec Brock Stevenson, William Yandell Elliott, and Nathaniel Hirsch. Nat Hirsch introduced his friends to his older half-brother Sidney of whom Louise Cowan has given an astonishing portrait:

By his very makeup an eclectic, he had so prodigious a

memory that he could recite a page of printed material
almost perfectly after a single glance. Along with this amazing faculty went a flair for the occult and a magnetic, dom-
inating personality, so that he always stood in need of an
audience. . . . His higher education had been . . . punctuated by trips from college to college, his family finally
acknowledging that so pronounced a genius must not be
intended to have a formal education. He ran off to the navy
for three years and afterwards travelled through the Far
East, his receptive mind soaking up Oriental art and mysticism. When he returned, his family secured for him a
tutor—a sculptor named Chase—who was acquainted with
and had taught numerous figures prominent in art circles.
Hirsch traveled abroad with Chase, enjoying the privilege
of moving in a world of celebrities. He stayed for a while in
New York as part of the company of such fashionable writers and artists as Percy Mackaye, Edith Thomas, Lorado
Taft, and Jock Whitney. In New York he had a hand in
several short dramatic skits and, after coming back to Nashville, in 1913 wrote and produced what *Collier's Weekly*
called "the most artistic and ambitious spectacle ever given
in the South," a Greek pageant entitled *The Fire Regained.*
Hirsch had become convinced that an esoteric symbolism
lay behind all great works of literature and explained the
Greek dramatic poet's method (which he attempted to
employ in his pageant) as a symbolical one. The whole
community had taken part in the production, much in the
spirit of a Panhellenic festival. Some of the features of the
performance were "a chorus of five hundred, a flock of five
hundred doves, a drove of three hundred sheep and a char-
iot race."[1]

The circle, dominated by this expansive gentleman, evolved into
a philosophic discussion group. Even after Davidson introduced
Ransom into the circle, their orientation remained philosophic,
but there was some interest in the "new poetry," particularly
that of Edgar Lee Masters. Somewhere along the line Davidson
recalls that Ransom read to him a poem he had written entitled
"Sunset." In that moment, Davidson felt, "was the actual dawn
of the 'Fugitive' movement." When the United States entered
the war Davidson and Ransom both happened to be stationed
for a time at Fort Oglethorpe, Georgia:

Again Ransom drew a manuscript from his pocket. This time it was a large sheaf of poems. . . . I carried with me to France, and back again, typed copies of some of the poems he had read to me—still admiring, but puzzled, wondering much. I could write nothing of that kind. . . . Then suddenly in 1920, as if the Muse herself had arranged our lives, we were all back at Vanderbilt again, teachers and students once more, the same group, with notable additions. The very first of these was Allen Tate in whom, much as if we had met "Cousin Poe" on some campus walk, we instantly knew the poet.[2]

In 1921 the young man who attended his first meeting of the group was slight in build. His fair hair was slicked back in the fashion of the 1920s; his expression when it was not hawklike was impudent. Flattered to be asked to come to a literary gathering where authors read poems and talked philosophy, he arrived with his guard up, but he was not particularly excited:

I remember the tone of the conversation; it was not very literary but philosophical and even philological; and I soon suspected why I had been asked to come. We had two hosts, Mr. James Frank, a cultivated business man of Nashville, and his brother-in-law, Dr. Sidney Mttron Hirsch, a man of vast if somewhat perverse erudition; and it was plain that I had been invited to hear him talk. He was a mystic and I think a Rosicrucian, a great deal of whose doctrine skittered elusively among imaginary etymologies. At that time I was not very consciously a poet. I was studying Greek and Sanskrit, and if I had behaved myself I should no doubt have gone the next year to the American School at Athens. But I had not studied Hebrew, and I never knew what Dr. Hirsch's middle name, Mttron, meant; I understood that it might be an archangel. He was a large man, an invalid who never moved from his *chaise longue,* and he always presided at our meetings. On this first evening he asked me what I knew about the Trojan horse. My answer must have seemed to him ignorant, for he brushed it aside and went on to explain that *woode* in Middle English meant "mad," and that the Trojan horse being the wooden horse must be the mad horse; and that since madness is divine, the Trojan horse is the esoteric and symbolic horse.

Shining pince-nez stood up on his handsome nose, and curled Assyrian hair topped a massive brow.[3]

Sidney Hirsch did not—indeed, could not—confine his philological romps to a Trojan horse. He reeled through dictionaries, playing with names such as Odysseus or Hamlet, releasing from them arcane meanings which he felt to be a scheme of veiled wisdom which all poets intuitively possess. His system extended to image and symbolism traceable "from the Ramayama to Homer to Sophocles to Dante to Shakespeare to William Blake"[4] and ultimately to Tate or Ransom or Davidson! One smiles to note that his theories were not very distant from William Butler Yeats's faith in a *spiritus mundi.* That he was unrepentant of his beliefs is evidenced by some of his talks at a reunion of the Fugitives in 1956. Within the space of a few minutes he had mentioned "a universal system of symbolism that is in all of the ancient poets"; had observed that Tate and Dante. had used the same symbol; and finally that "the word *spirit* is like a coaxial cable."[5]

The group met fortnightly on Saturday evenings at James Frank's house on Whitland Avenue, and Mrs. Frank customarily served the members supper at the end of the evening. The original members were, in addition to Davidson, Hirsch, Ransom, and Tate, Stanley Johnson, Alec Stevenson, Walter Clyde Curry, and two brothers, Milton and Alfred Starr. (William Yandell Elliott and William Frierson, both Rhodes Scholars at Oxford, were members *in absentia.*) The procedure was pretty much that of most such groups. Each of the members brought poems to read and discuss. Carbon copies were provided, and the author read his poems as beautifully, which is to say as *protectively,* as he possibly could. Much of the critical response was simply practical, technical advice. However, there were debates over the relative importance of "lofty subject matter" and modes of presentation and other aesthetic and philosophical issues. Still, what was effective for all of them was the direct challenge, line by line, word by word, of poems.

In addition, the colloquium was blessed by a singular and congenial variety. There were the passionate warriors, such as Davidson and Tate: Davidson arguing for a regional poetry, not, of course, just of the South, though he gladly supported that, but

of a somewhat romantic apperception of an heroic past; and
Tate arguing for an internationalism based on regionalism. In
contrast to these earnest polemical voices, Ransom's voice fell
dryly, skeptically, but with the kindness which characterized all
his relationships. Finally, the presence of Sidney Hirsch added
an indispensable ingredient. Not that he made much sense. Not
that he wrote well. And not because he criticized competently
—he labored always in a *cumulus* far above terrestrial criticism.
But he was indispensable because every literary movement, like
any healthy tribe, needs its high priest, its shaman, disreputably
giddy and resplendent.

As the meetings continued, manuscripts accumulated, and
finally Hirsch suggested that they publish a magazine. Poets seldom say no to such proposals. Immediately they wondered
about a name. Among the words whose hidden meanings Sidney
Hirsch had revealed was "fugitive." He had also used the word
as the title of one of his poems. When Alec Stevenson suggested
that the magazine be called "The Fugitive," everyone agreed.
In fact, so appropriate did the title seem that years later a number of the Fugitives, including Tate, quite incorrectly "remembered" that Hirsch himself had proposed it.

The first issue appeared in April 1922. And—forgive the critic's choleric heart—looking back at it now, one wonders why
anyone hoped for much from *The Fugitive*. The noms de plume
were amusing, yes. The resinous rasp of amateur earnestness
beseeched the ear on every page. But there were no really good
poems. Yet the very badness is instructive, for the poems which
least realized their aims were written by those with the most
considerable talents: by John Crowe Ransom, writing under the
name of "Roger Prim," by Donald Davidson under the name of
"Robin Gallivant," and by Allen Tate writing under the name
he had purloined from Hawthorne, "Henry Feathertop." Ransom's poem "Ego," which proposes to celebrate the magazine's
first issue, limps and, rather than being public, as one supposes
an occasional poem should be, is queerly private. The kinky
recoil, the grand absurdity of Ransom's later diction, is faintly
recognizable. But if one sees these traits in "Ego," it is because
he also knows how this diction eventually flowered in a masterly
and truly original style. It is doubtful that one could have spot-

ted the promise in 1922. Donald Davidson's poem "A Demon
Brother" admixes impulses of both high and low romanticism.
Here is a smudged fingerprint left by Blake:

> I heard, and was agape to see
> How like that piper was to me.

There is also something of Shelley's Doppelgänger religion, as
well as soft turnings reminscent of the Rhymer's Club. The
theme, however, is typical of Davidson in that it concerns the
unattainability of some aim or ambition submerged in an irre-
trievable past.

The first issue contained two poems by Tate, and they both
indicate assurance about what can be accomplished within the
boundaries of a specific mode. That one of them, "Sinbad,"
veers at times away from its model does not negate that assurance. "Sinbad," as others have remarked, is a Browningesque
monologue, blending an only partly revealed "plot" with a col-
loquial fragmentation of expression. What others have not remarked is that it moves at one point into something much more
akin to Elizabethan soliloquy than Victorian monologue:

> I sailed too long over that monstered ocean
> Ever to grapple with the sinews of an emotion
> Like this slave-girl's. If I could wipe the must
> From the mildewed jars of devilry, and the rust
> Off my lip, the taste of the red preserves
> Of love would be as honied as one deserves
> Who lusted with wormwood and with sickening myrrh,
> Buried with a magic wife.

That the extended analogy is lugubrious does not negate its
technical interest. Furthermore, the poem offers an example of
verbal play of the kind that would become popular twenty or so
years later:

> As I was saying: trickery, the one weapon I had,
> Led me to a blind valley . . .

The slippage from blind *alley* to *valley* is not spectacular and
may even seem insipid, but it is there with the arrogant cranki-
ness of an ancestral voice prophesying Dylan Thomas. Henry

Feathertop Tate's other poem "To Intellectual Detachment" is
more consistently faithful to a model:

> This is the man who classified the bits
> Of his friends' hells into a pigeonhole—
> He hung each disparate anguish on the spits
> Parboiled and roasted in his own withering soul.
>
> God give him peace! He gave none other peace.
> His conversation glided on the brain
> Like a razor honing in promise of one's decease—
> Smooth like cold steel, yet feeling without pain;
>
> And as his art, disjected from his mind,
> Was utterly a tool, so it possessed him;
> A passionate devil, informed in humankind,
> It turned on him—he's dead. Shall we detest him?

The poem is notable for its early evidence of an obsession with
the difficulty of attaining wholeness in life; more notable for its
calculated emulation of Edwin Arlington Robinson's themes and
techniques: the theme of strangulated pathos; the distant, ironic
approach; the mixture of formal and conversational language
bound together by tight iambics. One may wonder about the
terminal question, "Shall we detest him?" The way it falls with
an epigrammatic neutrality transports us to the eighteenth century, somewhere between Goldsmith and Pope. True, Robinson
could have written it; his admiration for some eighteenth-
century poets is plain. Yet his instinct ran against ending poems
with questions. Questions open a poem and he liked his closed.
The ending suggests an impatience on Tate's part with the
very formula which he had with considerable success managed.
He has himself written of his early attempts to costume his
verse in Robinson's "drab style." And though he admired
Robinson's verse, he found that there was nothing there for him
to build on. The point, however, is that in these early emulations we see that Tate worked as a craftsman. There was little
or no self-serving, little or no adolescent self-pity, no pretty but
weak dreaminess.

Malice forbids that one leave the first issue of *The Fugitive*
without mention of Sidney Hirsch's poem "The Little Boy Pil-
grim." Did all the mystical philology lead only to a monstrously

funny approximation of one of Shelley's worst poems, "The Cloud"? Two stanzas will suffice:

> I dance in the fragrance of living;
> I shriek till my nose is a-thrill.
> Then I see that the rustics are peeping
> From their boast of the common-sense hill.
>
> They who are slaves and the playthings,
> The manna for beetles and plant.
> They boast that their common-sense keeps them
> From all that is deemed elegant.

What one can say in summary of the first issue hardly explains the prestige which soon came to the Fugitives. Perhaps it is impossible now to read *The Fugitive* in the way it would have been read in 1922. There have been so many divagations, so many fits and starts in the century that it is getting difficult to look back at the poetry of the early twenties and recover what was new and ardent in it. One can observe that the Fugitives were modernistic in certain attitudes. If one forgets Sidney Hirsch's poems, one can say that they abhorred "sentimentality." They preferred the play of mind to simple lyricism. They believed in, but did not always practice, the techniques of suggestion as against direct statement. They were—bless them—pessimistic. But the only member who was much drawn to the mainstream of modern expression was Allen Tate.

Serious recognition came to the Fugitives mostly from outside Nashville, from *The Double-Dealer* which had been established in 1921 in New Orleans, from New York, and ultimately from London, Berlin, and the offices of *La Nouvelle Revue Française* in Paris. In Nashville the group received not so much recognition as notoriety. The South had been stung by H. L. Mencken's attack on the state of culture in the South, "the Sahara of the Bozarts," so that it gave an especially acute scrutiny to any regional manifestation of art. But scrutiny is not sympathy. In addition the South was wallowing in the troughs of change. All its aspirations and traditions were shifting and under question. Those Southerners who endorsed the idea of changing to a more nearly Northern kind of society seemed to the traditionalists to be Sadducees. To the Fugitives the new did not seem new and the old seemed dead. Ransom's introductory editorial to the first issue of *The Fugitive* singled out the philistine in mild terms:

> Official exception having been taken by the sovereign people to the mint julep, a literary phase known rather euphemistically as Southern Literature has expired, like any other stream whose source is stopped up. The demise was not untimely: among other advantages, THE FUGITIVE is enabled to come to birth in Nashville, Tennessee, under a star not entirely unsympathetic. THE FUGITIVE flees from nothing faster than from the high-caste Brahmins of the Old South.

If these words were mild, they nevertheless brought down suspicion. The Fugitives were often considered obscure, academic, not really acceptable. Professor Mims, who publically praised the group before Nashville clubs, privately urged caution. Could he really have feared that anything scandalous would come from a group to which John Crowe Ransom gave his allegiance? Local newspaper accounts of the magazine and the group tended by and large to be condescendingly encouraging or condescendingly satirical. From this situation John Bradbury deduced the notion that the Fugitives suffered from "alienation":

> For the Fugitives, neither the militant Fundamentalism with its anti-intellectual appeal, nor the new boosterism had any attraction at the moment. Their basic reaction, personified chiefly in Ransom, was much that of the Pounds, Steins, Joyces, and Eliots of a few years earlier, a sense of alienation. They tended therefore to shore themselves up in aesthetic-intellectualist preoccupations. They could not, and did not, ignore their immediate surroundings. Nashville, Vanderbilt, and Dr. Edward Mims were daily realities to most of them, and each of them contributed to the self-consciousness, as well as to the alienation, of the group.[6]

This is a bit glamorous. It seems unlikely that Ransom, fond of golfing and playing cards with friends who never paid much heed to the Fugitives, felt "alienation." Or Davidson who admired Mims' teaching, loved Nashville and Dan McGugin's football teams. It is true that Tate told Michael Millgate that he "felt a little alienated from my backgrounds, as I think everybody else did at that time; and our generation was just trying to find itself, and on the whole it was rather successful in that task."[7] But this statement is not grounds for seeing the Fugitives as a whole recessive and forlorn. Tate himself carried on a fairly glittering social life. It is not so very easy to feel alienated while dancing with a pretty girl.

After the appearance of the first issue Merrill Moore joined the group. Tate had known him slightly in connection with *Jade*, the campus humor magazine, but Moore had given no sign of interest in poetry. And so Tate was astonished when Moore, handing him the manuscript of a poem entitled "To a Fetish" during a casual encounter on the campus, asked for his opinion. Tate said he thought it was "wonderful," and immediately showed it to Donald Davidson. Moore, whose family lived in Nashville, was seventeen. Everyone has inevitably commented on Moore's prodigious production of "sonnets," something in excess of fifty-thousand before his death in 1957. It is doubtful, however, that his poetry improved much after his Fugitive days. His rather frontal talent is revealed by his contributions to *The Fugitive* as well as it is in any of his subsequent poetry. The immediacy, the charm, and canniness are evident qualities which he preserved even when creating sonnets—not altogether discreetly—from interviews with patients after he became a well-known psychiatrist in Boston. These qualities are not quite enough. What strikes one everywhere in his poems is a too great willingness to record the surface of existence, to see that surface as mystery, and to worry no further.

Before the second issue of the magazine appeared, Tate was separated for about nine months from the Fugitives. Threatened by tuberculosis, he was sent by his doctor to Valle Crucis, a village in the mountains of North Carolina. His stay there was of great importance to his literary career. With characteristic reserve Tate says of the sojourn: "I think I began seriously to study the writing of poetry, and I began to be a little more aware of the world, or at any rate of the literary world, at large."[8] Tate had in some ways already been more aware of the literary world at large than most of the Fugitives and more in tune with it than any of them. He had already responded to the synesthesial effects of Baudelaire, and in 1922 adapted with grave competence Baudelaire's "Correspondences":

All nature is a temple where the alive
Pillars breathe often a tremor of mixed words;
Man wanders in a forest of accords
That peer familiarly from each ogive.

Like thinning echoes tumbling to sleep beyond
In a unity umbrageous and infinite,
Vast as the night stupendously moonlit,
All smells and colors and sounds correspond.

Odors blown sweet as infants' naked flesh,
Soft as oboes, green as a studded plain,
—Others, corrupt, rich and triumphant, thresh

Expansions to the infinite of pain:
Amber and myrrh, benzoin and musk condense
To transports of the spirit and the sense!

One sees immediately how the psychological commitments of "Correspondences" extend a gossamer thread toward Mallarmé, Laforgue, Rimbaud, Pound and Eliot. Whether or not Tate saw these connections at the time he translated the poem, he soon did. For in 1924 he was to write in the April issue of *The Fugitive* that "Baudelaire's Theory of Correspondences—that an idea out of one class of experience may be dressed up in the vocabulary of another—is at once the backbone of Modern poetic diction and the character which distinguishes it from both the English Tradition and free verse . . . We think of this as Decadence, but in a wider sense, if it may be repeated here, it is Elizabethan. It is not direct continuity from the immediate past of English poetry. It is development out of the whole of it under French direction: and it is no more startling than the progress from Wyatt to John Donne." One is awed. At twenty-four Tate knew essentially everything that he needed to know of the dominant aesthetics of his century in order to become one of its spokesmen. But even before he voiced his insight—which was really an avowal, a dedication—he was cognizant of its possibilities, though perhaps not sufficiently well-read to be sure of them. Before he went to Valle Crucis, one of Tate's poems, "Euthanasia," was published in *The Double-Dealer,* put out in New Orleans. This fine little magazine's catholicity is suggested by its

hospitality not only to the likes of William Faulkner and Ernest
Hemingway but also to the likes of Ronald Firbank. "Euthanasia," subsequently revised, appears in Tate's *Poems* under the
title "Elegy, *Jefferson Davis: 1808–1889.*" The revised version
(1932) is sufficiently close to the original to preserve its essence
and sufficiently better to be preferred:

> No more the white refulgent streets,
> Never the dry hollows of the mind
> Shall he in fine courtesy walk
> Again, for death is not unkind.
>
> A civil war cast on his fame,
> The four years' odium of strife
> Unbodies his dust; love cannot warm
> His tall corpuscles to this life.
>
> What did we gain? What did we lose?
> Be still; grief for the pious dead
> Suspires from bosoms of kind souls
> Lavender-wise, propped up in bed.
>
> Our loss put six feet under ground
> Is measured by the magnolia's root;
> Our gain's the intellectual sound
> Of death's feet round a weedy tomb.
>
> In the back chambers of the State
> (Just preterition for his crimes)
> We curse him to our busy sky
> Who's busy in a hell a hundred times
>
> A day, though profitless his task,
> Heedless what Belial may say—
> He who wore out the perfect mask
> Orestes fled in night and day.

Tate had written to *The Double-Dealer* that he was
twenty-two and lived in Nashville, "of which two facts . . . the
latter is perhaps the more damning."[9] But why should he have
feared provincialism when in this one poem he had ceased to be
a citizen of a literary province and become a citizen of the literary world? Not many could have seen that at the time, but anyone can see it now. We can see how his language selects its

correspondences, gravitating toward the antiphony of "white refulgent streets" and "dry hollows of the mind" for the purpose of its bleak irony. One might as well observe, too, while he is at it, that the poem looks forward to Tate's "Ode to the Confederate Dead" both in its theme of the impossibility of fully apprehending the whole weight of the tragic past, and in its imagery—the aural effect of "death's feet round a weedy tomb," which is comparable to the sound of the silk worm in the "Ode." The language, the nervous shifts of image, and the predilection for a dry irony rather than heroic whoops attracted another poet to the poem. From Cleveland, young Hart Crane, almost as unknown as Tate, wrote to his Nashville brother-in-arms. As Tate tells it, Crane "said that my poem showed that I had read Eliot—which I had not done; but I soon did; and my difficulties were enormously increased. Anyhow from Eliot I went on to the other moderns, and I began to connect with the modern world what I had already learned from Baudelaire, first through Arthur Symons, then from Baudelaire himself. I mention this personal history because I believe it was through me that modern poetry made its first impact upon the doctors who gathered fortnightly in Mr. Frank's house."[10]

Fortified by the interest shown by *The Double-Dealer* and confirmed by Eliot's and Crane's work, Tate pushed forward on the bent he had intuitively taken. But he tended for a time to excesses of grotesque humor, reminiscent of Laforgue, as in "Elegy for Eugenesis" which appeared in *The Fugitive*, October 1922. The third quatrain:

> Dear Lady, it is revealed that you were twenty-six
> And died giving us an homunculus with bald head:
> May your black hair darken even the dark Styx,
> May your soul have no tears, forgetful of protoplasm.

There were other poems of the period written in a similar vein of burlesquing pastoral motifs. Such poems as "Non Omnis Moriar," "Bored to Choresis," "Lady Fabulous," and "To Oenia in Wintertime," do not come up to his elegy on Jefferson Davis.

Oddly enough no poems of the period seem to deal with Tate's illness. Only two poems, both dated August 1923, a year after Tate had left Valle Crucis, incorporate memories of his stay there. Even more odd, these poems are written with an openness and simple clarity quite uncharacteristic of Tate's work. The second of them, "The Wedding, Valle Crucis, North Carolina, August, 1923," describes a bride and groom coming from a church "like infants from the womb." It finishes:

> From the churchyard
> Down the listless and jagged single street
> The returning guests went home, but I remained—
> And remaining must ever seem pitiless
> To a stranger who saw the black
> Charred march of death from the same churchyard,
> Down the same road.

Clearly Tate makes of the "stranger" a revenant self from the past who is frozen in his knowledge of death, rather as Keats's knight in "La Belle Dame sans Merci" is frozen in the past. The convergence, too, of death and life is manifest, so that we feel the poem retains some of the strain Tate must have felt at the sanatorium. After all in 1922 the prognosis for recovery from tubercular infection was not good.

It would, however, be wrong to infer that Tate's stay at Valle Crucis was unrelieved gloom. Letters kept him in touch with the other Fugitives. Merrill Moore wrote chatty letters, giving Tate all the Nashville news, as well as detailed descriptions of the meetings of the Fugitives. Among the items of news which he was able to report was that the English poet Robert Graves had taken a "keen interest" in the Fugitives, especially in Ransom's poetry. Moore also sent copies of the poems read at the meetings and tactfully urged Tate to give up smoking.[11]

With Davidson, Tate engaged in the raptures of the perennial battle of the books; that is, the moderns versus the ancients. That he had taken Crane's poetry seriously is evidenced by his citing him as precedent for ignoring rhyme, imploring Davidson "not to ruin a good poem with a bad rhyme."[12] He even got Davidson to buy a copy of Eliot's poems. Davidson with a right good will responded by trying some of the new techniques. For a time he seemed almost a convert, but his heart was not in it; he sagged and finally wondered if the money paid for Eliot's poetry was "well spent."[13] A bit later he chastized Tate for obscurity, a lack of warmth, and for being too analytical—

approximately the objections that have always been raised against Tate's poetry. "I have always heard a lot of talk," he wrote, "about objectivity in writing, but I have never been able to conceive how in the world it can exist. . . . One must have an attitude toward his object; one must pity or scorn or accept; one cannot *simply* analyze."[14]

From this time on Tate and Davidson were to be divided on this issue, but it was not one which ever subverted their friendship. And it is unlikely that Davidson's words had much effect on Tate who by this time had moved too far into his own configurations to retreat. The poems which he was to write in the next year or two moved laterally, like artillery fire, across the target. When he was wide of the mark it was because he was drawn momentarily by some model. Occasionally a phrase sounded as if it had been given fiat by Ransom's mock-heroic smile, his nursery rhyme ease, his grave-gay tone. Sometimes Tate seemed to be trying for an innocence unnatural to him, as if he after all had been worried by Davidson's allegations of obscurity. Nevertheless, taken as a whole, the poems confirm the direction he had taken almost unconsciously in "Euthanasia," though it was to be a while before his poems would consistently rise to the power and unity of that poem. The reason for the lag is simple. He was less sure of a subject matter than of a technique. Nevertheless, a growing awareness of his proper subject may be documented.

The poems published in the year 1922 in *The Double-Dealer* were, in addition to "Euthanasia," "William Blake," "Parthenia," "Stranger," and "Hitch Your Wagon to a Star." These are bewilderingly diverse; none is entirely satisfactory. "William Blake" is a sophomoric mockery of Blake's mysticism. It is hard to believe that Tate ever wrote it, yet it anticipates his later concern with the role of poetry in life. "Parthenia" appears to be an imaginary and slightly allegorical narrative about a virgin who takes her own life rather than submit to a ritual deflowering. The phrasing is recognizably Tate's, but the poem does seem an exotic until we see that what surrounds her choice of death is her inability to find unity of flesh and spirit, a theme which in an evolved formulation dogs Tate's later poems. And it may have been the first of Tate's poems to derive from the dream fantasy he deployed in the late poems. For Merrill Moore reported to his friend at Valle Crucis that at the meeting of the Fugitives on July 1, 1922, the members thought it one of Tate's best poems and a perfect illustration of Robert Graves' theory that poetry derives from dream stuff.[15] "Stranger" tells about a man who enters a strange village while a funeral is in process. The streets are not quite funerary, for they contain one "gay with huckstering" and "sly wags." Like the poems written about Valle Crucis, then, "Stranger" juxtaposes death and life. "Hitch Your Wagon to a Star" is satiric in the way that many of Pound's and Eliot's poems are. It contrasts a vital past with a vitiated present. But that past cannot be resuscitated even though the poet enjoins: "Let ancient visions impinge the modern retina." And here we have the dessicated modern state of Tate's late poetry, coupled with an image, faintly scientific, of the eye. Thus, both important thematic and technical elements appear in the poems written while Tate was at Valle Crucis, important because they predict the direction of his mature poetry.

Though these poems are different from each other, a common ground becomes apparent, not so much of theme but of a basic attitude standing behind the theme. Blake cannot come to terms with life, nor can the virgin. Life and death are disparate entities in a village where the stranger stands. The past and present will not join, whether or not one hitches one's wagon to a star. The common ground, then, the common attitude, is that of awareness of discrepancies, of dovetailings that should but will not fit. Tate would ultimately strain to make them fit, but for the time being he was content to emphasize discontinuities, discrepancies, antiphonies. This he did with considerable success in the third issue of *The Fugitive*. His "Horatian Epode on *The Duchess of Malfi*" extends the technique of restless juxtaposition, surprising adjective, abrasive metaphors, and exorbitant analogies observable in "Euthanasia"; it concedes much to an alliance with wit; it teeters, as do many of Tate's poems, upon the sawhorse of an allusion. In revising the poem Tate cleaned up the language and changed the epigraph to one which emphasized that central allusion by calling attention to Webster's naturalistic view of life. The revised version follows:

The stage is about to be swept of corpses.

You have no more chance than an infusorian
Lodged in a hollow molar of an eohippus.
Come, now, no prattle of remergence with
the *ontos on.*

As (the form requires the myth)
A Greek girl stood once in the prytaneum
Of Carneades, hearing mouthings of Probability,
Then mindful of love dashed her brain on a megalith

So you, O nameless Duchess who die young,
Meet death somewhat lovingly
And I am filled with a pity of beholding skulls.
There was no pride like yours.

Now considerations of the void coming after
Not changed by the "strict gesture" of your death
Split the straight line of pessimism
Into two infinities.

It is moot whether there be divinities
As I finish this play by Webster:
The street-cars are still running however
And the katharsis fades in the warm water of a yawn.

The poem has been faulted often enough, and one is not obliged
to prefer it among Tate's works. After all the animadversions
have been noted, however, it is legitimate to ask how many
poets in their early twenties have written a more brilliant poem.
How many poets of whatever maturity can wrench into unity all
the disparate elements of past and present, form and chaos, feeling and learning? This unity—better to say this symbiosis, for the
parts live by feeding on each other—is obtained by the second
quatrain. The quatrain begins with an irony deprecatory of self
and indeed of the poem: "the form requires the myth," which
perhaps echoes Ezra Pound's line, "The age demanded an image" in the Mauberley sequence; then the quatrain sweeps far
away from that Duchess who is Duchess of Malfi still. It takes us
to the academy of Carneades (c. 200 B.C.) where it was taught
that human knowledge was an impossibility, though Carneades
believed that certain stages of clarity in human perception de-
served the term "probability." The girl who in Tate's poem kills
herself "mindful of love" implies a human contradiction to

Carneades' view, just as the Duchess who receives death "lov-ingly" contradicts Bosola's view of life as "a box of wormseed." In the end, neither view remains as the catharsis fades in physi-cal tiredness, delivering the poem to simple sensation, for one takes the warm water as the salivation which accompanies yawning. The resolution, characteristic of much of Tate's poe-try, forms a kind of theme beyond the theme. The resolution is the impossibility of resolution. It is no wonder that Tate soon was to begin upholding the virtues of Eliot's "ironic lyricism" to the Fugitive group. No wonder, either, that Davidson would scoff at the theory, for Davidson could only see it as a threat to the large, vaguely focused emotions he himself believed in.

By September 1922, Tate's health had improved to the point that he could leave North Carolina. On the way home to Ken-tucky he stopped off in Nashville for a meeting of the Fugitives. He describes himself at this time as intolerably conceited. "Had not *The Double-Dealer* written me a letter saying that they saw in me the White Hope of the South? Add to that the easy lesson in shocking the bourgeoisie that I had learned from reading French poets, and was relearning for American use from Ezra Pound, and you have before you the figure of a twenty-two year old prig as disagreeable as you could possibly conjure up, until you see in him several varieties of snobbishness, when he be-comes even more disagreeable."[16]

The September meeting was the last this priggish snob—with beautiful manners—attended until the spring of 1923. Once home in Ashland, Tate joined his brother Ben in the colliery business. The attempt to become a businessman proved a fiasco. On one day alone his commercial talents lost the company $600, and, with some alacrity, his brother agreed with Allen that his future must lie in some other field.

At this time—though doubtless the plan had been forming for months—he schemed to make a trip to New York late in the year. The praise of Hart Crane had held out to him a vista of a literary world beyond the boundaries of the "dear old Fugi-tives," as Donald Davidson was fond of calling the group. He wrote of his planned trip to Ransom who, though he feared Tate would abandon the Fugitives, wrote him a letter of introduction to Christopher Morley and observed in a fatherly way, "I think you are doing the inevitable thing in having a fling at New York, though I am skeptical about any good man's making his way there by literature pure and undefiled."[17] Hart Crane expected Tate to visit him in Ohio on his way back from New York and wrote to his friend Gorham Munson to alert him to Tate's impending visit. A month later Crane complained to Munson that he had not heard anything from Tate, and wondered if he were ill or deranged. The fact is Tate's trip fell through. He could not scrape together enough money and stayed for awhile in Cincinnati, later returning to Ashland.

At loose ends he began to reconsider the aesthetic views he had embraced in the past year. He wrote to Alec Stevenson that it was amusing to write in the modern vein, but that the traditional modes were "a unique satisfaction."[18] Out of this reconsideration came his first literary essay "Whose Ox" published as an editorial in the fourth issue of *The Fugitive*. His argument is of interest, for he apparently wished for some synthesis in his own mind of the traditional and the contemporary. He does not, however, state such a synthesis, but submits that what is formally appropriate to a traditional poem is traditional expression; and, as a corollary, what is formally appropriate to a modernistic poem is modernistic expression. He supposes that the two modes can coexist in the present literary age.

Meantime, Tate remained in the "abominable little town" of Ashland, Kentucky. Isolated and unhappy with his surroundings, he was nevertheless able to work and rework his poems. More and more he inclined toward configurations of wit and symbolism, which more and more brought him into a kinship with T. S. Eliot's poetry. At the same time he began an extended correspondence with Ransom. Ransom characteristically attacked what he felt was a discrepancy between Eliot's theory of tradition and his actual practice; Tate characteristically defended Eliot. Some of Tate's own poems written at the time, late 1922 and early 1923, Ransom found accomplished but disturbingly subrational. Among these was "Yellow River," which after revisions was published in the seventh issue of *The Fugitive* under the title "Screen." It shows how far Tate had gone in his pursuit of Eliot's methods—an exhausted persona and a narrative movement with pauses for meditation such as come from time to time to Prufrock. And he had adopted Eliot's device of mundane deflations:

> And afterward, like a brutal song
> Stabbing the young dusk to stillness,
> Comes the after-dinner hour.

The after-dinner hour arrives much as the taking of a toast and tea arrives for Prufrock.

In February 1923 Tate returned to Vanderbilt to complete the Bachelor's degree which his illness had interrupted the year before. He had to grind away at mathematics and chemistry. Davidson, who was in Oberlin, Ohio at his wife's home, kept urging him rather fiercely to "get that damned chem. & math., and make everything cocksure for the degree." He seemed to fear that Tate would disappear into an aesthetic maze and never become financially "independent."[19] Davidson's fears were groundless. Tate passed a tranferable chemistry course at Peabody College in Nashville and satisfied the other requirements. The Bachelor's degree was granted to the young Phi Beta Kappa scholar at the end of the summer, *magna cum laude*. By the kindness of the University his diploma was dated 1922, so that he technically graduated with his class. For a time, also, Tate felt immediate fame was within his grasp. He had gotten together a collection of poems which was accepted by a small company in New York, but the company failed before publication could take place.

Soon after returning to Nashville in 1923, he met a student who became one of his closest lifelong friends. He writes:

> One day in February 1923 (I think it was) I was typing a bad poem entitled "William Blake" on Walter Clyde Curry's typewriter. Dr. Curry gave the poets the freedom of his rooms. I became aware of a presence at my back and turning round I saw the most remarkable looking boy I had ever laid eyes on. He was tall and thin, and when he walked across the room he made a sliding shuffle, as if his bones didn't belong to one another. He had a long quivering nose, large brown eyes, and a long chin—all topped by curly red hair. He spoke in a soft whisper, asking to see my poem; then he showed me one of his own—it was about Hell, and I remember this line:

> Where lightly bloom the purple lilies . . .

> He said that he was sixteen years old and a sophomore. This remarkable young man was "Red," Robert Penn Warren, the most gifted person I have ever known.[20]

Red Warren soon introduced Tate to Ridley Wills, a friend of his who had written a first novel entitled *Hoax*. He had come back to Nashville, after a stint in the army, to complete a degree. He was also the cousin of Jesse Wills who had recently become a member of the Fugitives. Ridley was a mercurial, amusing person, and he and Tate and Warren took a room together in Wesley Hall during the spring term. "It was," Tate tells us,

> one large room with two double-decker beds, and Ridley and I being older than Red made him sleep above. In order to get into bed at night we had to shovel the books, trousers, shoes, hats, and fruit jars onto the floor, and in the morning, to make walking-space, we heaped it all back upon the beds. We stuck pins into Red while he slept to make him wake up and tell us his dreams.[21]

Tate tells us nothing of the dreams, but he does report on Warren as an artist. Red created on the walls four murals based on scenes from *The Waste Land*.

Warren's graphic homage to Eliot was soon topped by Tate and Ridley Wills one spring night when they went down to a student hangout and wrote before dawn a series of poems burlesquing T. S. Eliot's poetry. They entitled the whole series *The Golden Mean*. They parodied more than T. S. Eliot. Sidney Hirsch's magical etymology maunders through the footnotes. The title itself was satirical of Professor Mims who frequently adduced the phrase as a doctrinal panacea in his classes. The satire probably did nothing to improve Tate's standing with Mims. But then, Tate, Wills, and Warren exulted in his disapproval. Warren once wrote gleefully to Tate that Mims had characterized the two of them as "debauched aesthetes, whose one ambition was to die before the age of thirty-five with only a poem or two to live after them."[22]

Tate and Wills showed the manuscript of *The Golden Mean* to Merrill Moore who was, as Tate says, "pretty envious," and so he was told he might have a place in the book if he would write eulogies of the other authors. He did so, although Tate says, "his tongue was not where it should have been."[23] An air of pubic naughtiness hangs about a number of the poems. Still, they are endearingly youthful. And how well Tate knew Eliot's, poetry is revealed in his poem "The Chaste Land (Continued)," complete—or perhaps one should say replete—with footnotes:

> At the perspiring hour, when she lies for lack
> of other things to say, and the pristine prick of
>   gooseflesh waits
> intersected by quite hopelessly conflicting dates,
> at the perspiring dour and widowed midnight
> when she pulls the tangles of her hair outright°
> and walks in beauty like the night°°
> of loudless infants on a jag of murder:
> and only a demure and virtuous dole°°°
> succedent of a successful procrastination
> and bafflement of endocrines
> COO-COO
> fear death or a daughter°°°°
> when I was creeping through the vegetation °°°°°
> quite the most impassioned in the nation
> I became somedel aware of affectation
> and saw the muddy creeks behind the scenes
> betweens and ins and outs
> and I came to the point
>
> > *Shanty Shanty Shanty*°°°°°°

°   T. S. Eliot, *The Waste Land*, What the Thunder Said.

°°   George Gordon, Lord Byron. *She Walks in Beauty*, p. 508. Wks. of B., ed. by J. W. Lake, Philadelphia, 1836.

°°°   cf. Geo. Herbert, *Virtue.*

°°°°   cf. T. S. Eliot, *Waste Land*, The Burial of the Dead.

°°°°°   Ibid., The Fire Sermon.

°°°°°°   Prakrit slang for "the peace that surpasseth the pursuit of further ambition, i. e., the home."

The little book, dedicated to *The Fugitive*, was privately published in an edition of two hundred copies. It is a collector's item.

By this time *The Fugitive* had opened its pages to others than the Nashville group, among them Robert Graves, Louis Untermeyer, and Witter Bynner. It was also planned to conduct a public poetry contest with prizes. The group selected as judges for this contest Jessie B. Rittenhouse, William Alexander, and Gorham B. Munson. Tate served during the summer of 1923 as managing editor. His industry overwhelmed Jesse Wills who wrote to Davidson, "I never saw anyone who enjoyed writing letters as he does. . . . He's carrying on a personal correspondence with several of our contestants of both genders."[24]

During the summer *The Fugitive* engaged in a brief tiff with Harriet Monroe who in *Poetry, a Magazine of Verse* had dreamily suggested that Southern poetry ought to exude an attar of honeysuckle. Davidson replied in the June-July issue of *The Fugitive* in tones that were not exactly redolent of honeysuckle. Miss Monroe's assistant, a Miss Swett, wrote a letter defending Miss Monroe. Tate replied to her in the neutral tones of reason:

> We do not disagree with Miss Monroe when she emphasizes the artistic possibilities latent in the traditions of the Old South; nor do we feel called upon to object if she feels—as she evidently does not—that this tradition is the only genuine source for Southern poets to draw upon. . . . But we fear very much to have the slightest stress laid upon Southern traditions in literature; we who are Southerners know the fatality of such an attitude—the old atavism and sentimentality are always imminent. . . .[25]

As the tempest in a teapot subsided, a more serious storm arose. Tate and Stanley Johnson came to feel that the magazine which had operated from the outset under a general editorial board should have one responsible editor. They preferred Donald Davidson. Ransom, who was away in Greeley, Colorado, opposed the idea. Furthermore at this time Tate felt less than kindly toward Ransom; they were engaged in a public literary duel. Ransom had published an essay in the issue for July 14, 1923 of *The Literary Review* in which he voiced his dubiety about Eliot's *The Waste Land*. He found the juxtapositions of noble verse and vulgar argot incongruous and he doubted the importance of the poem. Tate posted off a riposte which appeared in *The Literary Review* for August 4, 1923. Without pondering the fact that he was addressing his friend and mentor, he slipped into the high polemical tone which had of late come easily and too intoxicatingly to him. He sent a copy of the letter to Ransom. Ransom, undoubtedly shaken by the imputation that he had been fuzzy in his arguments, countered in the issue for August 11 with a reply in which, quite falling out of character, he assumed a patronizing air. "The truth is," he wrote, "Tate has for two years suffered the damning experience of being a pupil in my classes, and I take it his letter is but a proper token of his final emancipation, composed upon the occasion of his accession to the ripe age of twenty-three." The exchange, as one contemplates it now, has its comic side, but it did not then. Tate thought for a time of severing all connections with Ransom, and indeed their relationship was for almost a year icy. In the midst of this unhappy situation, Ransom was advised of a palace revolution. He received a letter in which Davidson accepted the editorship in accordance with a resolution approved by all the Fugitives except Ransom, Merrill Moore who was incommunicado in Europe, and Ridley Wills who was honeymooning. Tate was named assistant editor. Ransom bowed genially to the coup.

Having no better occupation, Tate stayed on in Nashville during the fall, even though he had at the end of the summer been granted his degree. He had hoped to receive a scholarship, and would have pursued a Master's degree in classical studies. But he had exasperated important faculty members, and no scholarship materialized. He continued to give his energies to the magazine which had attracted considerable attention by this time, both for itself and for the contest which drew entries from all over the country. The results of the contest, announced in the tenth number of *The Fugitive*, December 1923, were probably galling to him. There had been entries from Hart Crane, Laura Riding, and Robert Penn Warren, of whom Tate thought highly, but the wide disagreements among the judges resulted in the prizes going to rather insipid poems. Not surprisingly, in the subsequent contest of the next year outside judges were not used.

The Fugitive had come a long way. The poets, at least many of them, had gained in muscularity, and some of Ransom's finest poems had appeared. But Tate's intimate relationship with the

magazine was drawing to a close. He still dreamed of making a
trip to New York and of pitting himself against the empire, not
the provinces of literature. He had published a number of
poems in various magazines. He had received encouragement
from Hart Crane, and of even greater importance, William Elliott had during the previous summer received a letter from T.
S. Eliot in which the master had praised poems of Tate's he had
seen in *The Fugitive*. This news made Tate feel like putting a
record on the gramophone. His earlier plan to visit New York
had bogged down for lack of funds. This time he planned better.
When, as a result of a teacher's illness, a job at a high school in
Lumberport, West Virginia, was offered him, he accepted. Enroute in late February he stopped in Louisville to call on Laura
Riding Gottschalk whose poems in *The Fugitive* had impressed
him. He found her as impressive as her poems. "Her intelligence
is pervasive," he wrote. "It is in every inflection of her voice,
every gesture. . . . But always you get the conviction that the
Devil and all Pandemonium couldn't dissuade her of her tendency."[26] Tate taught at Lumberport from March to June 1924.
Though he found the work pleasant and interesting, it was not
something he wanted to continue for long. He was kept informed of events in Nashville by Davidson and most faithfully
by Robert Penn Warren.

Warren's letters of the period reveal a deep attachment to
Tate, almost a hero worship, certainly a psychological depen-
dence. He had been too young when he entered Vanderbilt.
Even more, the strain of literary ambition, imposed upon him
prematurely by his association with the Fugitives, was difficult
to support. He fluctuated between elations and despairs. In the
spring of 1924 he wrote to Tate that he found himself in a situation which paralleled Tate's own relationship to Eliot. Having
not surpassed Tate, he could only imitate.[27] Under all of this
stress he became so ill in late May that he had to return home
to Guthrie, Kentucky.[28] Tate was alarmed, but Red seemed to
recover rapidly and soon was writing to ask Allen to spend the
summer at Guthrie. He thought he could obtain for them both
jobs doing construction work.[29] One pauses, slightly amused, at
the vision of the tall, gangling Warren and the small, slender
Tate engaged in building roads. The vision can be permitted to

fade, however, for the jobs were not forthcoming. Warren's mother also wrote, asking Tate to visit them during the summer; she hoped that Tate's presence would amuse "son" and keep him from reading and writing.[30] It may be questioned whether Tate was the right person to keep anyone from reading and writing. He did, however, join the Warrens that summer, but only after at last making his trip to New York.

Early in June 1924 Tate visited his mother in Washington and then went on to New York. Davidson wrote to him, hoping that he would be able to "overcome the siren attractions of Gotham, Gorham, and the Ghetto."[31] Tate's letters to friends at Vanderbilt were rather reserved about his experiences. He remarked that Hart Crane had treated him "royally." He found the literati of the city less immersed in theory, less "conscious of themselves as poets" than the Fugitives.[32] Even so, Davidson worried about Allen's being corrupted, and urged him to call upon people whom Davidson considered "right," as contrasted to Tate's "friends of the left." Davidson's letter finishes with an implication that Tate was having a hard time making up his mind whether or not to stay in New York.[33] Perhaps this uncertainty is what Hart Crane referred to when he wrote to Gorham Munson a bit later: "The boy left NY in a frightfully feverish state . . . and I am a little worried about what's happening to him since." But Crane also noted:

> Allen has a very good mind and a kind of scepticism which I respect. I got very few chances to really talk with him, but I suspect that at least we have established an idiom or code for future understandings which may make our correspondence at once a simple and more comprehensive pursuit. . . . it may well be that a place like NY means less to him than to the usual young literary man.[34]

During his short stay Tate met, besides Crane and Munson, Slater Brown ("Mr. B." in E. E. Cummings' *The Enormous Room*), Malcolm Cowley, Matthew Josephson, Edmund Wilson, and Louise Bogan. He moved bedazzled in the bohemian milieu of Greenwich Village, and when he left New York he was exhausted.

By the end of June, Tate was in Guthrie, Kentucky visiting

the Warrens. The summer was lazy and happy. The two friends swam, rode horses, and walked in the countryside. Another visitor was in Guthrie with her family that summer, a slender, dark-haired girl four years older than Tate. Caroline Gordon had been born at Merry Mont Farm near Trenton, Todd County, Kentucky. She was passionately interested in literature. Tate had known of her before meeting her, for she had written an article on the Fugitives in the Chattanooga *News* for February 10, 1923, under the headline "U.S. Best Poets Here in Tennessee." In October Tate returned to New York, and there on November 2, 1924 he and Caroline Gordon were married. They planned to live permanently in New York.

Tate continued to contribute to *The Fugitive*, though he had resigned as Associate Editor during the summer. However, in February 1925 he sought to resign completely from the association since he felt he would never return to Nashville. He was persuaded by Ransom to remain a member in inactive status. That was of little significance, for *The Fugitive* itself ceased publication with the December 1925 issue.

As little magazines go, *The Fugitive* had been spectacularly successful. There had been money troubles, but, underwritten by Nashville businessmen, it was solvent at the time of its demise. There had been quarrels and defections, but there was a durable bond of affection among its important members, Ransom, Davidson, Tate, and Warren. Neither quarrels nor money explain the death of *The Fugitive*. It died by the mutual consent of the founders. Donald Davidson ascribed its death to the need to defend the South against the hostility engendered by the Dayton "evolution" trial in 1925.[35] Ransom simply said in a final editorial that "The Fugitives are busy people, for the most part enslaved to Mammon, their time used up in vulgar bread-and-butter occupations. Not one of them is in a position to offer himself on the altar of sacrifice." Unquestionably these reasons are primary, but one can be added. In the space of three years, the important poets had ceased to be amateurs and became professionals. Many of Ransom's finest poems were written during the time and published in *The Fugitive*. Davidson would write somewhat better in future years, but the nature of his poetry was by 1925 clear. Tate had found his voice; Warren was about to find his. For them the magazine had done all that it could do. To all of them it gave, or confirmed, a respect for the design of art, respect for the contours of formal thought, and faith in the saving dignity of literature. Furthermore, it had led them to see what *The Fugitive* itself had neglected; namely, that all of these values must be sustained by a serious, responsible criticism. These were the tenets that eventually Warren would take to *The Southern Review;* Ransom to *The Kenyon Review;* and Tate to *The Sewanee Review.* In this way *The Fugitive* rose from its ashes to continue in the most powerful and sensitive voices in American culture for a span of three decades.

But in 1925 it was the present, not the far future, that pressed on Allen Tate, a young man newly married, penniless in New York, and driven by the most fierce and most cruel of ambitions, that of fulfilling himself as a poet.

CHAPTER THREE

❧ New York ❧

IN NEW YORK CITY, ALLEN AND CAROLINE RENTED A SMALL FLAT
at 30 Jones Street and turned to their literary careers. The years
1924 to 1928, spent mostly in New York in freelance writing,
brought Allen Tate fame. His production of both prose and poetry was impressive. For such journals as *The Nation, The New
Republic,* and the New York *Herald-Tribune,* as well as a few
little magazines, he turned out more than fifty reviews. Ranging
over a wide spectrum, from Edna St. Vincent Millay to Ernest
Hemingway, these reviews were a financial necessity. The com-
missions for them owed in part to his friendships with Edmund
Wilson and Mark Van Doren. Wilson and Van Doren chose
well. Tate's reviews are distinguished by that quality rare in reviews: they come forth from an intellectual center; they rise
above sporadic opinions. Besides reviews, he produced his biography of Stonewall Jackson and did much of the groundwork for
that of Jefferson Davis. He wrote the first of his poems to receive wide attention and published his first book of poems. Furthermore, it was during this period that his mind began to engage
the principles which later on became known as "Agrarianism."
In view of the yield, one would expect Tate to have lived as a
hermit. The opposite is true. His life was full, and he made
many of his rich, lifelong friendships during these years.

The decade itself was a time of manic enthusiasms, great spiritual searching as well as hedonism and squandered energies.
Still, there was an innocence behind all the nervous courting of

disaster. There was an innocent appreciation of spontaneity and simple "fun." With Hart Crane, Tate went often to the old Winter Garden burlesque shows celebrated by E. E. Cummings. And he became a formidable figure in the formidable group of people close to Hart Crane. But he also established friendships outside that rather bohemian group, in particular with Mark Van Doren, then a young teacher at Columbia University. They had been introduced at a luncheon in 1925, and they took to each other immediately. After lunch they discussed Wordsworth for hours in Union Square. It seems likely that Tate found in Van Doren the same gentlemanly seriousness about poetry that he had known among the Fugitives, and now missed. And perhaps in that initial conversation he found himself too eagerly assuming his old Fugitive role of polemicist, for he shortly wrote, rather touchingly, a letter to Van Doren in which he apologized for his callowness:

> I get very little "literary conversation," and I miss it. . . . There are few persons these days who do not mistake obsessions, missions, remedies, and purposes for ideas . . . To hear you speak as you did of Wordsworth was worth, in itself, a trip to town; there aren't ten people in America who have that feeling for *literature*. . . . Finally, let me be self-conscious and offer excuses for a long letter in this age of "hurry." But, you see, I am still very young and retain my enthusiasms; "letters" are not yet a routine, they are still a passion. But I am almost afraid to tell you that I am just twenty-five; the fact might shake some of the confidence which I very gratefully feel you have in me.[1]

His passion for letters kept him in touch with the Fugitives, especially with Davidson, Ransom, and Warren. And Warren was soon present in the flesh. After finishing a Master's degree at the University of California in 1927, Red came to New York to visit the Tates. In the following year he was studying at Yale and could therefore see Allen and Caroline from time to time. Andrew Lytle, a late comer to the Fugitives, whom Tate had not known at Nashville, was also studying at Yale. John Crowe Ransom gave him Tate's address, and that was the beginning of their friendship.

At the end of 1925 Tate boasted to Davidson of his ability to live by his literary wits, and Davidson expressed his elation at the news, but he was amazed that one could make a go of it.[2] In fact, Tate did manage to live by his pen, but not altogether by belles lettres. He took a job as assistant to Susan Jenkins Brown (the wife of Slater Brown whom Tate had met in June 1924) who was editing a pulp-paper love-story magazine *Telling Tales*, published by Clayton Publishers. His salary, as estimated by Malcolm Cowley, was about thirty dollars a week. The work, mostly copy reading, did not demand so much from him that it seriously interfered with his own writing. Some of the time the work was amusing. Mrs. Brown's job included the writing of teasers for subsequent installments of the stories the magazine serialized. On one occasion she had written: "Do not fail to miss the next installment of this thrilling . . . *etcetera.*" Tate did not catch the slip in his proofreading, and it appeared in the magazine. Hart Crane, gleeful over the error, was fond after that of denigrating something he disliked by advising people not to fail to miss it.

The office of *Telling Tales* on East Eleventh Street near University Place served also as a meeting place for literary friends. Crane stopped by frequently at five o'clock, hoping to tempt Tate and Mrs. Brown to join him for a drink at a place called "Poncino's," but which they renamed "the Punchino Palace." The specialty of this tiny speakeasy, at the rear of a delicatessen, was a dubious rum toddy, but it was cheap. The office was also used after hours as the editorial headquarters for the booklet *Aesthete, 1925*. This booklet, a *jeu d'esprit*, was gotten up in a week's time in February as a rejoinder to Ernest Boyd's crudely aimed haymaker "Aesthete, Model 1924" which had appeared in H. L. Mencken's initial issue of *American Mercury*, January 1924. The article had given a portmanteau sketch of the New York literatus as a precious college sort who had become an expatriate, toyed with Dadaism, and finally returned to New York to forge a literary reputation from a spurious learning and fake mysticism. Malcolm Cowley, Mr. and Mrs. Brown, Crane, the Tates, Kenneth Burke, Matthew Josephson, James and Susan Light, and Laura Riding (who had also recently come to New York) were the group behind *Aesthete, 1925*. They frequently joined for dinner in a basement speakeasy, John Squarcialupi's restaurant on Perry Street. They were all pretty much in their middle twenties and felt, as Malcolm Cowley puts it, "invulnerable." Over them hovered a phantom presence by the name of Mr. Hankel whom the group invoked as tutelary spirit and editor. Harold Loeb recalls being at one meeting at which Hart Crane read a section of *The Bridge* and then proclaimed he was giving up poetry forever; and Tate read a satiric poem entitled "The Earnest Liberal's Lament."[3] Malcolm Cowley has captured the gay and confident spirit of the dinners at Squarcialupi's in honest verse. His poem "The Flower and the Leaf" celebrates the "omni-colored crew" who gathered at the table, "happy as jaybirds, loud as puppies." One stanza clearly and fondly delineates the person of Allen Tate at twenty-five, one who was "studiously polite," whose good manners preserved "for him an inner hush":

> There was no hush that winter night
> when flown with Squarcialupi's wine,
> he made a funnel, then adopted
> the look of a greedy child and said
> in a five-beat iambic line,
> having flung back his enormous head,
> "All contributions gratefully accepted."

Andrew Lytle also noticed that in New York Tate seemed to preserve an inner self behind an armor of formidable manners. He recalls presenting himself at the Tate's apartment and being "met with a severe and courteous formality—it was as if the eyes reflected but did not see what was before them. Later I came to recognize this as a mask to keep the world at a distance, because of the artist's necessity to be saved interruptions while at work . . . Once a caller asked for Katherine Anne Porter . . . and was received with grave decorum and told, with a bow, 'The ladies of this house are at the riot in Union Square.' The bow, as well as the words, was a conscious emphasis upon the irony of his situation, the common situation of the artist living in New York, belonging to no cliques, and demanding that the profession of letters be accepted as a profession."[4]

Though projected as a magazine, *Aesthete, 1925* appeared only once, and by June 1925 the circle had deserted Squarcialu-

pi's in favor of trips to Pawling, New York where Slater and
Susan Brown had bought a pre-Revolutionary farmhouse. Allen
and Caroline visited them on July 4 and found suddenly that
they wanted to live in the country also. Tate had begun to complain that the city was "killing" him. The bright aura of New
York was fading for him, and Caroline by disposition loathed
large cities which seemed to her perpetually unreal. Forlornly
they looked at a small farmhouse near the Browns' place, that
could be bought for about $500. But Caroline ruefully observed
that they did not have the money even to "buy an extra dinner
plate at Woolworth's."[5] They were, it is true, strapped, and
their financial difficulties were not eased by Caroline's expecting
a child. Nancy Tate was born September 23, 1925, and the
Tate's had to move to a larger flat on Morton Street.

Even worse, Tate lost his job at *Telling Tales*. As Susan
Brown puts it, "he had committed the indiscretion of correcting
the grammar in an office memo from the boss."[6] Keeping an
apartment in New York City became suddenly impossible, and
the Tates thought again of the country where perhaps they
could live cheaply. The result was that in November they rented
part of an old house at Patterson, New York, about half a mile
from the Browns' place at Pawling. For ten dollars a month they
had eight partly furnished rooms, including the use of a kitchen
with the redoubtable convenience of a pump indoors—actually
less primitive than the plumbing at Slater Brown's farmhouse. In
the other part of the house lived the owner, Mrs. Addie Turner,
a widow of sixty, and her aunt. The rent was small, but Allen's
income, mostly from book reviews, was less than $100 a month.
Cowley laconically observes that "fortunately potatoes were
cheap that year, and Allen warmed himself twice, in Thoreau's
phrase, by sawing and splitting wood."[7]

What both Caroline and Allen hoped for was that, released
from the city, they would be able to get more writing done.
Caroline had previously written a novel that had foundered.
Now she wanted to try a second one. For Allen, Patterson gave
promise of stretches of uninterrupted time and, more importantly, relief from the pleasurable but erosive social life in Manhattan. He had arrived at an intellectual and spiritual crisis, and he
needed time and serenity to discover his way. For, if he had

come to New York to escape the fiefdom of Tennessee, he soon
discovered that the literary coteries of Manhattan were no less
provincial in their way than had been the circle in Nashville. In
addition, since many of the intellectuals in New York centered
their faith in "society," rather than "culture," in economics
rather than spirit, in political idealism rather than in life, Tate
found that the interior life of the individual counted for less than
his instinct insisted it must. And so, while he could tell himself
that if he had been born in New York City, he doubtless would
at this time quite naturally have been a "scientific humanist" or
a "Marxist," he was aware that he was neither. Indeed, his
whole background, his whole being, was under challenge.
What he turned over in his mind, therefore, was the meaning of
his background which he would either have to repudiate or pro-
tect; how much of that background, he wondered, was truly
available to him. So much did he implore from the mists of the
past that his need for a certified identity could not be realized in
any way that would satisfy him. From his failure to discover
himself in relation to his antecedents emerged his first truly fine
poems.

But if peace and quiet were what were required at Patterson,
the Tates all too humanly behaved like Poe's self-destructive
hero in "The Imp of the Perverse." They took in Hart Crane.
Without a job in the late autumn of 1925, Crane was living by
borrowing what money he could from friends. Tate had known
from the first of Crane's poems he had seen that Crane was greatly
gifted. In New York early in 1925 he had also immediately recognized the unique quality of Crane's "Voyages," and had tried
to get them published in *Guardian,* a magazine put out in Pitts-
burgh by Harry Potamkin who had published in *The Fugitive.*
Apparently they were never published there, though to Crane's
chagrin the magazine did announce that a future issue would
feature "Voyages," four "remarkable" poems by Allen Tate![8]
Allen and Caroline knew that for almost three years Crane had
been trying to finish *The Bridge.* In the naive hope that they
could all do their serious work together, they invited him to live
with them at Addie Turner's. He accepted the invitation, but
just before he left the city for Patterson his fortunes changed.
Otto Kahn decided to help Crane with a gift of $1000 and the

promise of another thousand later on. For several days and nights Crane celebrated his fortune in the manner which has endeared him to biographers and undergraduates. He finally arrived on December 12 at the Tates, bearing liquor, exotic groceries, and a pair of snowshoes.

The story of that winter has been told several times. Hart Crane's view of it is well detailed in his letters. It need not be detailed here. Sufficient to say that for four months—even though they were cramped for space because of the difficulty of even slightly warming more than three rooms—the menage went well enough. But the egos of three writers with very different temperaments could not blend indefinitely. And Crane—though he seems to have restricted his more exorbitant behavior to his occasional jaunts to New York City—was noisy and, if not contemptuous of the rights of others, at least unconscious of them. In mid-April there was a quarrel. The Tates communicated with Crane by slipping notes under his door. At the end of the month he left Patterson and sailed for the Isle of Pines with Waldo Frank. His phonograph had blared much of the night; he went south in the spring. The friendship was patched up later when Crane's first volume of verse *White Buildings* appeared. The publisher, Horace Liveright, had accepted the book on the condition that Eugene O'Neill write an introduction to it. O'Neill was willing put paralyzed by the very idea of critical prose. Tate offered to write the introduction to appear over O'Neill's signature. Eventually, the introduction was signed by Tate.

In retrospect the quarrel seems comical. It ought to seem something more, for in that winter two remarkable poets were deeply involved in composing remarkable poems. These poems are about as opposed thematically as two poems can be. Tate's "Ode to the Confederate Dead" was taking shape in his imagination. Crane completed the "Atlantis" section of *The Bridge* and refined his outline for the whole of the work. This much profundity went on in Addie Turner's house, and the writers eventually quarreled over something trivial.

Caroline and Allen stayed at Patterson through the summer and raised a vegetable garden. But it is characteristic of Tate that after a pastoral interlude he became bored and longed to return to the city he had fled. In the autumn they took a basement apartment in a brownstone at 27 Bank Street, in the Village. To pay for the rent Allen did some janitorial work in the building. Unhappily his friend Matthew Josephson encouraged a newspaper to send a reporter to get a story on the plight of a young poet driven by an insensitive society to stoke a furnace. Tate was furious and refused to permit the story. Josephson's account of Tate's anger—namely that he had become proud of his connection with the "First Families of Virginia" and was ashamed of doing menial work—was a crude mishmash of misinformation and puerile psychology.[9] Tate was not ashamed of the work. After all, among his forbears was an indentured servant. What was distasteful to him was the idea of publicity of the most vulgar variety. But Josephson was unquestionably right that Tate had been thinking about his relationship to his past, though not with the results Josephson assumed. Public events intensified Tate's thinking.

The Scopes "monkey" trial, with its panache of Clarence Darrow and evolution, in Dayton, Tennessee in 1925 again spiritually reunited Davidson, Ransom, Warren, and Tate, along with Andrew Lytle who could claim membership with the Fugitives by reason of having published a poem in the final issue. The scorn heaped by northern journalism on the South and fundamentalism smarted them as though it were a personal insult.

Tate refers to his and Ransom's having written at the same time in 1926—so that their letters crossed—of the need to do something "about the South." It must have been late in 1926 and perhaps it was early 1927. In any event early in 1927, largely under the fiery leadership of Donald Davidson, the Fugitives were hatching plans for some kind of defense of southern culture. A bit later they were thinking of lines of political action, of taking over newspapers and magazines. All of this was to reach a climax later in the 1930s, and Tate was geographically remote from his friends in Tennessee for much of the time. But he carried on a correspondence with them from New York and later from Europe. Significantly, the early foment of the movement ultimately known as "Southern Agrarianism" coincided with a pattern of ideas in Tate's mind.

The first element of the pattern is one which haunts the pe-

riod, indeed the century: the impact of the historical theses of
Oswald Spengler. During the twenties, Spengler's Ragnarok-
style, his doom-ridden charts paralleling the artifacts and
the intellectual and religious drifts of various great civilizations
of the past, burst upon the intellectual world. His basic theme
was that all *cultures* move through their youth with aim and
confidence and then come into a period of *civilization* where
these dynamic qualities wither. Finally the civilization becomes
dessicated, romantically mourns its "childhood," loses objectivity
or purpose, develops a deathwish, and dies. Toward such a
decadence Spengler held the western world was rapidly moving.
These fatalistic views affected the attitudes of many writers.
Hart Crane, curiously enough, could accept Spengler's theory as
true, while at the same time dismiss it as unimportant, probably
because he placed his faith in an inner vision which could trans-
form, he hoped, the chaotic and malformed into the beautiful
and triumphant. Allen Tate was more gloomy. He found it improbable that a dying age could produce a vital art. In his review of Spengler's *The Decline of the West* (*The Nation*, May
12, 1926) he argued only with Spengler's method and by and
large accepted his prognosis. Yet, like many affected by Spengler's thought, he was, it would seem, not quite willing to accept the inevitable conclusion; namely, that there was nothing
at all to do about it. Yeats sought to save his soul in art or private vision; Eliot to save his in the sequences of a willed Christian belief; on the West Coast Robinson Jeffers preached
"inhumanism" and observed that for the individual at least,
corruption had never been compulsory. Tate sought to find
some solution in different ways, ultimately in a balance within
the self, but for the time being in a relationship with the past,
yet no simple relationship, no romantic return to the past.

In his review of Spengler, by adducing the name of T. E.
Hulme, Tate leads us into a second element in the uneasy compound of his thought: his anti-romanticism. Anti-romanticism
would not hold up indefinitely for him, but in the 1920s he endorsed the views of T. E. Hulme. It is hard today to see why
Hulme could ever have claimed such strong allegiance as he did
in the earlier part of the century. His essay "Classicism and
Romanticism" proclaimed that what was wanted in poetry was

an end to the dewy, the optimistic, the infinity-addicted poetry
of romanticism with its emphasis on imagination. In its place
Hulme wanted a dry, confined poetry of classicism with an
emphasis not upon imagination but upon fancy. The distinction
between imagination and fancy derives, one supposes, from Coleridge. The main trouble with Hulme's view is that it poses
good classical theory against bad romantic practice. It scarcely
asks *whose* classicism, *whose* romanticism. It never faces up to
the fact that both classicism and romanticism evince many
manifestations and that both produce extremes of aberration.
Hulme, furthermore, could not see that though the twentieth
century was rebelling against romanticism, the rebellion itself
was romantic. Nevertheless, Hulme could claim allegiance because his principles did give philosophic support to modern poetry's predilection for the concrete image, the finite terrain, the
employment of wit, and, above all, spiritual and intellectual
scepticism.

Tate had accepted Hulme's theories rather early and had
brought them into the discussions of the Fugitives. These
theories supported his impatience with, say, Shelley or Whitman. In a way they ultimately separated him from Hart Crane's
view of poetry, even though Crane had some respect for Hulme.
But just as he could believe in and still be unaffected by Spengler, Crane could believe in and be unaffected by Hulme. What
Crane could both believe in and be affected by was some kind
of seraphic vision. For this reason he was drawn to P. D. Ouspensky's beliefs as set forth in the *Tertium Organum.* Insofar as
these beliefs affect the literary mind, they do so by reason of
Ouspensky's concept of a unifying reality underlying the surface
manifestations of reality. For Ouspensky this reality was not
exactly a Platonic construct, even though it sounds like it, but
an adaptation from modern physical science. It was the "fourth
dimension" which he offered as a unifying correction to the illusion of time and space. It needs to be added that for him the
glimpse of this reality or dimension was evanescent and, if one
may judge from his prose, it was ineffable. Crane adopted Ouspensky's vocabulary to the extent of discussing poetry in the
terms of *phenomenon,* or superficial chaos, and *noumenon,* or
the underlying principle of unity perceived through vision. Tate

also used these terms, but only to reject them. In a letter written shortly after Hart Crane's decampment from Patterson, Tate flatly insisted to Mark Van Doren that "there is no *noumenon* and Imagination doesn't exist." He asserted that his own view, which he called "neo-realism" found no meaning in either "phenomenon" or "noumenon." "Because," he continued, "of our saturation, by influence, in German philosophy we are apt to think these terms to be categories—necessary ways of thinking." He rejects their validity and goes on to say that he ignores "substance altogether as an abstraction impossible of concretion. . . . Events take its place, and poetry instead of being substance (*noumenon*) becomes quality, an *aspect* of *events*—'a prehensive unity' of those aspects. This I believe is classical as opposed to romantic; it remains the emphasis from the mind as individual victor over mechanical nature. . . . I daresay until Hulme wrote, about ten years ago, that view was utterly lost to thought."[10]

These views Tate refined and published in the first of his important essays—though not one he has chosen to collect, "Poetry and the Absolute," published in *The Sewanee Review* for January 1927. But what do these views signify? They signify that Tate had decided to put his chips not on Keatsian essences, but on classical universals. Essence, for a poet like Keats, involves subjective will power. It involves an insistence upon *imposing* order—no matter what kind of order, upon the random confusions of existence. Universals, in the classical sense, involve the objective discovery of what exists as order—if it can be found. Hence, for the young Mr. Tate, the "aspect of things" took on a problematical importance. It would be, evidently, through the objective parade of occurence that he would discover universals. And yet, he himself ineluctably must be the viewer. And so, he saw that as the viewer he was limited within a subjective boundary. From such a limitation there was but one escape, and that was through "tradition," for if there were a tradition—cultural, social, religious—that would in itself compose a universal to which the subjective viewer of the aspect of things would be ancillary. The subjective and the objective would coincide. That he did not see a viable tradition functioning in his contemporary society did not diminish the desirability

of tradition, but it left him suspended and thwarted. Hence, he
would have to search for an equivalent, while continuously falling short of finding it. His poems for five or six years detail this
search and this falling short. Thus, he saw modern poetry as a
catalogue of "failures." He could admire MacLeish's poetry, for
example, but still find it a failure. The same with Hart Crane's.
Clearly, this word "failure," which haunts his reviews and earlier essays, did not necessarily mean that the poet was writing
badly. It meant that his poetry could not find any equivalent of
universals, any support from a tradition of belief and feeling.

A final facet of Tate's complex cosmogony remains: his quarrel with twentieth-century "Humanism," in itself a subject almost as complex as Tate's cosmogony. Two of the most conse-
quential philosophic forces in modern conviction are those of
pragmatism, subtending from William James to John Dewey,
and of Bergsonian vitalism. As different as James's and Bergson's
views are—the one naturalistic, scientific, the other intuitional
and mystical—they nevertheless collude in the various manifestations of Humanism, offered to the century by Irving Babbitt,
Norman Foerster, and Paul Elmer More. For both the Jamesian
and Bergsonian schools assume eternal progress, which simply
means that they presuppose a continuum wherein all forms of
existence, consciousness, social ideals, and so forth, move
infinitely on toward a receding horizon, and everything gets better and better. Presumably, then, if anything is bad it can only
be a lower or earlier stage of evolution, but it would not necessarily be recognized as bad until it was in the past and
ineffectual. Likewise, what might be good could never be
known, for it would of logical necessity exist only in the future.
This analysis exaggerates but only to emphasize the abstract and
relativistic view of that once new religion which has engaged
many minds in this century and has led step by step to the emi-
nence of what is termed "social science" today. The exaggeration should also serve to emphasize how slippery the concepts of
good and evil are within such a system, and how in the near
absence of such concepts, the will, like a man in a condition of
weightlessness, has nothing to thrust against; it allows of no up
or down. The will exists, but what does it have for a guide? And
if nothing, then what is the purpose of will? Tate, in line with

T. S. Eliot, could only deplore the new positivistic religion, for it directly confronted his anti-romanticism (no lover of progress from John Stuart Mill to Marx to Bertrand Russell has quite been able to hate Shelley); it confronted his urgent need for the discipline of tradition; it left everything to individual velleity, hence everything to sensibility.

In 1927 Tate earnestly wrote to Herbert Read, praising his book *Reason and Romanticism,* offering to help find an American publisher for it. Tate disagreed with Read's reliance on psychoanalysis, but approved his Thomistic basis for attacking Humanism.[11] Eventually Tate was convinced that Humanism and naturalism could be considered an identity, an idea which he pursued in his essay "The Fallacy of Humanism," published first in T. S. Eliot's *Criterion* (July 1929) and republished in *The Critique of Humanism* (1930).

For Tate, Humanism was flaccid, therefore dangerous; it wanted tendon; it obfuscated the domain of morality; it denied the polarities of life, heaven and hell, God and Satan; which is to say, Humanism aimed to remove the sacred myths from life, thus from literature. Make no mistake about it, Tate's classicism, his sense of tradition, his belief in form demanded these polarities along with recognition and respect for the power of Satan.

This then is the composition of Tate's mind in the mid-1920s. These are the pluses and minuses, no more, no less consistent than the mental composition of most artists. Still his overriding view possessed one transcendent consistency. That was the insistence on center, a center to be apprehended in the pulls of counterpoised energies, sustained like a planetary system by gravity. The configuration would in time alter, but for the time being the faiths in tradition and religion and the repugnance toward romanticism and Humanism would inform most of what he was to write, even his Civil War biographies.

If the biographies do belong in the overriding pattern of Tate's thought in the 1920s, still some circumspection must direct one's approach to them, particularly the first, *Stonewall Jackson,* published in 1928. It must be remembered, first of all, that Tate was dependent upon writing for a living and he must have regarded the biographies to a degree expediently. The suggestion is not, however, that *Stonewall Jackson,* whatever else it is, is at base a potboiler; but, as will become clear shortly, decisions about the style of the book appear to have been dictated by a desire for a popular success. In the second place, his biographies were conceived as parts of a larger plan which had as its consummation a biography of Robert E. Lee. And so, they are pointing toward a biography on which Tate worked on for several years but which he abandoned before completion. Third and finally, *Stonewall Jackson* speaks often from a satiric basis.

If one will take the trouble to consult a copy of *Stonewall Jackson* in, say, the library of a large Midwestern university, he will in all likelihood find that the margins are glossed by generations of indignant students. The marginalia will consist of terse exclamation marks or "Tate!!!" and at times extended counterarguments, raw sarcasms and jovial indecencies. Alas, the indignation all too often results from an inability to read, for when Tate tries to capture how Southerners felt during the 1860s, it is taken as his personal assessment of the universal truth of the situation. Equally often, his tone goes unappreciated. Tate delights in calling the Northerners "rebels," for example. Again and again with deadpan demeanor he turns the sentimental clichés of the Northern view of the War 180 degrees. And in fact, the deflation of moral pieties and sanctimonious idealism is the most effective aspect of the book. There are aspects that are not so very effective.

Primarily one may be put off by a distressing tendency on Tate's part to gloat over the stupidity of Northern generals. The stupidity existed, but Tate too often loses the sense of the tragedy of a war which should never have been fought, which accomplished nothing good that time would not have accomplished, and did not succeed in holding—at least spiritually—the North and South together. That loss of a sense of tragedy debars *Stonewall Jackson* from any claim to high importance. Likewise, President Lincoln's dilemma is lost in unfavorable cartoons of him. Another defect issues from Tate's partiality to ponder what might have been the course of history, had some event been turned in a way other than what in historical fact it was. Doubtless, such indulgence in ineffectual prophecy is one of the pleasures of history, but it is not history. Finally, there is the matter of style. Fairness requires the observation that the style of *Stone-*

wall Jackson has its admirers, among them Meiners, Bradbury, and Stewart. One can readily agree with them that the narrative moves rapidly, clearly, and interestingly. Yet consider the following paragraph:

> It was a good place to read and think. You could hear only the water in the mill-race or the slow, steady trickle of the overflow of the dam. He lay in the shadow of the old grist mill. The mill stood at the nose of a peninsula made by the winding Monongahela River, in Lewis County, Virginia. About three miles north of the town of Weston the river turns dead east for a half-mile, then northwest. The land hemmed in by the water is black and fertile.

What is this style that is unlike any prose Tate had written before or would write again? Well, it is much like Ernest Hemingway's. At least it evinces several qualities that are associated with Hemingway's style: the monotony of simple sentence structure, the random clutter of detail, the arrangement by other than logical sequence. Now, Hemingway's style perfectly fits the consciousness of heroes who fear "thinking," or do not want to think if they can avoid it, or who have no capacity to think at all. But anti-cerebration is foreign to Tate, and this style cannot convey either his subtlety or his ratiocinative virtues. So that one feels in *Stonewall Jackson* that the surface of the style obscures something which is far more intricate than the language intimates. Perhaps for this reason, as much as the misinterpreted tone, the book has been thought a celebration of the Southern plantation past. That interpretation makes of *Stonewall Jackson* a contradiction of Tate's earlier essay "Last Days of a Charming Lady" wherein he had gently deplored the genial inadequacy of plantation culture. But there is no contradiction. The failures of the Confederate cause are blamed largely on the gentlemanly effeteness of President Davis and to a lesser degree on General Lee. Furthermore, Tate writes that if Jackson had lived until 1900 he would have seen "a whole people . . . sorely afflicted with the delusion of ancient grandeur." The key word here is clearly *delusion*. Finally, one must see that Stonewall Jackson's brilliance as a commander, his ability to act promptly, is associated with his *not* having been an aristocrat. It is his early poverty, his self-education, his pioneer qualities that Tate emphasizes. *Stonewall Jackson* could on the strength of this primary insight have been a superb book. But it is written with gusto rather than taste.

The opposite is true of the poetry which, chronologically speaking, surrounds *Stonewall Jackson*. That Tate was aware of his own advance over the poems published in *The Fugitive* is evidenced by his choice of poems for *Fugitives, an Anthology of Verse* (1928). Of the poems he selected—"Ignis Fatuus," "To a Romanticist," "Mr. Pope," "Death of Little Boys," "Obituary," "Idiot," "Procession," "Ode to the Confederate Dead," and "Causerie II"—only "Procession" had been published in *The Fugitive*, though three of them had been composed as early as 1924. This anthology represents the last official act of the Fugitives. Davidson had sought ways to keep the group alive after the demise of the magazine, thinking first of an annual publication of verse. Tate himself suggested the anthology and also, after considerable difficulty, secured Harcourt, Brace and Company as publisher. The anthology served to confirm the historicity of the group. And if it tended to exaggerate in the scholarly world a cohesion of interest among the members it also served to affirm the significance of the poetry of Ransom, Davidson, Tate, and Warren. The collection was widely, respectfully and sometimes enthusiastically reviewed. That was gratifying to Tate, but his own contributions show that he had moved well beyond the poems he had written in the comradeship of the Nashville group, even though they preserve sufficient of his earlier voice that his growth is not one of drastic change. At the same time these poems, which form the nucleus of his first book of verse, give earnest of the future poetic development.

Mr. Pope and Other Poems, published in the fall of 1928 by Minton, Balch and Company was an uneven book; but it is easy to forget the unevenness, and there is no point in dwelling on the inclusion of the kind of poem, such as "Prayer to the Woman Mountain," for which Tate had at best only slight talent. What is important is that the book contained important poems. Let the rest go. In later collections Tate himself let them go.

The title poem makes particular claims on our attention. "Mr. Pope" has puzzled readers, and the last line, syntactically amazing, may always puzzle readers. But let us see; perhaps that troubling last line falls—if we proceed with the proper assumptions—within the probabilities of the poem. It is well to begin with the knowledge that the subject of the poem is the relationship of a poet to society, superficially that of Alexander Pope to eighteenth-century society, but by extension of any poet to the world. One notices throughout the four brisk iambic quatrains how the world seeks to possess, in various ways but always in false ways, the poet. In the first quatrain ladies lean from their sedans to stare at the misshapen poet "more out of fear than pity." The second and third stanzas remark how the "bones" of the poet become in their urn "a frivolous rust."

> And he who dribbled couplets like a snake
> Coiled to a lithe precision in the sun
> Is missing. The jar is empty; you may break
> It only to find that Mr. Pope is gone.

The attempt to hold, to label the poet in an urn is pointless. And one should at this moment remark how strongly the strange but marvelously apt image of the snake's tension in the sun destroys with its vitality the very notion of capturing the reality of the poet in a funerary urn. And then the last lines:

> What requisitions of a verity
> Prompted the wit and rage between his teeth
> One cannot say. Around a crooked tree
> A moral climbs whose name should be a wreath.

The common ground in all four stanzas is that of pseudo-possession. The ladies think of Pope not as his poetry but as a hunchback; that is their fallacious way of trying to encompass his genius. In so doing they fail to touch the poetry. The urn similarly fails. At the end one assumes that the crooked tree is Pope the hunchback, and here another failure occurs, the substitution on the part of the world of a "moral" for a "wreath." Which is to say, the passion to possess, to encompass, to contain

the man rather than his poetry proceeds ultimately to rationalistic teleology (moral) rather than aesthetic acquiescence
(wreath). The nature of Pope's poetry cannot be found in the
discoverable man, yet the world would have it so. In one way
the poem seems precociously to announce the emphasis of what
was later called the "New Criticism": the emphasis on the poem
itself rather than the litorals of biography or history.

Many of the poems in *Mr. Pope and Other Poems* demonstrate
Tate's irritability toward an environment he detested. In general
that environment was the whole of the western world with its
many facets and its absence of any face. Specifically the environment was New York City. Malcolm Cowley tells us that one
evening he, Tate, and Hart Crane looked at the city's skyline
and felt it was their sacred duty to capture the beauty and terror of the century's spirit.[12] If so, Tate neglected part of his
duty. For his emphasis was not on beauty. In "Retroduction to
American History" (1925) he contrasts antiquity's use of myths
to "breach mortality" with the disintegration of myth in the
modern world where "Narcissus is vocabulary." The result of
this "vocabulary" is that we lack "language." Without myth,
without language he can only wonder "When shall I wake?" A
further deprivation derives from the debasement of myth. Religion dies, as Tate observes in "Causerie" (1925):

>   For miracles are faint
> And resurrection is our weakest clause of religion,
> I have known men in my youth who foundered on
> This point of doctrine: John Ransom, boasting hardy
> Entelechies yet botched in the head, lacking grace;
> Warren thirsty in Kentucky, his hair in the rain, asleep;
> None so unbaptized as Edmund Wilson the unwearied,
> That sly parody of the devil. They lacked doctrine;
> They waited. I, who watched out the first crisis
> With them, wait. . . .

The ambience of "Causerie" is set by an epigraph clipped from
a newspaper:

> . . . *party on the stage of the Earl Carroll Theatre on Feb.*
> *23. At this party Joyce Hawley, a chorus-girl, bathed in the*

nude in a bathtub filled with alleged wine.—New York
Times.

The most successful of Tate's poems in this vein and the one
which comes closest to capturing a beauty in the terror of the
great city is "The Subway" (1925). It should be read alongside
Crane's "Tunnel" section of *The Bridge*.

> Dark accurate plunger down the successive knell
> Of arch on arch, where ogives burst a red
> Reverberance of hail upon the dead
> Thunder like an exploding crucible!
> Harshly articulate, musical steel shell
> Of angry worship, hurled religiously
> Upon your business of humility
> Into the iron forestries of hell:
>
> Till broken in the shift of quieter
> Dense altitudes tangential of your steel,
> I am become geometries, and glut
> Expansions like a blind astronomer
> Dazed, while the worldless heavens bulge and reel
> In the cold revery of an idiot.

It is impossible to imagine improvements on this gravely powerful sonnet which skirts the wild heavens of Einsteinian relativ-
ism, then falters, diving like Lucifer to an accepted doom. "The
Subway" adumbrates Robert Lowell's poem written about
twenty years later about the Pepperpot Bridge in Boston.

While it is easy to categorize such poems as being coordinate
with others of the century, others which scratch the scab of civilization's apostasy from grace, one must also see that, with far
greater urgency than one finds in the early Eliot or Pound, Tate
seeks a solution. For after all is said, and even allowing for
Eliot's religiosity and Pound's macabre economics, Eliot and
Pound really very much enjoyed the decadence they recorded.
Prufrock loves—and isn't this precisely his power?—those streets,
those restaurants, those phantasmagoric parties. But Tate feared
that poetry itself could not rise above its era. He had, after coming to New York, decided that the verse of the Fugitives was too
pessimistic, that it ought to be more "triumphant," and he

wrote his friends in Nashville to that effect. Yet he himself could
not find the way to such felicity. It seems probable that this inability led him to his theory of a poetry restricted to "the aspect
of things," which translates simply, but not too simply, into a
poetry based upon a subjective vision of reality. The attempt to
write such a poetry led to two poems of consummate despair.
These are "Death of Little Boys" (1925) and "Ode to the
Confederate Dead" (1926).

"Death of Little Boys" opens with the observation that when
little boys die "the event will rage terrific as the sea." Nevertheless, the event cannot escape from its prison of feeling to the
freedom of exonerating meaning. Even nature only "extends a
fear to you / From one peeled aster drenched with the wind all
day." (The word "peeled" has stumped a few commentators.
But why, it is hard to say. It does not seem a particularly trying
use of language. It is late in the year; the color or vitality has
been stripped from the flower as, for example, the bright peel of
an apple can be peeled away.) Mourners visit the body, "turn
down / Their palms":

> and delirium assails the cliff
> Of Norway where you ponder, and your little town
> Reels like a sailor drunk in a rotten skiff.
>
> The bleak sunshine shrieks its chipped music then
> Out to the milkweed amid the fields of wheat.
> There is calm for you where men and women
> Unroll the chill precision of moving feet.

Two allusions apparently infiltrate these last lines. First, the allusion to the cliffs of Norway, which takes the reader into Edgar
Allan Poe's story "The Descent into the Maelström." Here Poe's
narrator contemplates the fury of the sea (surely Tate's third
line about the event's raging "terrific as the sea" foreordains
the allusion) and, both attracted and repelled, throws himself on
the earth for fear he will leap over the cliff. The second allusion
is that of the sailor drunk in a rotten skiff. This may, though the
allusion is less clear than the maelström, remind one of Rimbaud's poem "The Drunken Boat," or of Poe's demonic, self-
destructive hero in his novel *The Adventures of A. Gordon Pym.*

Whatever the case, the effect of these referent images is that of underlining a romantic and disordered subjectivity in the response to death, an excessive emotional terror, a suicidal mesmerism rather than intelligence or meaning in the event. What is left, then, in the way of "calm" is monotony, presumably of a funeral procession, but still a rather demented monotony of "moving feet." In an often quoted criticism of the poem John Crowe Ransom once wrote that Tate was "trifling with important substantives." The word "trifling" is interesting, if only for the reason that one of Ransom's own techniques is that of treating a profound experience with a skew lightness. And the word is not quite sympathetic to the realized intent of the poem; namely to record the failure of isolated feeling to recover anything meaningful from an event as terrific as the sea. The "Ode to the Confederate Dead," a profounder poem, follows in the same path.

By reason of its intrinsic importance the "Ode to the Confederate Dead" merits an approach as complicated as the poem and its backgrounds are complicated. To talk about it at all is like stripping an artichoke toward its heart. One begins at the outside because that is where one has to begin, and every bract is tipped with a thorn. The poem is the record of a failure, yet what caution must be observed with the word "failure." For it means an incompetence to create of experience, past and present, the kind of great and relevant expression which one associates with blossoming cultures, with the drama of Sophocles, for example. For Tate the age had no particular sense of purpose; its religion had deteriorated to social philosophy; hence he doubted that an artist could produce a statement incorporating a whole, steady vision. Thus he was stuck with only the possibly eccentric, probably small and scattered impressions of a subjective vision. Such was the extension of his belief that poetry should be concerned with "the aspect of things." But one must go back even further to his earlier intuitions about poetry. Tate had, it would seem, as early as 1922, begun to worry about whether art could fully succeed in embodying the age. But he hoped it could. In a not very good poem entitled "On a Portrait of Hart Crane," published in *The Double-Dealer* he asserts that though he has not yet "clasped" the hand of Crane he hopes to learn from him the way of "vision." "Vision" has an obvious relationship to "the aspect of things." What Tate ironically learned from Hart Crane was that a merely personal vision would not work well enough: that Crane himself could not weld together by vision a split view of America, could not hold together Whitman's democratic vistas and Poe's inverted image of the House of Usher. And so "vision," which is, after all, an aggrandizement of personality, failed. This failure partly accounts for Tate's concern with the past, for the past came to represent tradition. Tradition itself of course is seen to be significant because of continuities of idea, religion, and purpose in culture—all the things that Dante or Vergil could press into their art. But Tate could not fully believe in his own Southern tradition, for, as we have seen, it was, while preferable in his view to a New England tradition, fragmented and imperfect. Left with little confidence, he began to insist that great art could not be produced in the twentieth century. By 1927, Yvor Winters, with whom Tate had begun a correspondence, felt that he must chide Tate for feeling that the artist needed a total explanation of the whole universe. He further observed that this demand could only lead to paralysis, and that at any rate the view was absurd in one whose capacity to write significant poetry was of the highest order.[13]

Against this background of uncertainty and exasperation—not against a background of Southern Agrarianism—Tate wrote his ode. In it he does not celebrate the Confederate dead; he records his inability to celebrate. In short, he yields quite purely to a subjective treatment, or, to use the word Tate himself would have employed at the time, he yields to a poetry of mere "sensibility."

Tate has told us a number of valuable things about the poem in his essay "Narcissus as Narcissus" (1938). The essay originated in response to a request from Norman Holmes Pearson for commentary on the poem which he wanted to include in *The Oxford Anthology of American Literature* (1938). It grew beyond reasonable bounds for that purpose, though two paragraphs from the essay were published by Pearson as a note to the poem. Those paragraphs still serve their purpose:

> The structure of the Ode is simple. Figure to yourself a

man stopping at the gate of a Confederate graveyard on a late autumn afternoon. The leaves are falling; his first impressions bring him the "rumor of mortality"; and the desolation barely allows him, at the beginning of the second stanza, the conventionally heroic surmise that the dead will enrich the earth, "where these memories grow." From those quoted words to the end of that passage he pauses for a baroque meditation on the ravages of time, concluding with the figure of the "blind crab." This creature has mobility but no direction, energy, but from the human point of view, no purposeful world to use it in: in the entire poem there are only two explicit symbols for the locked-in ego; the crab is the first and less explicit symbol, a mere hint, a planting of the idea that will become overt in its second instance—the jaguar towards the end. The crab is the first intimation of the nature of the moral conflict upon which the drama of the poem develops: the cut-off-ness of the modern "intellectual man" from the world.

The next long passage or "strophe" beginning "You know who have waited by the wall," states the other term of the conflict. It is the theme of heroism, not merely moral heroism, but heroism in the grand style, elevating even death from mere physical dissolution into a formal ritual: this heroism is a formal ebullience of the human spirit in an entire society, not private, romantic illusion—something better than moral heroism, great as that may be, for moral heroism, being personal and individual, may be achieved by certain men in all ages, even ages of decadence. But the late Hart Crane's commentary, in a letter, is better than any I can make; he described the theme as the "theme of chivalry, a tradition of excess (not literally excess, rather active faith) which cannot be perpetuated in the fragmentary cosmos of today—'those desires which should be yours tomorrow,' but which, you know, will not persist nor find any way into action."

The essay also discloses the poetic procedures of the poem, the mounting rhythm, the varied lengths of the iambic lines, the shock tactics of unexpected rhymes. These disclosures are fascinating. It may be doubted that most readers could on their own uncover the ploys and gambits Tate extended. That is of slight

importance. As W. H. Auden has said, the poet himself is the
supreme expert on his own devices; no one can come up to him.
One is aware, however dumbly, of form, music, device and of
the organization of all of these things. One might be ignorant of
the turnings Tate lathed into the lines of the "Ode," but he
could not miss the severe music that falls and rises like the medieval *sequentia*. He might go innocent of the rhyme set like a
trap, but he does not go innocent of the shock of both sound and
image. Since Tate tells us as much as he does and speaks from
such incontrovertible authority, there is little to add. Here is
that little.

"Ode to the Confederate Dead" has been revised several
times. The version quoted here is the final one (1936)—a bad
choice with respect to chronology, yet a choice made inevitable
by the fact that the poem is what it became. Anyway, except for
the addition of a varied refrain, the emendations are not very
extensive. The refrain was added in 1930, as Tate tells us, to
pace the poem and render "quite plain the subjective character
of the poem throughout." It first appears as follows:

> Dazed by the wind, only the wind
> The leaves flying, plunge.

There are variations but all of them keep the wind-driven
leaves.

This leaf-refrain, though added almost five years after the first
draft of the poem, does not intrude some image which occurred
to Tate in greater maturity. On the contrary, the image may be
found in one form or another, even in this specific form, in
poems earlier than "Ode to the Confederate Dead." In the
fourth issue of *The Fugitive*, a sonnet entitled "These Deathy
Leaves" imagistically counterpoises the falling leaves against
love and rebirth. The autumnal theme and image are, of course,
too commonplace to constitute overpowering evidence of anything at all. Yet the image does seem obsessive with Tate. In the
very next issue of *The Fugitive* (February–March 1923) the image occurs again in the poem "Teeth," and here the context is
not that of rebirth but despondency and social decay:

> No music comes to sorrow like a thief,
> No twitter of birds, as in Spring, for eucharist;
> Only the soft thrust of a falling leaf
> And in the mind the bloodless lips of Christ.

The "bloodless lips of Christ" haunt Tate's poetry for two decades. The "soft thrust of a falling leaf" is ancestor to the leaves
that fall, plunging in the Ode. And the image means more in
Tate's poetry than it superficially seems to mean.

Throughout his verse, images of nature appear. These are
seldom simple or innocent—the peeled aster in "Death of Little
Boys" is exemplary of the kind. These images jut from the
poems with a curious sort of impertinence. Not that they do not
bring feeling to the poems, not that they cannot be justified by
various relationships, but that they are cold and ecdemic. They
are cold and ecdemic because they propose a nature that is
going its way alone, separate from man and from the passions or
sentiments of the poet. The natural observation can be emblematic of emotion or idea in Tate's poetry, but only by an *accident* of analogy. One may contrast this impression with that
which he derives from Frost's analogies between self and nature,
analogies which have about them an air of providence and inevitability. That may be a way of saying that Tate, unlike Frost,
has never admired Emersonian transcendentalism. Whatever the
reason, nature in Tate's poetry takes on an aspect of idiocy over
which he attempts to triumph with a universalizing adjective, a
fixative, one might say, as in the phrase "ambitious November"
from the "Ode." The attribution "ambitious," reminiscent of T.
S. Eliot's *depraved* May or *cruelest* April, is not pathetic fallacy
so much as ratiocinative fallacy, for it does not seek to draw
nature into a relationship of feeling; it seeks to set it apart in an
ideal attitude. One further observation on this score. The isolation from the natural environment is one which further isolates
the speaker in the "Ode" and therefore more certainly con-
demns him to his awareness only of the aspect of things. To
what degree the subjective isolation extends may be seen in the
third variation of the refrain, introduced by the line "You will
curse the setting sun":

> Cursing only the leaves crying
> Like an old man in a storm.

It is difficult here to avoid remembering King Lear and the subjective monomania in which he is imprisoned.

The speaker of the poem is imprisoned in the self and imprisoned therefore in darkness; the "Ode" is the darkest of Tate's poems, containing not a single image of light. That is noteworthy in a poem by a poet who is addicted to images of light. No, what one finds is "blind crab," "twilight certainty," "midnight restitutions," "willows without light." "Night is the beginning and the end," we are told. It is not surprising. As indicated earlier, the poem was written in a spirit of disillusionment in Hart Crane's faith in vision. But the disillusionment probably goes back at least a year earlier. The poem "Ignis Fatuus" (1925) shows a rejection of romantic vision. One says "romantic" because the fool's fire in the poem is associated with "fierce latinity." In the first stanza Tate writes:

> In the twilight of my audacity
> I saw you flee the world, the burnt highways
> Of summer gave up their light: I
> Followed you with the uncommon span
> Of fear supported and disbursed eyes

In the last stanza he writes:

> To the green tissue of the subterranean
> Worm I have come back, two-handed from
> The chase, and empty. I have pondered it
> Carefully, and asked: Where is the light
> When the pigeon moults his ease
> Or exile utters the creed of memory?

So much for vision at this point in Tate's career.

There is no light, then, in the "Ode to the Confederate Dead." Only the dark of self, which knows "the rage, / The cold pool left by the mounting flood, / Of muted Zeno and Parmenides," those Eleatic solipsists for whom reality was nothing more than illusion created within the mind. Two years before, Tate had feared that this might be the beginning and end of all poetry, for he had written in an editorial in The Fugitive for April 1924 that "the Modern poet might tell you that his only possible themes are the manifold projections and tangents of his own perception. It is the age of the Sophist."

If the "Ode," with its yielding to the theme of the self in an age without faith, is the blackest of Tate's poems, it nevertheless, by going down so deeply to the bedrock of his despair, prepared the way for future reconsiderations of the theme, efforts to dispel the shades of Zeno and Parmenides. Some of these efforts were to prove successful, and the more successful were to prove to be Tate's loftiest poems. Yet the impression must not stand that "Ode to the Confederate Dead" wants stature. One must argue its case at the highest level. Indeed, it belongs with some of the finest poems of the century, and it belongs with them because it shows with them its intense, though separate, treatment of the same thematic material. These poems must include T. S. Eliot's "The Love Song of J. Alfred Prufrock," Paul Valéry's "Marine Cemetery," and Wallace Stevens' "Sunday Morning." Each of these poems, though Eliot's is a dramatic monologue and Stevens' is a multi-voiced argument, is a meditation upon the relationship between subjective and objective worlds. For Eliot's agonist the inner world cannot pierce into an outer world. Valéry, like Tate, mentions "cruel Zeno" who freezes the world in subjective vision, but then goes on to suppose the subjective vision can give movement to existence. Stevens also ends confident of a subjective vision which he believes offers a metaphysics parallel to the clutter of objective phenomena, so that death is not only the *natural* but also the *mystical* mother of beauty. Tate's "Ode to the Confederate Dead" is bleaker than Eliot's poem, less humanly arrogant than Valéry's or Stevens', less willing to soften or dilute its theme. Though it was written later than the others, it should be read before them. For the theme behind his poem is the theme of the others, and it is an old theme: the *vanitas* about which St. Augustine knew everything.

Perhaps "Ode to the Confederate Dead" got too much attached to Tate's name—with the result that his finer poems have been disregarded. But it brought him early fame. This was a fame that Tate, the recipient of a Guggenheim award in 1928, took with him to Europe. He also took with him the unresolved dilemma of "Ode to the Confederate Dead," his question,

"What shall we say who have carried knowledge to the heart?" He meant, how shall the poetic self speak nobly and publicly of the past or present or of things to come? He had without knowing it answered his own question. At the end of the "Ode," he hears the silkworm eating mulberry leaves, and calls that creature a "gentle serpent" who is "Sentinel of the grave who counts us all." In "Narcissus as Narcissus" this serpent is explained as the universal symbol of "time." Of course it is, but if Tate had thought longer about his symbol he might have remembered that when Aeneas prays at his father's grave, a serpent wriggles up from the earth. That serpent was the spirit of his lineage, the spirit of the past, present, and future of the house.

CHAPTER FOUR

❧ Paris ❧

WITH HIS FIRST VOLUME OF POETRY BEHIND HIM, TATE COULD no longer rest content with writing a poem simply for the sake of writing a poem. He began to see that there was no point in duplicating performances. He expected his work to have continuity, yet he knew he must advance or be still. As a consequence, his production of poems fell off, although his production of essays increased. Tate was by this time nearing his thirtieth year, that difficult mark where the poet says goodbye to the easy time when poems tumble forth unbid, and says hello to the time when the poems come harder and—if he is lucky—come better. A little over a year after he wrote "Ode to the Confederate Dead," Tate wrote in the opening stanzas of "Fragment of a Meditation":

> Not yet the thirtieth year, the thirtieth
> Station where time reverses his light heels
> To run both ways, and makes of forward back;
> Whose long coordinates are birth and death
> And zero is the origin of breath:
> Not yet the thirtieth year of gratitude,
> Not yet suffering but a year's lack,
> All thanks that mid-mortality is done,
> That the new breath on the invisible track
> Winds anciently into my father's blood.

In the beginning the irresponsible Verb
Connived with chaos whence I've seen it start
Riddles in the head for the nervous heart
To count its beat on: all beginnings run
Like water the easiest way or like birds
Fly on their cool imponderable flood.

Then suddenly the noon turns afternoon
And afternoon like an ill-written page
Will fade, until the very stain of light
Gathers in all the venom of the night—
The equilibrium of the thirtieth age.

No matter apprehensions of the thirtieth age, Tate planned during his Guggenheim fellowship to finish his biography of Jefferson Davis and also to write a "long poem." The idea of a long poem—even though it was never finished—suggests that Tate was casting about for something deeper and more elaborate than he had heretofore tried. Something like that must have been his ambition when with Caroline and daughter Nancy he sailed for England in September 1928.

In London the American poetess Léonie Adams joined them and remained with them for the rest of their stay abroad. Just as in New York, Tate's circle of friends widened. He was taken by F. V. Morley to a *"Criterion* luncheon" where for the first time he met Herbert Read and T. S. Eliot, though he had previously corresponded with both. He writes:

> Read and I were nearly of an age and became friends as soon as his Yorkshire shyness allowed; this took a little time; but the twelve years between Mr. Eliot and myself were like the Grand Canyon that only after some years seemed to silt up until it was no wider than the Potomac above Washington; that is to say, about the width of the Mason and Dixon Line. I am sure that Mr. Eliot would not mind my saying that thirty-five years ago I felt closer to rural Yorkshire and to Herbert's grandmother, Jane Tate, than to Cousin Nancy Ellicott and the *Boston Evening Transcript*.[1]

Early in November the Tates went to Oxford where they met more of the British literary people and where they saw more of Eliot. Tate referred to him as "the prime cock who rules the roost." Still he found him a modest man, one who, if "he ever rode a high horse, he certainly doesn't now."² He felt little or no awe toward Eliot. His reaction to William Butler Yeats was a different matter. The English poet L. A. G. Strong in Oxford wanted to take Tate to meet Yeats, but, strange to say, Tate felt himself too callow and shyly refused the invitation.

The change of scene, new literary friends—and arguments— were stimulating to Tate, yet he felt an ambivalence about being abroad. The usual placebo for bemused travelers, that of sightseeing, would not work for him and Caroline. He confessed finally that he was no good at it, and wished "he were back in the United States."³ When, in late November, the weather in England turned damper and colder, the Tates with Miss Adams crossed over to France.

The Paris of 1928 was not quite the haven of the American expatriate that it had been a few years earlier. It was not quite the world of *The Sun Also Rises*. But most of the atmosphere and many of the people remained. Tate saw a good deal of Julian Green (with whom he shared Southern roots), Valéry Larbaud, Adrienne Monnier, Mario Praz, Morley Callaghan, and Sylvia Beach. At Sylvia Beach's Shakespeare Book Shop in the rue de l'Odeon, he noticed a large, dark "boy" whom he thought to be Hemingway. (Hemingway's picture was then appearing in advertisements for *A Farewell to Arms*, soon to be published.) Miss Beach introduced them, and Hemingway immediately suggested that they go to the Cafe Voltaire. As they walked along, Hemingway said, "You were wrong in that review. I've never read Captain Marryat." He was referring to Tate's review of *The Torrents of Spring* in *The Nation*, in which Tate had implied that Hemingway's style owed something to Marryat and Defoe. Over coffee at the Voltaire, Hemingway proceeded to vilify Ford Madox Ford who, as is now well known, had helped a younger Hemingway. Tate eventually surmised that Hemingway could not bear the idea of ever having been influenced or even aided by any other writer past or present. The two men were not temperamentally alike, yet they saw a good deal of each other in the next year. Tate recalls that "in the fall of 1928 he persuaded me to go one Sunday to the bicycle races at the Velodrome d'Iver. I didn't want to go, and I

went every Sunday of that winter. He could communicate his
enthusiasms more completely than any friend I have ever had."[4]

The salon of Gertrude Stein was still the center of literary
prestige. One day Tate received a note from Miss Stein, saying,
"You *will* come to tea next Thursday." He went. He remembers
clearly that famous apartment in the rue de Fleurus. "As you
entered the room on the right there was a little dais where Miss
Stein sat, her visitors sitting slightly below. The ladies who
might be present or who were coming in with us were whisked
off to the back of the room where Miss Alice B. Toklas had a
wonderful American chocolate cake. I never got any of it because I was always kept in the front of the room, at Miss Stein's
feet. That went on for some months, in fact for nearly a
year." On one occasion Ernest Hemingway came to the Tates'
pension and said "Gertrude has taken me back into favor."
Apparently she hadn't been speaking to Hemingway, and now
that she had decided to receive him again, he was "scared to
go and see her alone." And so he asked Tate to go along with
him for protection. That evening Miss Stein delivered a lecture
to the gentlemen at her feet, "nothing less than a kind of synop-
sis of the history of American literature from Emerson to about
1930. Emerson was the great forerunner because he had a genius for abstraction. He was not particularly concerned with experience. Hawthorne was practically impossible because he was
still European. Emily Dickinson was fairly good. Whitman was
on the right track. Henry James was really awfully good because
the design of his novels showed a genius for abstract construction; but alas, Henry James was also partly European. He was
bogged down in 'experience.' The climax, of course, of the lecture on American literature was that Miss Stein was the climax.
The genius for abstraction had finally realized itself in her." At
one point when Miss Stein paused, Tate, feeling that the silence
was embarassing made a remark which Miss Stein took as a contradiction. "Nonsense, my dear Tate," she said. "Nonsense!"[5] To
Mark Van Doren he wrote of this occasion: "She is really a delightful woman and mad as the March Hare. She says the only
thing she wants to see in America is the five and ten cent store.
She believes without much pretense to modesty that she is the
culmination of American literature—a theory of little intrinsic

interest; it shows what megalomania will do."[6] Tate did not really take to Miss Stein.

Tate could not believe that artistic talent and modesty were incompatible. He had the model of John Crowe Ransom in his past; the profounder friendships he made in Paris were with two men distinguished by modesty and kindness: Ford Madox Ford (Hueffer) and John Peale Bishop. Tate had made the acquaintance of Ford in 1925 in New York—Ford made many trips to America—and found him at that time "uninteresting" and "surrounded by sycophants to whom he played a role."[7] Still, Tate was a beneficiary of Ford's kindness, for it was Ford's recommendation that got him the Guggenheim award. And anyway Tate found him a different person in Paris. They became very close friends, and Tate frequently presided at sonnet-writing contests at Ford's apartment. Almost every night, as a matter of duty, he accompanied Ford to the Cafe des Deux Magots where Ford liked to play Russian Banque and drink brandy before retiring. Ford, in his mid-fifties at this time, was a bit lonely. His career had been long and diverse. He had written his first novel before he was twenty and was intimately associated by family relationships with a good deal of late nineteenth-century English literary life. He had known Henry James; he had—fantastic as it now seems—collaborated with Joseph Conrad on two novels. His own production was vast. Much of it was slack, yet he had written several extraordinary novels. He always thought of himself as one of the avant-garde. To the end he was deeply interested in new writers. And he liked to help them in practical ways. When Tate feared that he was going to run out of money long before the end of his planned year abroad, Ford took the Tates and Miss Adams under his wing—expecting, to be sure, little attentions in return. But his demands were of short duration since he sailed on January 30, 1929 for America and turned over to the Tates his apartment at 32 rue de Vaugirard rent-free for the next six months.

Tate had also met John Peale Bishop in New York. They were introduced by Kenneth Burke on a date Tate was not likely to forget—September 23, 1925, the date of his daughter's birth. But he did not get to know Bishop at the time, and did not see him again until 1928 in Paris. Tate shared with Bishop, who had been born and raised in West Virginia, a Southern heritage. However, Bishop had received most of his education in the North. He graduated in 1917 from Princeton where he had been a close friend of F. Scott Fitzgerald and Edmund Wilson. He had collaborated in a lugubrious hodgepodge of verse and prose with Edmund Wilson: *The Undertaker's Garland* (1922). He had worked for *Vanity Fair* and Paramount Pictures in New York City, but in 1926 he settled with his wife into a somewhat re- tired life in a chateau in Orgeval, about twelve miles outside Paris. He seemed in his isolation a bit abstracted and wanting in energy. He wished to write, but wrote very little. None of his literary friends, Hemingway, Fitzgerald, Wilson, or MacLeish, took him very seriously.

One evening in December 1928 Tate and Robert Penn War- ren, then a Rhodes Scholar who had come from Oxford to visit Caroline and Allen, spent an evening with Bishop over a bottle of scotch. Shyly, Bishop showed them some of his recent poems. Unlike his other friends, Tate and Warren were impressed. And Bishop dated from that evening a change in his life. Indeed, he wrote to Tate a few years later to say that he owed to that eve- ning hardly less than his life.[8] The friendship between him and Tate, who was seven years Bishop's junior, was for both of them a source of strength. To look through their correspondence is to discover how fully each trusted the other, and how fresh their friendship stayed. Their criticism of each other's work was never the usual harmless compliments which old friends seem to deliver almost as a reflex action. It was very careful criticism; they often suggested specific emendations of words or lines to each other. Upon occasion they wrote "companion pieces," poems which were variations on one of the other's poems or themes.

It was Bishop who introduced Tate to F. Scott Fitzgerald at a dinner party to which Tate arrived late:

> When I walked in and was introduced, he said, "Do you enjoy making love?" and I said, "It's none of your damn business." I told Bishop about this later in the evening, and he said, "Well, no matter what answer you give him you are convicted. It's heads I win, tails you lose. Fitzgerald asks everybody that, and he's not interested in your answer.

He's watching you very closely—the expression on your
face—to see how you deal with a disconcerting situation."[9]

Once settled in Ford's apartment Caroline and Allen turned
to their literary tasks. Caroline, finding that Ford's generosity
released her from many domestic cares, worked on her novel
Penhally. Tate worked alternately at his long poem and his life
of Jefferson Davis. The poem did not go well for him. Late in
January 1929 he wrote to Mark Van Doren:

> I fiddle and fuddle every morning with my poem which is
> doing very well so far as quantity goes—five hundred lines.
> But the trouble is I can't understand the lines I wrote two
> weeks ago. I oughtn't to be writing a long poem. It is un-
> fortunate, of course, that I didn't see that before I was
> given a salary to write it. I've got to write it, but no one I
> daresay will force me to publish it. There's hope of sanity
> in that. Some of the short poems are better, but they are
> something that the world will not willingly recognize, and
> for the first time I believe the world will be right.[10]

Why did Tate find writing a long poem so difficult, so alien?

Up to this point, the discussions of Tate's poems may have
been misleading. The emphasis has fallen upon appropriateness
of image and upon the complex of feeling and idea, which we
call "meaning." None of this is about to be retracted, but any
impression that Tate always began a poem with a clear, conceptual outline for which he recruited suitable devices is not true.
His poems in their finished states may look as if that is how they
were written; the best ones certainly do. But many of them began only with an image or a clot of language or only an ominous
cadence in a phrase. One wonders if Tate ever paused to ask if
the cool, classical, dry poetry that Hulme demanded could
evolve from such beginnings. The point here, however, is that a
long poem—say a poem of 1000 lines—has only the slightest
chance to emerge and build successfully from cryptic whispers.

As to the short poems Tate mentions in his letter, while his
deprecation seems harsh, it is true with one exception ("The
Cross"), that the poems he wrote in late 1928 and in 1929 do
not rank with his best. Of course, it is not clear from the letter
what poems he was thinking of, or even if he was thinking of

poems which he later chose to preserve. But probably he included among them "Mother and Son," a poem which confirms
the hypothesis that Tate's works begin in uncertainty and attain
meaning only during composition. He tells us: "This poem was
written in Paris in 1928, one morning when suddenly the first
line came to mind, without warning of what the poem would be
about; the first draft was very rapid."[11] "Mother and Son" is a
baroque mixture of subjective passion and universal theme. But
the subjectivity is not "autobiographical" or "confessional." The
theme is, generally, the great theme of love and antagonism
between mother and son. The two engage each other only with
the silent weapon of psychological pressure:

> The falcon mother cannot will her hand
> Up to the bed, nor break the manacle
> His exile sets upon her harsh command
> That he should say the time is beautiful—
> Transfigured by her own possessing light:
> The sick man craves the impalpable night.
>
> Loosed betwixt eye and lid, the swimming beams
> Of memory, blind school of cuttlefish,
> Rise to the air, plunge to the cold streams—
> Rising and plunging the half-forgotten wish
> To tear his heart out in a slow disgrace
> And freeze the hue of terror to her face.

Of the latter stanza Tate writes:

> The cuttlefish, symbol of memory, has puzzled a few read-
> ers. This disagreeable creature blinds its prey by squirting a
> black fluid into the water, in which it hides: a man in emo-
> tional danger withdraws into his private mind where not
> even maternal love can follow him and where he becomes
> mysterious and menacing.[12]

How strange, one says, for this poem to intrude itself upon
Tate in Paris. Not that the visitations of the muse are so very
orderly, but they usually have some connection with the present
as well as the past. But the minute one says "the present," the
poem opens, and "the present" can be seen. The emotional dan-
ger, the retreat into mind or memory, attached in the poem to

the mother-son relationship, occurred to Tate in Paris because
he suffered, as he had in England, from cultural disorientation.
Along with disorientation came a graceless intellectual guilt. It
is relevant that at this time Tate was engaged in correspondence
with Donald Davidson and other Fugitives on the subjects
which led to the Southern Agrarian Movement. The mother-son
relationship in the poem offers a symbolic dramatization of his
separation from the homeland of his art, a separation from a
duty as demanding as the duty owed a mother. But of course
this analysis, open to charges of case-making and ingenuity, does
not suggest that the poem is *about* being separated from America, or that it at any point should be approached with that
theory in mind. No, one does not read a poem for its primary
cause. The poem is as it appears; it is about mothers and sons.
This analysis merely attempts to see the poem in relation to
Tate's mode of composition and in relation to a dominant mood
of cultural shock and homesickness.

   In the latter respect we are on surer ground with another
poem of the Paris period. "Message from Abroad" is addressed
to Andrew Lytle and dated "Paris, November, 1929," but the
poem was begun almost a year earlier and so is temporally close
to "Mother and Son." It opens with an epigraph from *Traveler
to America* (1799): "Their faces are bony and sharp but very red,
although their ancestors for nearly two hundred years have
dwelt by the miasmal banks of tidewaters where malarial fever
makes men gaunt and dosing with quinine shakes them as with a
palsy." In the poem Tate thinks of the red-faced men as his ancestors, therefore as his tradition; he thinks in Paris of how tradition of any sort comes down to the present. Some cultures,
"Provence, / The Renascence, the age of Pericles" come down
clearly, their history known, their art preserved. Others, wanting
"poetry and statures," are mute, lost, undiscoverable, though
Tate seems to suggest that such cultures may retain a virile
power that more artistically florid cultures sacrifice. At any rate
Tate observes that here in Paris his awareness of the red-faced
man, that westering pioneer, who had dogged him in the past,
has been lost:

>   The red-faced man, ceased wandering,
>   Never came to the boulevards

> Nor covertly spat in the sawdust
> Sunk in his collar
> Shuffling the cards . . .

M. E. Bradford in his sensitive study *Rumors of Mortality* accurately notes that being unable to "see" the red-faced ancestors is equivalent to being unable to see the dead soldiers in "Ode to the Confederate Dead." Bradford continues:

> Here, in Tate's steadiest meditative vein, the way of James and Joyce (the way followed by so many Americans in this decade) is rejected: aestheticism seen into and through. A few "centuries broken, divided up, and claimed" will not serve. . . . Return to America, it is implied, he must. Drifting the cold sea and (spiritual) drowning or the greater emasculating perils of the already remarked aestheticism are the alternatives.[13]

To these observations may be added that the poem is impelled by an equivocal guilt which involves the contrast between the incorruptible silent ancestor and the articulate cultures of Europe. But the guilt does not rest in an implication that Tate feels he is bad because he is in Europe or that he would be good if he were in Kentucky. Indeed, does anyone who is quite convinced that he is bad really feel guilt at all? The emotion of guilt—and make no mistake, guilt is one of the great emotions—rests upon uncertainty. To the same period belongs the extraordinary poem "Records." It shares an ancestral obession with "Message from Abroad." Since its significance lies, however, in other directions, it will be considered in a later chapter.

At this moment one may with exasperation demand: Why all the bother? Why all the to-do over soldiers dead in a war fought in another century? Why all the fuss over ancestors? A Middle Westerner like Hemingway was not asking these questions. Nor was Fitzgerald. Nor MacLeish. Nor Robert Frost—he went out and manfully cleaned the pasture spring or picked too many apples or mowed the hay around islands of flowers and birds' nests. Why should Tate worry the past? Perhaps no Northerner can give an answer. He can approach an answer by marking the fact that it is from his feelings as a Northerner that the question arises. That is to say, the Northerner views the past as a contin-

uum in which the Civil War is only one of many episodes. For
the Southerner the past is not a continuum, and the Civil War
represents a break after which the aim of southern culture wa-
vers. In feeling a fracture in the past, the time before that fracture becomes to the Southerner peculiarly precious. That is
where much of his spiritual loyalty lies, and it is no paradox that
the Southerner is far more patriotic both in peace and war than
the Northerner. His patriotism involves the protection of a past
which, because he is exiled from it, is especially sacred.

In Europe Allen Tate continued to think about tradition with
the same intensity he had brought to it since 1924. And a slight
but nevertheless meaningful shift took place in his attitudes.
Even before going abroad a change was implicit in his consideration of Emily Dickinson in an essay published in *Outlook*
(August 15, 1928). Yvor Winters wrote to Tate to say that he
considered the essay without reservation the most brilliant criticism of the era.[14] Well, its brilliance depends to a great degree
on Tate's alignment of Dickinson's poetry with his own concern about tradition. He sees her as a poet of "ideas," a statement which has misled some to suppose that he thinks of Dickinson as an intellectual poet. Nothing could be farther from his
intent, for these "ideas" are not her creation, nor are they very
rationally maintained. They are her tradition or inheritance
from the theological autocracy of Puritanism. Her ideas or assumptions of truth sustain her and her poetry. She need not
think about them; and, indeed, Tate says that she "could not in
the proper sense think at all."

> . . . and unless we prefer the feeble poetry of moral ideas
> that flourished in New England in the eighties, we must
> conclude that her intellectual deficiency contributed at
> least negatively to her great distinction. Miss Dickinson is
> probably the only Anglo-American poet of her century
> whose work exhibits the perfect literary situation—in which
> is possible the fusion of sensibility and thought. Unlike her
> contemporaries, she never succumbed to her ideas, to easy
> solutions, to her private desires.

Now, the fusion of sensibility and intellect is exactly what Tate
would seek in his future poetry. The absence of such a fusion is

exactly what he lamented in "Ode to the Confederate Dead." It is noteworthy, therefore, that he finds the fusion in a New England poet. Indeed, he sees this same New England tradition as the basic fortune of Melville and Hawthorne:

> The important thing to remember about the puritan theocracy is that it permeated, as it could never have done in England, a whole society. It gave final, definite meaning to life, the life of pious and impious, of learned and vulgar alike. It gave—and this is its significance for Emily Dickinson, and in only slightly lesser degree for Melville and Hawthorne—it gave an heroic proportion and a tragic mode to the experience of the individual.

Tate, one sees, is speaking primarily of a religious tradition—not of economics or politics. This aspect of his essay on Emily Dickinson predicts the true nature of Tate's commitment to the Agrarian Movement in which he would shortly be embroiled. One may speculate as to whether Tate might not have begun to consider religion the primary quality of a unified culture.

Certainly in his own life, Tate was pondering the necessity for religious dogma. Early in 1929 he was writing to Herbert Read with the primary purpose of pursuing their mutual disagreement with Norman Foerster's Humanism, but Tate's focus was very often on religion. Read caught the religious overtones, and Tate felt compelled to explain himself: "I am not," he wrote " 'in the arms' of any church; though I am convinced there is only one church capable of meeting us with a really warm embrace."[15] And Tate was more explicit in his letters to Donald Davidson, to whom he mentioned his gloominess over the disunity of the modern world, so that Davidson felt compelled to beg him not to follow T. S. Eliot in a religion of Anglican conservatism, which Davidson thought not "good enough" for his friend.[16] And John Gould Fletcher, whom Tate had met in New York in 1927 and seen again in London where he lectured Tate on the virtues of the British middle class, observed later that he thought that Tate had by instinct always been a Roman Catholic.

Nevertheless, it is true that Tate was not at this time in the arms of any church. It is also true that religion kept emerging as a possible answer to various questions. The absence of religion was the error of the Humanists; religion might bring unity to the modern world. And so forth. However, these postulates were intellectual. If he felt the need for religion he could not quite feel religion itself. Christ's lips remained "cold." All of this complex of urgency and indecision is documented in his best poem of the period. "The Cross," interestingly enough, was first called "The Pit." Like "Mother and Son," it began without any conscious impression as to where it was going to go. It was written rapidly in the space of about three hours on November 8, 1928.[16]

> There is a place that some men know,
> I cannot see the whole of it
> Nor how I came there. Long ago
> Flame burst out of a secret pit
> Crushing the world with such a light
> The day-sky fell to moonless black
> The kingly sun to hateful night
> For those, once seeing, turning back:
> For love so hates mortality
> Which is the providence of life
> She will not let it blessèd be
> But curses it with mortal strife,
> Until beside the blinding rood
> Within that world-destroying pit
> —Like young wolves that have tasted blood,
> Of death, men taste no more of it.
> So blind, in so severe a place
> (All life before in the black grave)
> The last alternatives they face
> Of life, without the life to save,
> Being from all salvation weaned—
> A stag charged both at heel and head:
> Who would come back is turned a fiend
> Instructed by the fiery dead.

R. K. Meiners discusses the poem intelligently and affectionately, correctly pointing out its unities. Some of the dissonances of the poem also need to be pointed out. One can paraphrase the general meaning of "The Cross" as follows: the emergence of Christianity placed before mankind the vision of immortality, and, as young wolves who have tasted their first warm blood are never content with mere flesh, man will "taste no more" of death. On the latter part of the poem Mr. Meiners comments: "We, as the heirs of the Christian tradition, have become 'blind' to the 'world'—it no longer nourishes us. . . . We have in a sense been 'buried with Christ,' in the words of the formula, but we have been buried to a form of living death, not to the 'new life' which baptism is meant to symbolize. . . . In such a condition the last alternatives of life are faced. The alternatives are, of course, the questions of life and death in a supernatural sense. But still 'without the life to save': the meaning of 'life' has shifted from the previous line. The usage of a single word with double meanings is typical of Tate; here, the life which cannot be saved is life in *this* world. This is one more insistence on the impossibility of returning to a pre-supernatural life. Such a return might be comforting, but it is historically and psychologically impossible."[18]

These responses to the poem are valuable, and Tate's correspondence with Meiners indicates that in general he approves the interpretation. A doubt nags, however. For the imagery of cosmic light and death, of lupine greed and beleaguered stag, of fiend and fiery dead all confer severe strains upon the poem; like a world *crushed* by a vision of immortality, it staggers under the burden of Christianity. The chances, the alternatives of Christianity, thus, seem cruel. And life has not been simply "life" since the advent of Christ who brings the concept of damnation as well as salvation. If these relationships are true, "The Cross" is not a "Christian" poem so much as a psychological poem, documenting the nearly unbearable strains of Christianity, the very strains Nietzsche felt Christianity had imposed upon Western man. It seems, therefore, not so much a devotional poem as one which merges a history of Christianity with a private religious ambivalence and weariness. The speaker of this poem would as gladly lief be rid of religion as he would be immersed in it. Yet conversion is sometimes preceded by acedia. It may therefore be that Tate was inching toward religious confidence. For the time being, however, he tended to view religion somewhat intellectually as a counterforce to a dark trinity of humanism, positivism, and science. In addition, his religious ideas were

layered between the strata of his concerns with his familial past
and southern history.

On July 14, 1929, the last day the Tates stayed in Ford's
apartment, Allen completed his life of Jefferson Davis. It is in all
respects a better book than *Stonewall Jackson*. Its style is
wedded to the subject matter; it is quiet and dignified; there is
no effort to intimidate the reader with sentences shaped like
bricks. Nor does *Jefferson Davis* contain the outrageous burlesque
of its predecessor. Abraham Lincoln, for example, is no longer
caricatured. In fact, he is regarded somewhat as Tate regarded
Emily Dickinson, Hawthorne, and Melville. His is given a "sublime" and "mystical" character which the Northern industrialists
exploited by identifying it, according to Tate, with their less
than sublime and mystical cause. At the same time the Southern
Cause is seen as lost through various failures that center ultimately in Jefferson Davis himself. For Davis cannot transfer
what he knows to vigorous action. The biography opens not
with Davis's early life, but like an epic, *in medias res*, with Davis's farewell to the Senate, January 21, 1861. Tate plays upon
contradictions in the man:

> A glance at this man would have revealed his possession of
> absolute self-mastery. Looked at more closely, he might
> have seemed less harmonized than self-conquered; as if he
> had suppressed a certain instability of temperament by will
> alone, and then ignored it. One would have supposed that
> the man could understand people intellectually, by a com-
> parison of their ideas with his own; but not emotionally. He
> seemed to lack emotional subtlety; while of every logical
> and intellectual subtlety he was the master. His gaunt as-
> cetic face and withdrawn eyes betrayed a haughty and
> impatient pride; he would expect ideas to settle the course
> of events, and not quite grasp the necessity of cajoling men
> into sharing his desires. A great statesman, perhaps the
> most disinterested statesman in American history, he
> seemed too remote and uncompromising to be a politician.
> As he stood at his desk about to speak, he must have struck
> the detached observer with a certain inflexibility of pose.

In his inability to bring intellect and emotion together, Davis is
a distant relation, is he not, of the speaker in "Ode to the

Confederate Dead"? Yet he is not identical, for in the "Ode"
emotion or sensibility dominates, whereas in the character of
Jefferson Davis, emotion is stunted:

> The farewell was one of the most characteristic speeches
> Davis ever delivered: it betrayed the curious separation of
> his intellect and his feelings. Beneath the beautifully coher-
> ent defense of the secessionists ran a note of regret for what
> he was about to leave behind; it was something more than
> the loss of the habits of fifteen years, though these, for a
> rigid character, must be hard to break; it came down, in
> the end, to an emotional timidity, a fear of changing the
> objects of one's attachment, a kind of inertia that no
> amount of intellectual conviction could quite remove. He
> was emotionally undeveloped; and for this reason he could
> not altogether get at the motives of men.

As Tate sees it, the imbalance in Davis resulted in an ineffectual
idealism. "All of Davis' thought ran on a plane considerably
higher than the reality of human conduct, and it is certain that
he would have been moved by a vindication of abstract principle anywhere. He was very much the saint in politics. While the
fire-eaters were motivated by a single and powerful desire to be
rid of the United States at any price, and were thus not so much
vindicating an idea as asserting a desire, Davis was always the
American standing for the *principle* of local self-government."
And so, unable to fire this abstract intellectuality with emotion
or even self-interest, Davis' life compounds a series of impotent
ceremonies, lofty pronoucements, leading to defeat for the South
and for Davis himself, to anticlimax and gray denouement. On
Davis, then, as the epitome of the idealist who tests life on ideas
rather than ideas on life, Tate blames in large part (he was re-
serving a share of the blame for Robert E. Lee) the loss of what
he saw as good in the antebellum South. What he saw as good
were the political principles of Calhoun and a society at ease
with itself and certain of its language.

M. E. Bradford interestingly calls the two Civil War biographies "Plutarchian,"[19] and in an important sense he is right.
Tate focuses in each upon some flaw of character which leads
to calamity. Stonewall Jackson, unsure of his birthright, his education, his religion, his "place," develops by way of compensa-

tion an eccentric, imbalanced individuality which leads him into an excess of personal bravery. Paradoxically, this makes of him too "good" a soldier, one who never disobeys an order. Jefferson Davis is too sure of his noble assumptions to suppose they will not prevail. He might be compared with a number of Melville's "bachelor" characters, like the narrator of "Bartleby the Scrivener" or Captain Delano in "Benito Cereno," characters who cannot see evil when it is right in front of their faces. Presumably, an inability to recognize evil is linked with emotional infantilism. In one important way the biographies are not Plutarchian. For the calamity of defeat is not Jackson's and it is not Davis' in these biographies. It is the South's. Tragedy is shifted from an individual to a culture. We read then of an impetuous Coriolanus who fails to deliver his nation from bondage. We read of a well-meaning Brutus who, neglecting to act decisively, fails to save the threatened republic.

After Ford Madox Ford's return to Paris, the Tates spent the remainder of the summer in Brittany at Concarneau, not far from Quimper. There on July 19 Tate received a cable from his brother Ben to tell him that his mother had died two days before at Monteagle, Tennessee. In September the Tates returned to Paris, staying at the Hotel de la Place de l'Odéon. On January 1, 1930, they sailed for New York.

CHAPTER FIVE

❧ The Agrarians ❧

THE NEW YORK TATE RETURNED TO IN JANUARY 1930 WAS NOT THE New York he had left. While there were few signs of economic depression, the stock market had crashed, and the confident façade of the boom days was beginning to erode. Already literature and criticism had shifted toward the political left. Some of Tate's literary acquaintances seemed to be erecting new careers on Marxist footings. Such shifts Tate found cynical yet symptomatic of the times. He began to doubt that he wanted to stay in New York. Beside, he had no money, and the prospects of making a go of it in New York City were poor. The Tates stayed in a flat on West Twenty-second Street for only a month, then left early in February for Tennessee.

In April something happened that deeply affected the course of Tate's life. His brother Ben bought for him a beautiful antebellum house with about a hundred acres of farmland and woods overlooking the Cumberland River near Clarksville, Tennessee, fifty miles northwest of Nashville. They moved there in June 1930.

The weathered brick house is of a design seen frequently in farming country in England and Ireland: a simple oblong with massive chimneys at each end. This basic design has been, in the Tates' house, altered slightly in recognition of the hot southern summers. On one side columns support twin galleries or porches which command a view of the river. The house has been built into the slope of the land, so that the dining room windows are at ground level. The front grounds are planted with lilac, rose of Sharon, and crepe myrtle. A narrow lane runs between junipers for a hundred yards or so from the Clarksville road to the house. Caroline and Allen called the house "Benfolly." The name probably derives in part from the title of Caroline's recently completed novel *Penhally* which dealt with her forbears who settled in the Clarksville region. More obviously it pays amusing tribute to Benjamin Tate and his generosity. Malcolm Cowley was an early visitor at Benfolly and reported to Mark Van Doren that the Tates lived in a mansion with a great central hall and a dining room big enough for Stonewall Jackson's staff.[1]

After the apartments in Manhattan, the farmhouse at Patterson, the hotels and apartments of Europe, Benfolly gave the Tates stability—at least for a few years. There were disadvantages. It took money to keep the house running. The farmland was not very good, and the economic situation was not only depressing the value of produce but was also making reliance on "tenant farmers" less and less feasible. In addition, though Caroline loved to garden, Allen was scarcely suited for the ordinary chores necessary to keep even the house and grounds trim. He might, as Caroline observed of a character in one of her novels, have made a splendid botanist but never a gardener. Still, these disadvantages counted for less than the feeling of anchorage. And living within driving distance of Nashville gave Tate the opportunity to see John Crowe Ransom and Donald Davidson from time to time. Andrew Lytle, living at Monteagle, was also within driving distance. And Robert Penn Warren returned from Oxford at midyear to take a teaching post at Southwestern University in Memphis.

Tate and Warren soon found themselves embroiled in the "defense of the South" which Ransom and Davidson had already begun: Ransom with an essay "The South—Old or New," published in *The Sewanee Review* (April 1928); Davidson in an essay "First Fruits of Dayton: The Intellectual Evolution in Dixie," published in *The Forum* (June 1928). Both Ransom and Davidson attacked northern industrialism and sought to find a way to preserve from its encroachment a southern culture which they felt was more "European" (a line that Tate also took in his biography of Jefferson Davis) and less materialistic than that of the North. In September 1929 Ransom continued the attack with "Classical and Romantic" in *The Saturday Review of Literature*. Here he probed the fetish of scientism and "progress" in American life, and like Tate suggested that only a core of religion could culturally unify society. These ideas form the foundations of Ransom's book *God Without Thunder* published in the summer of 1930.

Early in 1930, Davidson and Ransom began recruiting contributions for a proposed symposium intended to support the southern, that is to say, Agrarian way of life. Although they had hoped for a wide and varied range of intellectual representation, some prospective contributors proved unsympathetic, so that the volume turned out to be largely by people connected with Vanderbilt, and the nucleus was the Fugitive Group. As summer drew to a close *I'll Take My Stand* was being printed. Ransom and Davidson had chosen the title. Tate and Warren suddenly decided that "A Tract Against Communism" would be more appropriate. But it was too late to change the title, and one suspects also that Davidson liked the Civil War tone of the original. In addition to Ransom, Davidson, Lytle, Warren, and Tate, the contributors were Frank Laurence Owsley, Professor of History at Vanderbilt; Lyle Lanier, Professor of Psychology at Vanderbilt; Herman C. Nixon, member of the Department of History at Tulane University, but formerly and later at Vanderbilt; John Donald Wade who was teaching English at Vanderbilt; Harry Blue Kline who had recently finished a master's degree at Vanderbilt; Stark Young, the drama critic; and John Gould Fletcher whose reputation as a poet was fading as the prestige of the school of Imagism faded.

Looking at *I'll Take My Stand* at the end of the 1960s, one may well find it a rather mild collection of essays and wonder at the derision and vituperation which greeted its publication in 1930. Perhaps one can attribute this reception to the fact that *I'll Take My Stand* was not a book which could hope to claim allegiance from any specialized modern mind—the economist, the sociologist, the political scientist. In addition, the essays were uneven in quality and dispersed in effect. This was evident to Ransom, who tried to impose upon the book a semblance of unity by a statement of principles which precedes the essays. His principles may be summarized as follows:

1. Without any intention of starting a new civil war the South should avoid becoming a replica of the industrial North.

2. The South should join with other sections of the country whose preference is for an Agrarian rather than an industrial economy.

3. There is no quarrel with abstract science, but applied science, exempt from reason and criticism, is held the culpable force behind the evils of industrialism.

4. The laborer under modern industrialism backed by applied science does not receive greater leisure or enjoyment from his work than does a farm worker.

5. Labor-saving devices assume that work is an evil rather than a source of happiness.

6. Industrialism leads to overproduction, unemployment, and inequality in the distribution of wealth.

7. Industrialization will lead to the government's setting up "an economic super-organization which in turn" will "become the government, a system not very distinguishable from communism."

8. Under industrialism "manners, conversation, hospitality, sympathy, family life, romantic love" deteriorate, and man loses his "sense of vocation."

9. Religion cannot flourish in an industrial society because nature subdued and simplified loses its aspect of mystery.

10. Without religion, art cannot flourish.

11. Education cannot help, for no one knows what anyone should be educated for.

12. Modern Humanism in seeking to force individual life into conformity with an abstract idea cannot ameliorate the wrongs of industrialism.

13. The concept of continuing progress is illusory.

14. Against industrial evils is set the Agrarian view whose theory "is that the culture of the soil is the best and most sensitive of vocations, and that therefore it should have the economic preference and enlist the maximum number of workers."

The principles finish with the ring of a manifesto: "If a community, or a section, or a race, or an age, is groaning under industrialism, and well aware that it is an evil dispensation, it must find the way to throw it off. To think this cannot be done is pusillanimous. And if the whole community, section, race or age thinks it cannot be done, then it has simply lost its political genius and doomed itself to impotence."

In his contribution to the symposium, "Remarks on the Southern Religion" (later entitled "Religion and the Old South"), Tate makes a plea for the "short view" of history and a view of the "whole horse," by which he means a concrete view of history and of religion. He has, one notes, moved away from Spengler's attitudes. He deplores an analogistic history wherein Greek and Roman civilizations appear identical. He deplores a comparative religion that has "no reason to prefer Christ to Adonis." Working from this base, he proceeds then to contrast "abstract" New England and the "concrete" South: "The Southern mind was simple, not top-heavy with learning it had no need of, unintellectual, and composed; it was personal and dramatic, rather than abstract and metaphysical; and it was sensuous because it lived close to a natural scene of great variety and interest." Nevertheless, Tate perceives an inadequacy in the southern religion:

> They had a religious life, but it was not enough organized with a right mythology. In fact, their rational life was not powerfully united to the religious experience, as it was in medieval society, and they are a fine specimen of the tragic pitfall upon which the Western mind has always hovered. Not having a rational system for the defense of their religious attitude and its base in a feudal society, they elaborated no rational system whatever, no full-grown philosophy; so that, when the post-bellum temptations of the devil, who, according to Milton and Aeschylus, is the exploiter of nature, confronted them, they had no defense. Since there is, in the Western mind, a radical division between the religious, the contemplative, the qualitative, on the one hand, and the scientific, the natural, the practical, on the other, the scientific mind always plays havoc with the spiritual life when it is not powerfully enlisted in its cause; it cannot be permitted to operate alone.

Except for the very last words of this paragraph Tate's essay conforms to the principles set forth by Ransom, but here he seeks in a characteristic way to find the flaw in the past, just as he sought in his biographies of Jackson and Davis to find flaws that would account for historical failures. To the degree that the statement trembles on the brink of supporting a Catholic view it does not support the fundamentalism that Ransom was willing, if not determined, to defend. But his minor heresy did not portend a break with Agrarianism. On the contrary, the principles continued to occupy him for the next ten years, though after 1936 with diminishing intensity.

The public resistance to *I'll Take My Stand* did not discourage the Agrarians. That Northerners hooted was to be expected. That southern establishmentarians repudiated the group was also to be expected. But the group was dismayed that the book did not sell well and that criticism focused on the paucity of economic theory. More than the others, John Ransom took the criticisms of Agrarian economics to heart. He had publicly debated the principles of Agrarianism with Stringfellow Barr shortly before publication of *I'll Take My Stand* and he had been made aware of the effectiveness of Barr's sarcastic assault on the Agrarians' economic naïveté. While Davidson, Lytle, Tate, and Warren concerned themselves with the tenets of Jefferson and Calhoun, Ransom took to studying contemporary economics. Indeed, on a Guggenheim grant from 1931 to 1932, Ransom spent a good deal of time in Wales, studying British economists.

In these early years of the movement, Donald Davidson seemed always to feel that the world was about to be "delivered," in the Old Testament phrase, into Agrarian hands. But Tate had been at the outset dubious of the ability of the group to effect reform, and he could not ever quite believe that the world would be delivered to them. Yet he believed the Agrarian credo was right and he enjoyed the atmosphere of crisis and polemics. As the Great Depression deepened even his hopes rose. When in the spring of 1932 he became southern editor of *Hound and Horn,* he hoped to be able to further the Agrarian views through that excellent journal. He was not notably successful in that aim, although one of Davidson's Agrarian essays

did appear in *Hound and Horn.* However, another publication
suddenly offered hospitality to the group. Seward Collins,
blessed with a private fortune and a passion for cultural analysis
which he had picked up from his teacher, Irving Babbitt, in
1932 bought *The Bookman* and renamed it *The American Review.* His editorial policy of sponsoring a *radical* reconsideration
of American life from a *traditional* point of view was one which
had something in common with Agrarianism. Collins, through
the editor of *The Sewanee Review,* W. S. Knickerbocker, met
and conferred with the Agrarians at Andrew Lytle's farm in
Alabama, with the result that they were given an open invitation to publish their ideas in *The American Review.* Davidson
published a number of partisan essays, some frenetic in tone, in
the magazine; Tate's and Ransom's contributions were more
moderate both in tone and quantity. Altogether, Tate published
only four essays in the magazine. "The Problem of the Unem-
ployed: A Modest Proposal" appeared in May 1933. As its subti-
tle suggests, the essay is grim and a bit lugubrious. His "Notes
on Liberty and Property" (March 1936) fancifully supported the
Agrarian concept of a morality based on the personal ownership
of land, as did "What is a Traditional Society," his Phi Beta
Kappa Address given in June 1936 at the University of Virginia
and published in *The American Review* in September 1936. His
final contribution to the magazine in February 1937 was not
political: "Modern Poets and Convention." In addition to these
essays Tate reviewed Herbert Agar's *The People's Choice,* W. T.
Couch's *Culture in the South,* and Oswald Spengler's *Tract
Against Liberalism.* The magazine itself was eventually taken to
task for certain articles sympathetic to fascism, an occasion
which engaged Tate in some painful correspondence in *The
New Republic.* Samuel Eliot Morison in his *The Oxford History
of the American People* refers to *The American Review* simply
as the voice of American fascism. It does not deserve the label.

Tate's review of Herbert Agar's book led him to write to Agar
toward the end of 1933, suggesting that he support the Agrarian
position by articles in *The American Review.* Agar, the London
correspondent for the Louisville *Courier,* had already developed
a sympathy for the British equivalent of the Agrarians—the Distributists, led by G. K. Chesterton and Hilaire Belloc. The Dis-

tributists believed in fragmenting large industrial corporations and distributing all property among small subsistence farmers. They also dreamed another medieval dream, hoping that in such a society, the authority of the Roman Catholic Church would once again become pervasive. In the summer of 1934 Agar returned to America and gave a series of lectures. Meeting Tate along with other Agrarians in Tennessee, Agar enthusiastically joined forces with them. He took an editorial position on the Louisville *Courier,* so as to be near the thick of things. By December of that year he and Tate were making plans to establish a political weekly which would appeal to both the Midwest and the South. Nothing came of that, but no matter, other plans were at hand. And they were extensive plans, based on Agar's view that unless they were able to "capture" the New Deal by the end of Roosevelt's second term, the country was doomed to slavery.[2] They hoped to make common cause with groups in the Far West, which they believed was being sucked dry, like the South, by an industrialism centered in New York City. As the plans became more ebullient, however, internecine suspicions developed. In fact, from the first Davidson had not wanted Agar in the cadre. When Agar proposed a conference in Nashville to confederate various reformist groups, the Agrarians were less than enthusiastic about the "outsiders" Agar invited. Similarly, when Agar and Tate began plans for publishing a collection of essays by Agrarians and Distributists, Owsley and Davidson felt that the southern character of the "Cause," as they called it, was being diluted. Nevertheless, the symposium entitled *Who Owns America?* finally appeared in 1936.

Who Owns America?, though more patiently edited than *I'll Take My Stand,* adds very little to the picture of Agrarianism. Those contributors who had originally written for *I'll Take My Stand* pretty much follow the pattern of the earlier essays. There were newcomers. Sociologists, such as David C. Coyle, spoke more blandly than had the original founders of Agrarianism, yet all in all the conceptual loyalties were almost identical with those principles Ransom had enumerated in *I'll Take My Stand.* Tate's contribution, "Notes on Liberty and Property," reprinted from *The American Review,* repeats his belief in the evil of large corporations and the virtue of limited, private land holdings. It is neither his best nor most subtle statement on the subject.

Who Owns America?, though less scorned by reviewers than *I'll Take My Stand*, failed to change the world. In later years Tate spoke of the Agrarians as "being rather like the French Encyclopedists. We issued certain ideas, reaffirmed the Southern tradition or standards. Well, the Encyclopedists turned out to be, according to the way you look at it, a great success. They brought on a revolution, or at least they provided the ideas for the revolution. And the Agrarian ideas didn't have such success. I think that's about all you can say about it."[3]

Perhaps one can say a bit more. Certainly it is true that after the publication of *Who Owns America?* the Agrarian-Distributist movement lost force. Probably the reasons were largely historical. Capitalism altered its course by a few degrees and did not collapse. And the world began to watch the wild growth of fascism in Europe. Tate remained faithful to the tenets of Agrarianism and served in 1939 as one of the editors of Herbert Agar's short-lived magazine *Free America*. He was, like Davidson, hurt when John Crowe Ransom publicly repudiated Agrarianism in 1945. No doubt he was disappointed by the general ineffectuality of the movement. It is wrong, however, to postulate, as has John L. Stewart,[4] that the failure of Agrarianism was for Tate anything like an insufferable blow. Granted Tate was easily attracted to a good fight, literary or otherwise, but, unlike Davidson, he knew when to quit. As it happens, for two years prior to 1936 he had been planning to lessen his prominence in the Agrarian movement. In 1936 he wrote: "I feel that my political career is over. In the last two years it has consisted solely in efforts to get Herbert Agar—a very high-powered person—identified with the Agrarians. I've succeeded. He is the leader. I will follow from now on at a literary distance."[5] There is no reason for not taking this letter at face value.

There is a more basic reason for discounting the idea of Tate's being overwhelmed by the failure of Agrarianism. The views he believed in were not precariously based upon the journalist's pinpoint of time. The views were as old as civilization. One may remember that before Socrates begins to analyze the nature of the republic, he says that the best state is one where a farmer and his wife and children sit down together to a simple meal. When the objection is raised that the farmer's "society" is dull, Socrates says that if it is life lived at a fever pitch which interests his companions, he will proceed to consider society in an advanced state of "civilization," which he sees as second best. Much of the time Tate and his friends were speaking about the farmer's irenic board while their critics were talking about life lived at a fever pitch. Commentators have been happy to shoot down Agrarianism with "facts." But any philosophical view can be shot down with facts. Anyway, what happens if one allows the truth of the facts? Does the virtue of an Agrarian Eden disappear if we agree that poverty existed in the old and new South? Or if we allow that industrialism has resulted in the distribution of more common goods to more people? Or that life on a farm is no guarantee of cultural vitality? After all these facts have been shot forth, they are still ineffectual, for what lies behind Agrarianism is the stubborn belief of mankind in innocence; just as, what lies behind industrialism is man's belief in progress. The two beliefs will never be compatible, but they are inseparable, for they create each other. The myth of progress will generally dominate, but only so long as it is tempered by the Edenic myth. Criticism of Agrarianism written from 1930 to 1960 now seems freighted with irony. The radical call once again is for breaking up industrial might, for saving one's soul by living in agrarian communes. Once again that voice will probably die out, but its presence, its resurgence, should bring humility to absolutists of any persuasion.

This account of the Agrarian movement has been allowed to run on so that it might be seen with some historical coherence. The movement obviously bears a relationship to Tate's literary accomplishments. He himself has claimed that "some of [his] best verses [were written] during the Agrarian phase in the 1930s." And not because his mind was divided between public policies and poetry. On the contrary, he believed with Donald Davidson that *I'll Take My Stand* constituted "as much a defense of poetry . . . as a defense of the South."[6]

From 1930 to 1936 Tate worked intermittently on two prose manuscripts, a biography of Robert E. Lee and a novel entitled *The Ancestors* or *Ancestors of Exile*. Both of these projects were ultimately discarded, but the work was not entirely a waste, for both stand behind his novel *The Fathers*. In addition, one notes that in this same period Tate wrote even more reviews, primarily for *The Nation* and *The New Republic*, than he had during his New York phase. And his literary essays, in addition to Agrarian pieces, continued to appear in such journals as *Hound and Horn*, *The Nation*, *The New Republic*, *Poetry*, *The Southern Review*, and *The Virginia Quarterly*. Moreover, his *Poems: 1928–1931* was published in New York and London in 1932. *The Mediterranean and Other Poems* appeared in 1936. In the same year his first collection of essays, *Reactionary Essays*, was published.

The poems Tate wrote between 1930 and 1936 often reflect his intellectual and spiritual commitments to Agrarianism. But one is aware of these commitments not as doctrine but as mood. Agrarianism does not displace his older concern with the pursuit of integrity, the theme which created his first important poem "Ode to the Confederate Dead"; the older theme exists under the new Agrarian concern. And there is something else, some personal engagement with evil. In fact, Tate seems determined that man's duty is to find the evil within himself, know it, and live with it.

Early in July 1931, Tate found himself exhausted by the completion of nine sonnets. These were, he found, "the most personally forthright poems" he had ever written. He had begun the sequence without any intention of writing a sonnet; indeed, he had just been "fumbling" around with a pencil. But before he had written the second sonnet "the others came crowding in so fast that [he] could barely get each preceding one done in time."[7] These sonnets were eventually given the title "Sonnets of the Blood." To most readers they seem more "personal" than "forthright." The references to family past and present are tantalizing rather than clear or helpful. And it is tempting to assume that Tate is hinting at frightful family secrets. That assumption gets us nowhere. The poems are concerned less with particular evil than with general evil as it permeates generation after generation. One may read them as a Gothic elaboration of the old Roman belief in the *genius* of the family or house. There are, however, particulars. "Sonnets of the Blood" does reflect

Tate's return to the South after an absence of six years; it reflects the death of Tate's mother in 1929; and it reflects a new closeness or an attempt at a new closeness between Tate and his brother Ben. The sonnets are addressed directly to Ben and they consider in a general way how two brothers whose lives are dedicated to entirely different things, to art and commerce, share an identical past, a past which includes:

> a Virginian
> Who took himself to be brute nature's law,
> Cared little what men thought him, a tall man
> Who meditated calmly what he saw
> Until he freed his Negroes, lest he be
> Too strict with nature and than they less free.

The Virginian, whom one could probably identify but should feel no need to identify, and other instances of personal and historical tradition bind the different brothers together. For the blood is a "fire that warms the deepest grave . . . to which our blood is the indentured slave." Throughout, Tate praises the blood as a fire, yet a fire that is now burning low:

> Thank God the fuel is low, we'll not renew
> That length of flame into our firmament;
> Think too the rooftree crackles and will fall
> On us, who saw the sacred fury's height—
> Seated in her tall chair, with the black shawl
> From head to foot, burning with motherly light
> More spectral than November dusk could mix
> With sunset, to blaze on her pale crucifix.

The eighth sonnet does pose a question of familial guilt, but consider the terms.

> Call it the house of Atreus where we live—
> Which one of us the Greek perplexed with crime
> Questions the future: bring that lucid sieve
> To strain the appointed particles of time!
> Whether by Corinth or by Thebes we go
> The way is brief, but the fixed doom, not so.

The guilt of the noble families in the Greek sagas is, after all, a pagan equivalent of the doctrine of original sin. And whether one goes to Delphi by way of Corinth or Thebes, the oracle will speak of retribution. That much admitted, the final sonnet turns to the brother, one of the captains of that very industry which, like a barbarian invasion, threatens "culture":

> Let you, brother, captaining your hour
> Be zealous that your numbers are all prime,
> Lest false division with sly mathematic
> Plunder the inner mansion of the blood.
> The Thracian, swollen with pride, besiege the Attic—
> Invader foraging the sacred wood . . .

One wonders if Tate intends in his "prime numbers" to invoke the reverence that the ancient mathematicians and natural philosophers gave to numbers indivisible except by themselves or unity. The property of prime numbers gives Tate a cerebral metaphor by which to argue against division—division of the self first of all; and of the house or culture after self. It is therefore a metaphor which ties together the theme of "Ode to the Confederate Dead" with the concerns of Agrarianism. The sestet of this terminal sonnet employs the metaphoric implications of "prime," so as to associate it with tradition, and finishes with a warning:

> Yet the prime secret whose simplicity
> Your towering engine hammers to reduce,
> Though driven, holds that bulwark of the sea
> Which breached will turn unspeaking fury loose
> To drown out him who swears to rectify
> Infinity, that has nor ear nor eye.

The sequence, as we see, carries two burdens. One burden is that of tradition symbolically inclusive but particularized in the family. The other burden is the breaking of that tradition through the emergence of some new drift in the familial ego. No easing of these two burdens comes, no resolution of their opposition, but the "fury," like the furies who pursue Orestes, watches. "Sonnets of the Blood" then is made by myth less "Southern" than any easy glance at the poems would suggest; it is made through myth not so much a confession of familial guilt as a confession of universal guilt, universal sin.

While sin is not pursued in Tate's poetry, the recognition of its presence constitutes virtue. We are made aware of this rather

Manichean posture by a poem like "Last Days of Alice," written, as was "Sonnets of the Blood," in 1931. Alice, "grown mammoth but not fat" gazes from the looking glass into which she has disappeared while:

> Above in the dozing leaves the grinning cat
> Quivers forever with his abstract rage . . .

Lewis Carroll's Alice represents not solely the narcissism of modern life, not only its abstraction, but even more importantly its ignorance of evil, an ignorance supported by ego and abstraction and science:

> —We too back to the world shall never pass
> Through the shattered door, a dumb shade-harried crowd
> Being all infinite, function depth and mass
> Without figure, a mathematical shroud
>
> Hurled at the air—blesséd without sin!
> O God of our flesh, return us to Your wrath,
> Let us be evil could we enter in
> Your grace, and falter on the stony path!

One is stunned by the extension of the poem's single conceit in the continuing analogy between life and the plight of Alice marooned in the looking glass. One is aware that the poem is one of the first of the century to make use of the terror in children's literature. One thinks of Randall Jarrell's mining of fairy tales two decades later. Insofar as the poem detains us in its argument, we obtain the idea that it is better to be capable of sin, thus to be human, than lost in the mathematical refractions of glass, of vitreous science. This concept binds "Last Days of Alice" to "Sonnets of the Blood," as well as to the poem "Idiot" and "Sonnets at Christmas" (1934). At the same time "Last Days of Alice" tells us what the word "blood" means to Tate, how its palpable warmth, its darkness, its mortal fallibility contrast with abstraction all the way through his poems, culminating finally in the imagery of "The Buried Lake." It also adds a dimension to Tate's probing of the past, his pondering of the blood lines, literal and figurative, of his life before his life.

To this amalgam of intensity over the past belong such poems as "The Traveler," dedicated to Archibald MacLeish because the relentless pressure of time couples it with MacLeish's "You, Andrew Marvell." Possibly "To the Lacedemonians" belongs here also. Probably it is an anomaly and belongs in no category, for it is the only poem Tate ever wrote for an occasion; namely, a Confederate Soldiers Reunion in June 1932. It was commissioned by the Richmond *Times-Dispatch*. To Donald Davidson who had lamented the absence of the Confederate dead in "Ode to the Confederate Dead" this poem gave delight. Few others have liked it. One can say with more confidence that "The Ancestors" belongs in this pattern. It is a conscious companion-piece to John Peale Bishop's poem of the same title, also written in 1932. Bishop's poem is the clearer and better work; just as Bishop's masterpiece "Perspectives are Precipices" is better than Tate's "The Robber Bridegroom" which was written in a daze of admiration for Bishop's atmospheric balladization of the Bluebeard story. But neither "The Traveler" nor "The Ancestors" is the best of Tate's poems in the ancestral vein. The best is "The Oath," written in 1932 and dedicated to Andrew Lytle. The conversational ease of the poem is remarkable as the reader is drawn to the fireside "with not much untold / By two old friends when neither's a great liar." The friends meditate silently for awhile

> Then Lytle asked: Who are the dead?
> Who are the living and the dead?
> And nothing more was said.
> So I, leaving Lytle to that dream,
> Decided what it is in time that gnaws
> The ageing fury of a mountain stream
> When suddenly as an ignorant mind will do
> I thought I heard the dark pounding its head
> On a rock, crying: *Who are the dead?*
> Then Lytle turned with an oath—By God it's true!

The poem has been thought to say that the antebellum South is more alive than the present-day South. That view is hasty. "The Oath" is more nearly a poem of eerie derangement than it is one of definite meaning. The whole setting of dusk deepening into night yields meaning. The question "Who are the dead?" by necessity asks also "Who are the living?" The precedents for

this poem stretch deep into the past, as far back at least as Euri-
pides who wrote:

> Who knows but what we the living are really the dead
> And our death but life to those who have passed it?
>
> (Fragment 638)

Of "The Oath" Tate himself has written:

> I had for years been impressed by W. W. Jacobs' story
> "The Monkey's Paw." I wished in my poem to dramatize a
> supernatural intuition which cannot be reduced to lan-
> guage: Are the living really living, or are the supposed dead
> the actual living? This is a question universal in any Chris-
> tian society, and it has nothing specifically to do with the
> South. The only way such a question can be actualized is in
> its effect upon people who are aware of it. In Jacobs' story
> we do not see the dead son knocking at the door; we see
> the *effect* on the mother and father.[8]

At the same time as Tate was exploring the corners of the
ancestral house, he kept his belief in a theory of poetry as
"knowledge." His earlier epistemological poems had illuminated
the failure to attain complete knowledge. The fragmented world
would not support a whole view. The "Death of Little Boys,"
for example, had concentrated upon the knowledge that comes
from feeling only. "The Cross" had attempted to broaden mere
feeling through a religious emotion, as does the later poem "The
Twelve" (1931), yet both of them suffer from a cold impersonal-
ity. Another formula which his poems investigated was the substitution of a personal tradition for an unfulfilled or unrealized religious emotion. That is true of "Sonnets of the Blood," true of
the two parts of "Records" (1928) or "Emblems" (1931–33).
Among the earlier poems his most successful is that one in
which he admitted failure to bring heart and head and action
together—"Ode to the Confederate Dead." But another brilliant
success of this kind emerged in 1931, "The Wolves":

> There are wolves in the next room waiting
> With heads bent low, thrust out, breathing
> At nothing in the dark; between them and me
> A white door patched with light from the hall
> Where it seems never (so still is the house)

A man has walked from the front door to the stair.
It has all been forever. Beasts claw the floor.
I have brooded on angels and archfiends
But no man has ever sat where the next room's
Crowded with wolves . . .

                              Now while
I have looked for the evening star at a cold window
And whistled when Arcturus spilt his light,
I've heard the wolves scuffle, and said: So this
Is man; so—what better conclusion is there—
The day will not follow night, and the heart
Of man has a little dignity, but less patience
Than a wolf's, and a duller sense that cannot
Smell its own mortality. . . .

Now remember courage, go to the door,
Open it and see whether coiled on the bed
Or cringing by the wall, a savage beast
Maybe with golden hair, with deep eyes
Like a bearded spider on a sunlit floor
Will snarl—and man can never be alone.

Though the end tells us we can never be alone, "The Wolves" is
a very lonely and terrifying poem. The source of terror lies in
man's vulnerability to his animal self, and the vulnerability is
enhanced by the absence of religion. The man is lost in his intellect which can brood on angels and archfiends but which cannot
make them a part of the whole being. Hence, the isolated intellect breaks down, and the last line compounds a supreme irony.
The isolated intelligence is driven to the brute for company.
Hawthorne would have liked this poem.

Little wonder that Tate during this period sometimes felt that
his gift for poetry must itself fail along with a vision that
seemed then so partial and imbalanced. Little wonder that he
often told his friends that his "latest" poem always theatened to
be his "last." Nor is it any wonder either that in "The Eagle"
(1934) and "The Meaning of Life" (1935), he sought escape from
epistemology altogether, celebrating a vision of a simple urgency and spiritual force—life rendered immune to the clogs of
metaphysics, imagination, intellection, religion. From "The Eagle":

Think not the world spins ever
(Only the world has a year)
Only the gaunt fierce bird
Flies, merciless with fear

Lest air hold him not,
Beats up the scaffold of space
Sick of the world's rot—
God's hideous face.

In the early part of 1932 Tate was occupied in working up a "Southern" number for *Poetry, a Magazine of Verse*. That is mildly astonishing. His relations with Harriet Monroe had not been quite cordial in the Fugitive days. Furthermore, Miss Monroe in the previous October had asked Tate to review a book by George Dillon and then withdrew the assignment on the grounds that she did not want to risk a negative review![9] It is likely, however, that Tate saw a southern number as a way of helping the cause both of letters and of his friends.

Of more importance, Caroline's first novel *Penhally*, published in 1931, had received respectful reviews, and she was awarded a Guggenheim grant in 1932. In July of that year she and Allen went to France, leaving Nancy with an aunt of Caroline's. Allen, on the advice of John Bishop, who was still living in his chateau outside Paris, took along his Model A Ford. The automobile doubtless made it easier for them to live in the villa which Ford Madox Ford found for them on the French Riviera: the Villa Les Hortensias at Cap Brun, Toulon. Ford himself lived nearby in Villa Paul, although part of the time he was away in Germany.

The Tates moved happily into their villa, and Allen got down to work again on his biography of Robert E. Lee; he also wrote his story "The Immortal Woman" here. In September, Bishop and his wife came down to visit them and they splurged at Monte Carlo together. When the Bishops left, however, Tate was assailed by a feeling of utter boredom and futility. The spell continued for over a month, and on October 26, 1932 he wrote to Bishop, humorously suggesting that they form a "suicide club" or "a club against suicide":

I have got to the place you seemed to occupy a few years
ago. Perhaps it is the crisis of the middle thirties. You
probably know something about that. It is very difficult for
me to convince myself that what I am doing holds together
. . . We all get into these hollows of the spirit; I think I
was due for one and the upheaval of this trip to France
landed me in it.

Four days later Tate sent Bishop a new poem, one of the best he
ever wrote and one of the truly memorable poems of the entire
modernist period. The circumstances immediately behind this
poem, "The Mediterranean," are well documented. Shortly after
settling in at Villa Les Hortensias, Allen and Caroline had gone
with Ford and perhaps fifteen others on a picnic at Cassis. The
picnic was held in a small cove approached through a narrow
channel or *catalque* navigable only by small fishing boats. All
about the shingle beach rose the dark red cliffs typical of the
Riviera. The sky was utterly blue. The picnickers had a great
feast. There were cocks boiled in wine and in great cauldrons a
sumptuous bouillabaisse, a towering salad, a pile of cheese and
fruit. An old man, known as Monsieur l'Hermite, came by foot
down the cliffs, bringing the wine—sixty-one bottles. As they ate
Ford remarked to Tate that it must have been in such coves that
Aeneas and his band had stopped to eat. Tate bought a copy of
the *Aeneid* the next day in Toulon and re-read it for several
weeks. In September he began to compose "The Mediterranean."[10]

The rhythmic push and drag of the poem, the repetition of
words and phrases impart to "The Mediterranean" a tidal determination. At first the poem seems primarily descriptive; then in
the third stanza we are told:

> And we made feast and in our secret need
> Devoured the very plates Aeneas bore.

The reference is to the *Aeneid*, Book VII lines 115–27, where
Aeneas' son jokes about eating their food on slabs of bread. "We
are eating our tables," he cries. Then Aeneas remembers that
Anchises had prophesied that when they have so little food that
they will eat the tables, their hardship is finished, they have
found their new home. Tate continues upon the momentum of

an ironic contrast between the opulent picnickers and Aeneas:

> Where we feasted and caroused on the sandless
> Pebbles, affecting our day of piracy,
> What prophecy of eaten plates could landless
> Wanderers fulfil by the ancient sea?

At the end he asks:

> What country shall we conquer, what fair land
> Unman our conquest and locate our blood?
> We've cracked the hemispheres with careless hand!
> . . . .
> Westward, westward till the barbarous brine
> Whelms us to the tired land where tasseling corn,
> Fat beans, grapes sweeter than muscadine
> Rot on the vine: in that land were we born.

The poem comes back—like a mind coming back from immediate pleasure to a thought that worries it—to the center of Tate's social beliefs, his uneasy Agrarianism. It comes back like a picnicker returning to his daily cares. Yet all of Tate's views have been broadened in his poem. The ancestors here are the common ancestors of Western civilization. Faceless industrialism has been converted to the westward course of empire.

In "The Mediterranean" Tate for the first time discovered a tradition in which his intellect and sensibility could make a home together. This is so because this tradition is Western man's. Similarly, Tate's "region" is for the first time fused with a universality that accommodates "tasseling corn" along with a Mediterranean cove. Later Tate would be able to employ Dante as he had Vergil to widen his vision—which is a way of saying that he learned that myth and great art would work where the simple historical sense had to fail because history itself was failing.

And, of course, Tate has his dessert; his sense of irony is satisfied in "The Mediterranean," for Aeneas' somber journey had as its aim the discovery of a new homeland, or at least the recovery of an ancestral home. Tate's picnickers have not only reversed the westward direction of civilization—but they are searching only for spiritual roots, not for land. "The Mediterranean" is the best of Tate's poems written before his fortieth year. It so completely realized itself that there was nothing much left for its twin "Aeneas at Washington." And yet Tate did not at first realize the merit of "The Mediterranean." In a letter to Bishop he passed the poem off as "not one of my best, but it has a few nice phrases."[11] Bishop's response encouraged him, and he wrote a week later about the poem then called "Picnic at Cassis": "By the way isn't Arnold's feeling for the Mediterranean nearly perfect in the last two stanzas of The Scholar Gypsy? I don't think I have anything quite that good. Perhaps the idea underlying my poem is a little more realistic—less committed to the illusion that there was ever a paradise, but my writing is not so good."[12] Soon, however, the friends to whom he had sent the poem inundated him with praise, and he later wryly observed, "I hear so many people say 'It's your best poem—so unlike your other work.'—a discouraging elegy."[13]

Though "The Mediterranean" is one of the high points in Tate's art, Tate produced little at Cap Brun. He was restless, just as he had been in France in 1929, even though he had the greatest affection for French civilization. Of course, his ordinary existence was never free of economic worry. At Toulon he complained of "dire poverty because every cent we have got hold of for four months has gone home to creditors." By mid-November he decided it would be better to be "poor & working in Paris," where there were books, "than idle and poor in Toulon."[14] They remained in Paris, however, only until late February, then sailed for New York, where they visited old friends. Enroute to Tennessee, they stayed for two weeks with Phelps Putnam in Maryland and then spent another two weeks in Nashville conferring with Davidson and other Agrarians. In April they visited at Caroline's family farm in Kentucky. As soon as they were again at Benfolly, Allen found that Europe seemed "very far away, remote, and unattainable . . . all the emotions of this country clicked back into place, and life now goes on."[15]

Life did go on with the same old urgencies to create, the same passions to place the Agrarian view before the world, and the same difficulties with money. A whole host of new troubles beseiged him, climaxed by the death of his father in Kentucky on October 21, 1933. Struck down on the street by a taxi, Mr. Tate lingered on for awhile after the accident, but died finally of heart failure. "He was seventy-one," Tate wrote to Bishop, "died in poverty after a reckless life, but gallantly; with his last words he rallied the nurse about her good looks."[16] Death, it would seem, assuaged the son's bitterness. To Van Doren he wrote, "In the most important respects he was a perfect father, but there was no way for me to tell him so."[17] It is an old story.

Late in 1933 Tate was awarded the Midland Authors Prize by *Poetry, a Magazine of Verse* primarily for his "Sonnets of the Blood," published in that magazine in November 1931. He felt "buoyed up" by what he referred to as "Aunt Harriet's prize money."[18] But he could not have been buoyed up very high or long by $100. Nor could the three articles on poetry he finished in October for *The New Republic* have helped much. The Tates' Christmas that year consisted of a "glass or two of home-made sherry and some rounds of charades, besides Nancy's Christmas tree."[19]

Matters did not improve in the new year. On April 1, 1934 Tate had an automobile accident which demolished his car, so that he had to go further into debt to replace it. At this time his life as a freelance writer came virtually to an end. He turned, as many another writer in this century has, to college teaching. Robert Penn Warren had decided to leave his post at Southwestern University in Memphis in order to join Cleanth Brooks at Louisiana State University and start *The Southern Review*. Tate took Warren's place at Southwestern as a lecturer in English. They rented a house at 2374 Forrest Avenue in Memphis.

Tate had many qualities that suited him for teaching: a beautiful voice, mental agility, sympathy with others. Yet his two years in Memphis were far from happy. Toward the end of the first term he looked back bitterly on the whole year, observing that "this will be a particularly futile year for me. My debts oppressed me so that I could write nothing."[20] A bit later he sent Bishop a copy of "To the Romantic Traditionists," terming it the sole output of the whole year. That may have been a bit dramatically put—there are other poems that date from that year. But certainly it had been a melancholy period, and his creativity had flagged. Still, the Tates were cheered at Christmas, for with Andrew Lytle they joined the Warrens and Bishops in New Orleans.[21]

In July 1935 Tate made the first of his many appearances at a writers' conference. Joseph Brewer, the very young president of Olivet College in Michigan, who had instituted an Oxonian tutorial system there, decided to increase the prestige of Olivet by emulating the Breadloaf Conference held yearly at Middlebury, Vermont. Whatever Tate thought of Brewer's scheme, he certainly felt the honorarium was too good to pass up. As it turned out, Brewer was not quite able to scrape up the whole of the fee he had promised,[22] but that did not keep Tate from returning the next year.

In 1936 Tate decided he could see no future for himself at Southwestern, and determined that if nothing better turned up he would resign and return to the economic uncertainity of a freelance. In June, the Tates said goodbye to Memphis. Mark Van Doren got Allen a job that summer as a lecturer at the Columbia University Summer School where among his students was the young John Berryman whom he found to be "somebody to talk *at*."[23] But after this stint of teaching he settled down to writing his novel *The Fathers* at Benfolly.

CHAPTER SIX

❧ The Fathers ❧

ONCE THE AGRARIAN SYMPOSIUM *Who Owns America?* WAS IN print and the ardors of the movement began to subside, Tate found more time and serenity for creative work. Nevertheless, his energies were devoted to prose. With his return to Benfolly from Memphis in June 1936, he worked steadily on *The Fathers* for the next two years. No poems, at least none that have been published, date from this period. He did, however, put together his *Selected Poems*, published in 1937. And he wrote but one essay, "Narcissus as Narcissus."

Benfolly was as usual warmly hospitable to guests. In the spring of 1937 Ford Madox Ford, having been in Europe for a year and in New York since December 1936, again visited the Tates. He found "consorting" with them "an exhausting intellectual undertaking," but kept to his regimen of writing a thousand words each day on his *March of Literature*.[1] During this visit Tate and Ford were drawn into the academic conspiracies and recriminations that marked John Crowe Ransom's departure from Vanderbilt University. Ransom had been offered a position at Kenyon College but was vacillating about leaving Vanderbilt. Tate wrote letters to the newspapers, calling attention to the scandal of letting a man as great as Ransom be lured away from Tennessee. At a testimonial dinner for Ransom, Ford as toastmaster suggested that Ransom ought to leave in order to administer a lesson to Vanderbilt. Ransom jokingly observed later that as a result of these remarks, he had no choice but to go. Ransom's departure was no joking matter to Tate. He never quite forgave Vanderbilt for permitting both Robert Penn Warren and Ransom to leave its faculty.

Just before Ford arrived, Robert Lowell, entirely unknown and in flight from home and Harvard, came to Benfolly looking for Ford. He gives a charming memoir of the occasion:

> The Tates were stately yet bohemian, leisurely yet dedicated. A schoolboy's loaded twenty-two rifle hung under the Confederate flag over the fireplace. . . . After an easy hour or two of regional anecdotes, Greenwich Village reminiscences, polemics on personalities, I began to discover what I had never known. I, too, was part of a legend. I was Northern, disembodied, a Platonist, a puritan, an abolitionist. Tate handed me a hand-printed, defiantly ginger-snap-thin edition of his *The Mediterranean and Other Poems*. He quoted a stanza from Holmes's *Chambered Nautilus*—"rather beyond the flight of your renowned Uncle." I realized that the old deadweight of poor J. R. Lowell was now an asset. Here, like the battered Confederacy, he still lived and was history. . . .
>
> I came to the Tates a second time. Ford Madox Ford, the object of my original visit, was now installed with his wife and secretary. Already, their trustful city habits had exhausted the only cistern. On the lawn, almost igniting with the heat, was a tangle of barked twigs in a washtub. This was Ford's Provençal dew-pond. The household groaned with the fatigued valor of Southern hospitality. . . . Instantly, and with keen, idealistic, adolescent heedlessness, I offered myself as a guest. The Tates' way of refusing was to say there was no room for me unless I pitched a tent on the lawn. A few days later I returned with an olive Sears-Roebuck-Nashville umbrella tent. I stayed three months.[2]

In July, Tate again took part in the writers' conference at Olivet College and arranged also for Ford to teach at the conference. Together with Ford and Robert Lowell the Tates drove to Olivet. Among Tate's students at this session was Theodore Roethke, then as unknown as Robert Lowell. The Canadian poet A. J. M. Smith had brought him to the conference. Both Roethke and Lowell became firm admirers of Tate's poetry and established personal friendships with him: Roethke as a life-long correspondent, or perhaps more appropriately, as a life-long long-distance telephonant; Lowell as a personal friend who could say in 1959 that "in a sense" he had never left the hospitality given him when he first came to Benfolly.

Ford returned to Olivet to teach during the regular term. Tate went back to work on *The Fathers* in Clarksville, but was suddenly offered a post at The Woman's College in Greensboro, North Carolina. The Tates moved there to a house at 112 Arden Place in January 1938. The job was one which Tate exultantly reported brought a "fabulous salary." Both Allen and Caroline taught three hours per week in the writing program.[3]

Once again Benfolly was left to the care of Mr. Norman, the tenant-farmer. Once again Caroline doubtless observed that she would not see the spring bulbs flower that she had planted the previous fall. Neither of them could have known then that they would never live in their "antebellum mansion" again. Tate went to Greensboro with elation over a job he considered good, but he did not go free of worry. He had written little or no poetry for a year, and he feared that he might never get back to it. He also knew that the energy he had given to the Agrarian cause had had no public consequence. Hence his life seemed to lack "justification." In this mood he wrote to Bishop on January 11, 1938:

> I suppose one difference between a poet and a reformer is that the latter thinks he can fill up his void with any sort of odds and ends; the poet must take the punishment. That, by the way, may be a quality I share with Baudelaire: he took his punishment and didn't pretend it was Society. I would agree with him that somebody is to blame, and his name is Satan, or Evil. It is so simple few of our contemporaries can believe it.

This identification of Satan in a cosmic lineup was not new for Tate, but it is worth noting that as he was writing *The Fathers* he was staring with particular intensity into these dark, purgatorial fields.

When Tate moved to Greensboro *The Fathers* was moving toward completion. And yet he was still baffled by technical problems. The structure bothered him, and he kept changing his mind as to whether it should consist of two or three parts. At times his doubts had involved more than problems of structure. Sometimes the whole novel had seemed to him a hopeless fiasco, a "fake" which he, as he put it, would have been "happy to throw away this moment if I were not a sharecropper who must pay back the advance from his landlord."[4] Nevertheless, by the spring of 1938, while still uncertain about the partition of the book, he could see the end and determined to finish it as rapidly as possible, perhaps before the end of the school term. He did not have large hopes for the book:

> I know exactly what the reviewers are going to say about my book—which relieves me of the bother of reading them. They will say that the narrator beats about the bush for a hundred thousand words but never comes to grips with the characters. Of course, that was what Dorothy [Van Doren] had in mind, and she was right. But what can I do without having the patience and gifts of Flaubert? He would have thrown it all away, and started again. I care just enough about the book to finish it as it is, not enough to rewrite it. Caroline got quite excited and fearful about Dorothy's criticism, which she feared I might adopt; she won't mind it at all the moment it gets into type. She will then tell me what is wrong with all the things that she has been telling me are right.[5]

Doggedly Tate planned to finish the novel and have a summer of rest in West Cornwall, Connecticut at the "Scoville Cottage" which Mark Van Doren had found for the Tates, near the Van Dorens' own summer place. The prospect of being close to friends whom they loved filled Allen and Caroline with happy anticipation. As excited as a boy, Tate wondered if Van Doren's boys would go fishing with him; he doubted that their tender-hearted father would be interested. Or, perhaps, if the boys shared their father's scruples, they would like to play tennis. He warned the boys in a letter to their father that "Nancy is bringing along with her a companion, a professor's daughter who breeds white rats and discusses socialism at the age of twelve."[6]

The novel was still incomplete when the Tates arrived at West Cornwall in the third week of June. Nothing can be reported on fishing or tennis, but Tate worked hard on *The Fathers* for a month and was able to announce to Bishop that he had finished it on July 21, 1938. He was amused to note the coincidence of the book's final episode's taking place on July 21, 1861. G. P. Putnam's Sons, the "landlord" who had given Tate the "sharecropper" an advance, published the novel early that fall. And, despite some reviews of the kind Tate had predicted, the novel enjoyed a critical success, and, reissued after World War II, is still in print. Despite Tate's perturbations and doubts, *The Fathers* is a novel of extraordinary strength. It has some indebtedness, some echoes, but, taken as a whole, there is nothing quite like it in its genre.

No one is likely to improve on Arthur Mizener's reading of *The Fathers*. His essay "*The Fathers* and Realistic Fiction," first published in *Accent* in 1947, is clear and true. Later readings must acknowledge Mizener's as fundamental. But perhaps one can add something by placing the novel in a context of emotion and thought, a foment of evolving obsessions with which Mizener was not concerned but which may help to illuminate the book.

In 1932 Tate was engaged in writing a biography of Robert E. Lee, which he had conceived in 1927. Yet something appears to have shaken his confidence. His theory of Lee's character appears in a letter of October 19, 1932 to John Peale Bishop, in which he says that worry over "the problem of Lee" has left him with "a few gray hairs." He continues:

> The whole Southern incapacity for action since 1865 is rationalized in the popular conception of Lee. It is time this was broken down. . . . Lee did not love power; my thesis about him, stated in these terms, is that he didn't love it because he was profoundly cynical of all action for the public good. He could not see beyond the needs of his own salvation, and he was not generous enough to risk soiling his military cloak for the doubtful salvation of others . . . you know Lee pretended all along that he had no connection with politics—a fiction that won him applause because it seemed to mean that he was above intrigue. . . .

A most fascinating thesis, with enough debunking in it to have
made Americans angry and the book popular. Even more fascinating is the fact that in the same letter Tate admits to possessing
the same cynicism toward "all action for the public good";
though we read this statement against a background of Tate's
involvement in Agrarianism, we pause with the implication that
Tate himself had perhaps begun to displace Lee in the biography. The implication is further documented by a reply from
Bishop, asking what did it matter if the Lee of the biography
were really Tate; the biography, Bishop felt, might be all the
better for that fact.[7] Any concern with a fusion of Tate and Lee
is academic. The biography was never finished. But possibly a
reason for its not being finished is that it had begun to turn
into a species of autobiography or even of fiction.

Tate temporarily put his work on Lee aside in those early
months of 1932 in order to take up a new project in prose, a
project more frankly autobiographical and fictional. But his
word for the book was neither "autobiography" nor "fiction,"
but "genealogy." He told Bishop that he planned to write about
"his own ancestry, beginning with Robert Reade in Va. about
1638, and bringing it down to my brothers and myself, who are
fairly good types of modern America, absolutely different but
motivated by the same blood traits." He conceived the book as
delineating two contrasting figures in each generation, so as to
emphasize the difference between the stability of the Virginia
Tidewater culture and the chaotic energies of the pioneer. The
book seemed all formed in his mind. He thought in February
1932 that he could finish it up by summer.[8]

More than a year later the book was not finished, but it had
developed further in Tate's mind. It also by this time bore a title *Ancestors of Exile*. We obtain some impression of the scheme
of the book from a table of contents which on May 31, 1933
Tate sent to Ellen Glasgow with whom he had corresponded for
a number of years:

> Chapters I, III, and V deal with the growth of a family in
> Virginia, and its fall in the war. Chapters II and IV deal
> with the wanderings and final settlement in Kentucky of a
> typical Scotch-Irish family. Chapter VI deals with the fu-
> sion of these two strains in the chaos of the Reconstruction:

the Virginians go west to St. Louis, and the Kentuckians go there; so that we get a typical modern combination, no longer based upon the land, but committed to the disorder and competitive struggles of modern capitalist society. Chapter VII, "Anonymous Confession", is the chaotic protest of a woman produced by the union of the Tidewater and Scotch-Irish strains—her protest against the aimless life to which she is committed without quite understanding why it is aimless. Through her I am offering my judgment upon the modern mind.

It is clear from the letters to Bishop and Ellen Glasgow that Tate was engrossed in an intricate problem in which personal tradition, his own life and that of his brothers, was to be fitted into a polarized public tradition or history in which the formal society of antebellum Virginia contrasted with the sprawling culture of Kentucky. Equally, it is clear that his ultimate focus was the modern American, not the American of the past. One wonders what such a book would have been like. We shall never know; in the early fall Tate abandoned *Ancestors of Exile*. The step was no easy one, for he wrote:

> I've been in a crisis. I have out of heroism or cowardice (take your choice) thrown over the ancestry book forever. The agony was great, but the peace of mind is greater. It was a simple problem that I could not solve. The discrepancy between the outward significance and the private was so enormous that I decided that I could not handle the material in that form at all, without faking either the significance or the material. A couple of years were wasted, but I learned a lesson, how valuable depends on whether I make the same mistake again. I feel a great release of spirit, but for the moment at least a good deal of sheer exhaustion.[9]

One notices that his abandonment of the book did not mean that he had abandoned the material. Some of the material ultimately found its way into *The Fathers*. And in another way some of *Ancestors of Exile* was preserved.

In 1934 Tate published in *The Yale Review* a short story entitled "The Migration." It is narrated in a laconic style rather like a softened Defoe's by one Rhodam Elwyn, the son of an eighteenth-century Irish-Scottish immigrant, evidently modeled on Tate's own ancestor who was apprenticed in Port Tobacco, Maryland. Much of the story describes the migration of the family from Virginia to North Carolina, thence to Tennessee in about 1800. The observations of frontier life are convincing. In one spot where we are given a description of the religious neurosis of people in a wilderness hardly touched by civilization, the observations are particularly vivid:

> It was in the spring of 1801 that the great camp meeting was held in Logan County, Kentucky, about forty miles from our farm. . . . This was the first time I had seen the jerks, and though I derived great spiritual benefit from the mighty sermons of many godly preachers, I looked upon this jerking exercise with astonishment. Many fell down under the burden of sin, as men slain in battle, and lay for hours in a nearly breathless and motionless state, sometimes for a moment reviving with symptoms of life, giving deep groans or piercing shrieks; and thus did they obtain deliverance from evil. . . . A grove of saplings had been cut down breast-high, and at each post a zealous Christian took his station, so that when the time came he would have something to jerk by. At these posts pretty girls and sober matrons waited, and it was wonderful to see my sister Emily Maxey jerk and kick so powerfully that the earth under her feet looked like a hitching place for horses in fly time.

In its total effect "The Migration" creates admiration for the courage and vitality of the westering folk. Though they are a humorless lot, they do seem like giants.

Except insofar as *The Fathers* is concerned with an aspect of American energy, none of the subject matter of "The Migration" enters directly into it. But there is another link. "The Migration" is told by an old man who is "remembering" the past. That is true of *The Fathers*. In a way it is also true of Tate's other story "The Immortal Woman," for while the narrator is not old, he is distanced from the story by illness; and while he does not "remember" the story, he nevertheless tenders others' memories of incidents which happened long before.

"The Immortal Woman" was written earlier than "The Migration." It dates from 1932; a version of it was sent to Bishop while Tate was living at Toulon. The story is strange. The narrator, a Pennsylvanian by the name of Hermann, wounded ten years before in World War I, is confined to a wheelchair and a room in a house in Georgetown where he lives with his Aunt Charlotte. She takes in sewing. He has not been, he tells us, exactly "right" since his wound. The neighborhood where he and his aunt live is decaying but had obviously once been splendid. From his window Mr. Hermann can see an elegant deserted eighteenth-century house. From time to time for ten years he has been aware of an old lady who comes down the street, sits on a bench and looks up at the house, always staying until she is taken away by a man the narrator supposes is her husband. The husband, we are told, never looks at the house. We are also told that upon one occasion, not the husband but an old man, supposed by the narrator to be a doctor, had come for the old lady. He had been driven in a Victoria by a Negro boy who calls the old lady "Miss Jane." All this has been in the past. Now, as Mr. Hermann again watches the old lady seated on her bench tying pieces of twine together, he listens to a narration coming from the next room where an elderly woman, Mrs. Dulany who is being fitted by Aunt Charlotte, speaks of Georgetown and people who had lived sixty years or so before. As Mr. Hermann listens to Mrs. Dulany and at the same time watches the old lady in the street he tells us that "I suddenly knew that I had been hearing the voice all this time, the words from the sewing room forming a single moment with the image in the street." By this intersection of image and sound the reader is instructed to follow Mrs. Dulany's narrative for a clue to the old lady's identity. Would that it were easy to follow! All that one finally knows is that two Southern families have been brought into an interrelationship by marriage after the Civil War. None of it is very clear. However, we are led to identify the old lady, "Miss Jane," with a "Jane" in Mrs. Dulany's narrative. She had been crazy; she had a habit of making balls of twine; she had died a long time ago, although it is remarked that no one "saw her laid

out." But there remains the possibility that we are to see her not
as the crazy woman but as her niece "Little Jane," who had visited her each day in her room in the now deserted house. Ultimately we cannot be sure which "Jane" is intended. Nor can the
reader confidently say whether or not Jane is a ghost, along with
her "husband" and the "doctor." One thinks so, however, for
the decor or a Victoria carriage, the clothing belong to the past.
Ultimately we decide the matter on symbolic grounds. She is a
ghost, for "she had no place to die. She could neither die nor
live." At the end of the story she is taken away neither by the
husband nor the doctor, but by a young man, handsome and
sure of himself. The reader may guess that she has loved him in
the past, though in what way one cannot be sure, nor can he be
identified in Mrs. Dulany's narrative, though like the old lady
herself, he wears glasses with very thick lenses. All, then, that
one can say with certainty about the story is that some evil
event or events once transpired in the house in Georgetown and
that as a result Miss Jane never knew her true identity, her
proper roots; hence, having had no life, she has had no death.

John Peale Bishop found the story obscure. Tate replied to his
comments in such a way as to confirm what one can on his own
derive from the story:

> Mrs. Dulany's monologue worried me vastly, mostly in
> point of credibility. Now I see that I did not think enough
> about its being comprehensible: I thought that the reader
> wouldn't take it all in, but would let it sink into the general
> atmosphere of time and change—except at the end, where I
> wished to emphasize the old lady's connection with the
> crazy woman, Jane. But since you felt that you *had* to get
> the connections all through straight in your mind, they
> must be made clearer: for if the reader demands that, he
> must have it, or else the writer must keep him from de-
> manding it, which I didn't do.[10]

Though in a final consideration "The Immortal Woman"
teases rather than satisfies the reader, it nevertheless bids for
interest on curious grounds: Mrs. Dulany's mystifying reminis-
cences of the past contain a scene duplicated in *The Fathers* as
well as references to the main characters in the novel. George

Posey, the crucial character in *The Fathers*, appears, and the deserted house in "The Immortal Woman" is, one suspects, the house in Georgetown where much of the decisive action of the novel takes place. Furthermore, *The Fathers* is narrated by Lacy Buchan who becomes a doctor and is the son of Major Buchan. In Mrs. Dulany's monologues, reference is made to Lacy Beckitt, a doctor, the son of Major Beckitt. The madness of the old woman, "Miss Jane," in the story is probably in Tate's mind connected with the displacement of the woman raised in one tradition and exposed to another, which, we remember, was once entered into the design of *Ancestors of Exile*. And that also is the fate of Lacy's sister in *The Fathers*.

One can assert with some firmness, then, that the basic material of *The Fathers* was being sifted and shaped in Tate's mind as early as 1932. Probably earlier, for he had been interested in genealogical materials prior to this time. This interest is corroborated by the fact that Major Beckitt mentioned in the story and Major Buchan of the novel are based upon a forbear on his mother's side, a Major Bogan. Interestingly enough both the short stories enter into *The Fathers* in the matter of style. The deliberate, shrewd and cautious voice of the narrator in *The Migration* is quite different from the slight disorientation, the quavering involutions of the narrator of *The Immortal Woman*. The former, as was mentioned earlier, might suggest Defoe; the latter might suggest Henry James in his Gothic moments. In fact, Donald Davidson found "The Immortal Woman" repulsively Jamesian.[11] But as different as these styles are, they seem to mingle and unify with improbable ease in the voice of Lacy Buchan in *The Fathers*. Was this reconciliation of extreme verbal modes part of the lesson that Tate learned when he abandoned *Ancestors of Exile*?

One other element presses in upon our suppositions about the style and inner intelligence of the novel. This element is an acting version of Henry James' *The Turn of the Screw*, which Tate completed in collaboration with Anne Goodwin Winslow just before he turned to writing *The Fathers*. Tate met Mrs. Winslow—a Southern bluestocking who in 1934 was about fifty years old—when he was teaching at Southwestern. She suggested to him the idea of a dramatic adaptation. They finished their

version in the spring of 1936. Tate tried from time to time to
have it acted, even sent it to T. S. Eliot to see if he could help
get it produced. Eliot's reaction was rather odd. While he liked
the play, he felt that the imposition of evil on children would be
unbearable in the visual bluntness of the stage. The play was
finally produced in May 1962 at the University of Minnesota
Theatre. The press recorded no cases of hysteria in the audience.

Entitled *The Governess,* the play preserves many of the nouvelle's speeches intact, and it commits no violence on intentions,
or at least on the intentions which James ambiguously makes
possible. Yet the emphases of the play assert a simpler line than
does the story. Rather more certainly than in James' version,
Tate's and Mrs. Winslow's governess creates the ghosts of Peter
Quint and Miss Jessel. Rather more obviously, too, the governess
is fascinated with evil and with the possibilities of "badness" or
"corruption" in little Miles. Tate's governess attains a perverse
stature as a puritan who is in love with evil. Little clues are introduced into the play to suggest that some early frustration,
some blunted love motivates her. She remembers, for example,
once having been dressed as a bride when she was a child. She
mentions the death of a younger brother. But if she is in love
with evil, she is also in love with the Master. One thinks that
this is the case in James' story, but one *knows* it to be the case
in Tate's adaptation. The Master is as much to blame as the
governess for the death of Miles. For he abdicates, refuses his
authority, allows a world to exist where he (God) will not show
his face, so that this world is ruled by fanaticism. In such a
world all ultimately is perverse, all ultimately corrupt. Even
though the ghosts emerge from the thwarted psyche of the governess, they are "real" in the sense that their evil is real. Hence,
the children are truly corrupted by these presences. Miles dies
from the insufferable precocity of his corruption—he knows evil
before he can understand it.

The adaptation is brilliant and seems all the more so when
one considers that in 1936 *The Turn of the Screw* was not encir-
cled by excesses of scholarship and interpretation. Edmund Wilson's notorious naturalistic interpretation had appeared. Little
else. Tate's insights were original. These insights in a very broad

way correlate with his insights in *The Fathers*. In both, evil is recognized as a force in life, a force *centered* in life, but it is also recognized as a force whose energy is released by a social situation where an uncertainty about authority obtains.

Though Tate in the throes of finishing his novel had contemplated a structural revision which would employ a two-part scheme, the published version of *The Fathers* has three parts: "Pleasant Hill," "The Crisis," and "The Abyss." These subtitles put before us a broad relationship among the parts, a relationship which is both thematic and structural. That is to say, the movement from an isometric life to a life of angular disorders—from "Pleasant Hill" to "The Abyss"—this movement traverses "The Crisis" or the rise of the Civil War.

"Pleasant Hill" is the name Tate gives to the estate where his ancestor Major Lewis Bogan once lived. The ancestral house burned during the Civil War, but Tate spent part of the summer of 1917 with cousins who lived in a farmhouse on the property. In the first part of *The Fathers* Pleasant Hill embodies the values of order and stability, which the reader soon perceives to be threatened. What we know of these matters, as well as what we know of the whole of the novel, comes to us through the viewpoint of Major Buchan's youngest son, Lacy. But Lacy speaks at the beginning of the novel as an elderly man who tells about events which had taken place fifty years earlier. He is a retired doctor, haunted by memories, some of which are still incomprehensible to him:

> Is it not something to tell, when a score of people whom I knew and loved, people beyond whose lives I could imagine no other life, either out of violence in themselves or the times, or out of some misery or shame scattered into the new life of the modern age where they cannot even find themselves? Why cannot life change without tangling the lives of innocent persons? Why do innocent persons cease their innocence and become violent and evil in themselves that such great changes may take place?

The statement delivers the theme in a plangent way while warning us of the insoluble mysteries.

As the narration progresses in the first part, the distance of
the narrator, who is in effect partitioned off by his advanced
age, diminishes, and he becomes an adolescent boy in 1860. He
is only vaguely aware of the two opposed worlds of his father
and his brother-in-law George Posey. In effect, then, *The Fathers*
employs a dual viewpoint, the boy (who is gentle, virtuous, and
lovable) and the old man that the boy becomes. If some
diffusion attends the viewpoint, so also does a distinct advantage. The boy lives for the reader in the bewilderment of events,
in the scalding demands of his youthful loyalties. These are
brought to the reader with the immediacy of time contemporary
rather than time remembered. Yet, the old narrator enters, like
old paint bleeding through new, to comment from time to time
from his distance with the purged consciousness that cannot
belong to the young narrator. Thus Dr. Lacy Buchan functions
somewhat as a chorus. He seems a choral commentator on the
boy Lacy Buchan who is almost a stranger to him. And the
viewpoint is even more intricate. For the boy himself becomes a
rememberer. The first section contains an extended memory on
the part of the boy, and it seems *his* memory, not that of the old
doctor, even though one is finally aware that it is the memory
of what it was like to remember just at the age when memory
first becomes an important dimension of life.

The Fathers opens with the funeral of Lacy's mother, an occasion which in its emotional and social requirements tests the
natures of those who are still living. All the kin collected at
Pleasant Hill know their parts in the ceremony of grief, all, that
is, except the tall, handsome George Posey who violates the ceremony by riding away from the funeral. This unconventional
gesture both astounds and exhilarates the fifteen-year old boy
who worships the virility and ruthless power of his twenty-six
year old brother-in-law. (Posey, by the way, perfectly understands that he is worshipped. Again and again he says to the
boy, "You're my friend, Lacy boy.") The boy thinks as Posey
prepares to ride away, "In my boyish delight I would have any
day followed him over a precipice, just for his bidding. I know
distinctly that I thought of him always boldly riding somewhere,
and because I couldn't see where, I suppose I thought of a precipice. Yet I am sure he had never done anything crudely bold

that would arrest the attention of a boy." The reference to a
precipice surely portends the third section, "The Abyss."

The mercurial power of George Posey is brought to the reader at the same time that he becomes aware of his flaws. We discover that Lacy's older brother Semmes, who had introduced
Posey to the family, is also under his spell. Just after Posey
leaves the funeral Lacy talks with Semmes alone in their room.
Semmes criticizes their father for his inefficiency, his refusal to
sell any of the slaves, even though "twenty negroes are too
many for this place." The major considers it immoral to sell the
Negroes whom he maintains more as a courtly retinue than as a
source of slave labor. As Semmes speaks the boy reveals the
schism in his loyalties:

> The image of papa rose up before me, strange for the
> first time—his head bowed in humiliation as if he had been
> accused of wrong; that at least was the rôle I thought in my
> ignorance that Semmes had put him in. It struck me that I
> ought to hurt Semmes' feelings if I could; I sulked in my
> chair, and the double wrong, the criticism of my father by
> my brother, the violent behavior of George Posey on the
> day of my mother's funeral, came out in—
> "Brother George swore at Sister and rode off."

In this scene Tate miniatures the divided loyalty of the boy and
indeed of the novel. But the divided loyalty is made larger in
the boy's memory of George Posey's courtship of his sister Susan
two years before. The memory contains several instances of Posey's unconventional behavior, instances of the fact that he does
not belong to and has no patience with the way of Virginian
"aristocracy." All of this is dramatized in the scene where Posey
makes known his intention of marrying Susan. The Major, it
should be observed, is like one of Randall Jarrell's characters
who has become indistinguishable from his environment. He
thinks of Pleasant Hill not as real estate but as the "place"
where his family, including the slaves, will always live. In this
place they will all forever comprehend each other perfectly.
They will always know what they are doing and why. Births and
deaths will be normal joys and normal sorrow—they will not
create traumas. Hence, all problems can be handled and solved
by the laws of manners. And so, in the confrontation between

the man of tradition and the new man, Major Buchan supposes
that he can defeat George Posey by a cold courtesy. In response
to George's statement of his good intentions toward the family,
the Major observes, "Now that is kind of you, Mr. Posey. I tell
you, sir, that we do not deserve your kindness—why we've done
nothing *to* deserve it . . ." It does not work. George Posey does
not crumble; he keeps a relentless and somewhat ominous pressure on the major, finally announcing that he intends to marry
his daughter.

The same strength—which is, incidentally, the advantage a
barbarian enjoys against a civilized man—surfaces in a subsequent
episode of the "Annual Tournament," which Lacy remembers.
The tournament, a contest in which the aim is to capture a ring
on a lance while on horseback, represents the relationship of the
Southern culture to the European. That the description of the
tournament's formal pageantry sounds almost as if Sir Walter
Scott had written it need not surprise. Some such similarity is
intended. George Posey wins the tournament, but when he is
pushed aside by the drunken bully who in the past has usually
won, he assaults him with unnecessary violence. Yet when the
bully, John Langton, insists on a duel, Posey avoids it by knock-
ing Langton out before either of them can use the dueling pistols.
And so one sees Posey as a man who is prone to violence while
at the same time he has no love of violence. The reader learns
something else about Posey during this episode. He is good at
"business," but he does not know the "value" of anything. Unlike
the Major, he feels no compunction about selling his slaves. In
fact he has just sold Yellow Jim who, as the reader discovers
later, is his own half-brother.

To the ingredients of strength, violence, and ruthlessness in
Posey's character one more must be added. It will help us to
understand why Posey impetuously flees from the funeral. Lacy
gives us the reason. "My new brother George had needed in-
tensely to leave, to escape from the forms of death which were,
to us, only the completion of life, and in which there could be
nothing personal, but in which what we were deep inside found
a sufficient expression." This reason should be understood in the
light of another episode. On the morning after his confrontation
with the Major, Posey goes with him to the stable where they

see a young bull attempt to mount a cow. The Major remarks that though young the bull is probably "equal to the occasion." But Posey "was blushing to the roots of his hair. He looked helpless and betrayed." The Major gives him a "sharp, critical glance" and finds an excuse to send him back to the house with Lacy. The point is that for Major Buchan the bull's action is only an ordinary part of existence, just as death is. But Posey cannot bear life any more than he can bear death; he cannot accept death as it is because he cannot accept life as it is. Thus, everything that happens to Posey is as singular as a new phenomenon; nothing is part of a whole; all things are merely parts. This being so, he is at the mercy of phenomena, and to this condition may be attributed his ruthlessness and violence. For the man who has no ordered world will try to create a different world. He will never know exactly what he will do in the real world from one moment to the next, for while the real world is the world in which he acts, the world in which he conceives his acts is one of fantasy. With such a man the fate of the Buchan family is inextricably woven. After his marriage to Susan, Posey takes legal control of Pleasant Hill. That action is the superficial emblem of something more profound. When we understand how profound we begin to understand Lacy's love of George Posey.

The escapist tendency in Posey is attractive to the boy Lacy. He, too, wishes that he could ride away from the funeral and, as he admits this fact to himself he thinks—and this is very significant—of the motto which Edgar Allan Poe attributes to Joseph Glanvill in his story "Ligeia": "No man need succumb to death utterly except by his own feeble will." A hideous notion, really, and far more frightening than death. But it is exactly the kind of demonism which recommends itself to those who see disparate relationships of cause and effect rather than a broad design in life. Because Lacy perceives this demonism and is shocked as well as elated by it, when he goes to arrange for Posey's horse to be saddled, he puts a piece of strap which he spies on the ground in his pocket. Later, at the time he thinks of Glanvill's motto, he touches the strap. Very late in the novel he remembers the strap as an object he has thrown away. Commentators have made rather a lot of this strap. Certainly it is symbolic. Yet it seems the kind of symbol that Henry James was fond of using, the kind of symbol which is surrounded by accident and guilelessness. James was not above offering corrupting charities to his readers; that is, symbols which his characters do not need, but which delight his readers. Perhaps Tate intended to suggest a "search for identity" or a "search for maturity." Yet these phrases tend to destroy the literalness of the symbol. A strap is after all something that holds or is held onto. And that is precisely what Lacy requires as he becomes dimly cognizant of a demonic force affecting his life, his Pleasant Hill, where he comes to know that "our lives were eternally balanced upon a pedestal below which lay an abyss that I could not name." But the abyss could be named "Posey's Inferno"—or possibly the "workaday world of Edgar Allan Poe." The reader is welcome to make what he will of the similarity of the two names.

The first part of *The Fathers* ends with the interment of Lacy's mother in April 1860. The second part, "The Crisis," is at first concerned with the incipient storm clouds of the Civil War. In this stretch Tate lapses not very happily into a historical style reminiscent of his biography of Jefferson Davis. As the storm intensifies and secessionist sentiment grows, Major Buchan retains his Unionist sympathies. Thus, when Lacy's elder brothers, Semmes and Charles, join the Confederate cause, Major Buchan sends Lacy to stay at the Poseys' house in Georgetown within Union territory, so that the boy will not be able to follow his brothers' lead.

The Posey household, Roman Catholic, is more refined, Lacy tells us, but less civilized than that of Pleasant Hill. Refined, yes, and very strange. Posey's father, Rozier Posey, who died when George was a child, had a reputation for "secrecy of action and brutality of character." Posey's mother, despite her excessive refinement, had "once late at night" when her husband "had come home intoxicated . . . spread the sheets out at the top of the stairs" and "tripped him with a poker, and as he lay there in a stupor, she had sewed him up in the sheets and then horsewhipped him into sobriety." This story, which italicizes the chaotic temper of the family, appears also in Mrs. Dulany's narrative in "The Immortal Woman." The brutal husband's younger brother, "Mr. Jarman," almost entirely lacking in will, is just the opposite of Rozier. A failed man of letters, he is likened to

Poe's Roderick Usher. He "looks down" (like Poe's Satan in "The City in the Sea") upon the world from his dormer windows at the top of the house and never leaves his room. Aunt Milly is as much a recluse almost as Mr. Jarman. Even Posey's young sister Jane whom Lacy loves hopelessly shows something of the same recessive nature as the others. It is very much as if the Poseys do not *live* in a house but have only happened to take rooms in the same house. The second section of the novel ends with the beginning of the war.

"The Abyss" converts the brooding, premonitive motifs of the earlier sections into destiny. George Posey is away from the house much of the time. He is running guns from the North to the South, but he is doing it not for the profit but as if he were hypnotized by a role. Profit and loss take the place of life and death—or tradition—for him. While he is away his half-brother, Yellow Jim, whom it will be remembered Posey has sold, returns, a runaway. He resumes his place in the household where he had virtually reared Jane. Yet Jane, a curiously vapid girl, is now frightened of him. Several years have passed since she had seen him, and she has grown up. At the same time, Lacy's brother Semmes, now a "rebel," has fallen in love with Jane. Susan, stretched to breaking between the Poseys and Pleasant Hill, humiliated in different ways by both houses, determines that no Buchan again will marry a Posey. Because of her determination one suspects that in some way she maneuvers and manipulates either the circumstances or the appearance of circumstances so that Semmes is prevented from marrying Jane. All the reader knows is that Lacy is wakened in the night by a scream, that he finds Jane's mother in her room dead, and Jane herself unconscious in her room while Yellow Jim crouches in the hall. It is all circumstantial, but Susan nurtures the suspicion that Yellow Jim has raped Jane. The very next day Susan arranges for Jane, a ruined woman, to enter a convent. But there is no evidence of rape. Susan is interested in Yellow Jim's being killed only until Jane is sent to the convent and safely excluded from marriage. Then she would have Yellow Jim saved. He is not saved. George returns and with Semmes and Lacy takes Jim "up the river," a phrase in sarcastic contrast with Jim's having been sold "down the river" earlier. Semmes shoots Jim, and George, discovering that he had never intended to kill his half-brother, then shoots his brother-in-law. Senseless violence begets senseless violence. Posey disappears and Lacy crosses the river and makes his way back to Pleasant Hill. As he makes his way home exhaustion and terror disorient him, and he experiences a vision. Walking along the Ox Road he thinks that he sees his grandfather Buchan:

> His black silver-buckled shoes printing the brown dust; the black stockings below the tight broadcloth knee-breeches, black too; the buff waistcoat under the bottle-green tail-coat and, impossibly high, the white linen stock rising to the pompous and kindly face that radiated the correct, habitual mixture of warmth and indifference; then, at last over the long chestnut hair the black cocked hat, silver-buckled; and after seeing it I heard the shining silver of the shoe-buckles, the knee-buckles, the hat-buckle like a song. . . . Presently we came easily to a two-barred gate and we stopped to look over it and saw a big fat man standing in a dog-run, his hair stringy above the cold gray eyes. When we were standing on the porch and I was getting a drink from the cedar bucket he gave me a crooked stare. It is a good thing I thought that I have somebody to look to for guidance on this road, and then the man spoke: "The State of Virginia ain't in the Union no more. The people voted her out yestiddy. The Yankees are comin'." My grandfather and I said nothing but thank you as we turned away and, going out, leaned a while to rest upon the bars of the gate. I couldn't see anything; I heard a noise in the air, but it was only the fat man talking in a language that I could not understand.

Now, the identical experience appears in the first part of Tate's poem "Records" which was written in 1928, ten years earlier. The first part is subtitled "A Dream." It is the dream of a "sickly" boy of nine:

> The boy-man on the Ox Road walked along
> The man he was to be and yet another,
> It seemed the grandfather of his mother,
> In knee-breeches silver-buckled like a song,
> His hair long and a cocked hat on his head,

A straight back and slow dignity for stride;
The road, red clay sun-cracked and baked,
Led fearlessly through scrub pines on each side
Hour after hour—the old road cracked and burned,
The trees countless, and his thirst unslaked.
Yet steadily with discipline like fate
Without memory, too ancient to be learned,
The man walked on and as if it were yesterday
Came easily to a two-barred gate
And stopped, and peering over a little way
He saw a dog-run country store fallen-in,
Deserted, but he said, "Who's there?"
And then a tall fat man with stringy hair
And a manner that was innocent of sin,
His galluses greasy, his eyes coldly gray,
Appeared, and with a gravely learned air
Spoke from the deep coherence of hell—
The pines thundered, the sky blacked away,
The man in breeches, all knowledge in his stare,
A moment shuddered as the world fell.

One could hardly miss the telling similarity of details, the knee-breeches, the cocked hat "silver-buckled like a song," the two-barred gate, dog-run, and so forth. And of course, the "tall fat man with stringy hair" and cold gray eyes. The second section of the poem "A Vision" treats a similar experience when the boy is twenty and "strong." He once again meets a spectral figure with stringy hair, but this time he is not fat. He is thin and frenetic and says, "I'm growing old . . . you have no choice." One takes the poem as a whole as a vision of the intensity of Tate's feeling about his ancestors: their secret bond with each other; the way that one generation dies into the birth of the next; and the way all the generations are bound together by love . . . and evil. That Tate repeats the first section of the poem in his novel confirms that intensity and affirms the impression gained on all sides that his immersion in such themes began very early in his career. The repetition of the poem in *The Fathers* is also witty, a joke for those who know his poetry to share. One is reminded of André Gide's autobiographical puns in his *Theseus*. Yet Tate's joke is most serious; the vision offers occasion for a sermon from the grandfather who tells Lacy about Posey:

No, it was not the intention of your brother-in-law to kill your brother. It is never, my son, his intention to do any evil but he does evil because he has not the will to do good. The only expectancy that he shares with humanity is the pursuing grave, and the thought of extinction overwhelms him because he is entirely alone. My son, in my day we were never alone, as your brother-in-law is alone. He is alone like a tornado. His one purpose is to whirl and he brushes aside the obstacles in his way. My son, you are a classical scholar and you have read the epic of Apollonius of Rhodes, the Alexandrian scholar who pieced together from many older authors the pathetic tale of Jason and Medea and the Golden Fleece. . . . It was Jason's misfortune to care only for the Golden Fleece and the like impossible things, while at the same time getting himself involved with the humanity of others, which it was not his intention but rather of his very nature to betray. . . . And when Medea discovered his perfidy she killed her children, and went mad, becoming evil; whereas Jason caused all the evil by means of his own privation of good.

The myth fits. It offers a final comprehension of Posey. It encourages us to believe that little Jane has been deliberately sacrificed as were Medea's children.

Beyond this point the novel dives to its culminating violences. Major Buchan hangs himself when he finds that he cannot keep Pleasant Hill safe from the Northern troops. And Posey, who with Lacy joins the Confederate Army, responds to an insult by shooting to death the very John Langton he had refused to kill at the tournament. Consequently, Posey leaves the troops and returns to Georgetown. Lacy decides he will return to the army. "I'll go back and finish it. It won't make any difference if I am killed. If I am killed it will be because I love him more than any man."

Why should Lacy love the man who has killed his brother and driven his sister insane? He loves Posey because his unpremeditated evil is evidence of his life. Even his passion for commerce, a passion based not on greed but the need to act, is evidence of life. Major Buchan is not quite alive. He is the continuation of a form of life rather than life, and toward the end of the novel the boy sees that his father is beautiful the way pure forms are beautiful, but that he also is foolish and "arrogant." One must remember that Tate's brother Ben, highly successful in business, served as model for the character of Posey. And Posey is, finally, not a man in the Civil War but a modern American. If anything is to be loved it must be that which lives and is therefore becoming; not that which has become and is therefore dying. Certain critics have solemnly asserted that Tate would return us if he could to a plantation society. That view forgets that Tate has always insisted that one cannot understand America unless he acknowledges the importance of a frontier vitality in its composition. Such critics do not know—though a close reading of *The Fathers* would tell them—that Tate considered the antebellum plantation order imperfect and somehow silly. Not silly at the time it existed, but inevitably silly to a contemporary mind.

All of this analysis makes the book seem too doctrinaire. But *The Fathers* seldom loses subtlety. It never preaches for the reason that meaning occurs with incident, and the narrator never wholly understands his own story. In a way then one can say that *The Fathers* is a triumph of the Jamesian viewpoint. Yet to say so obscures the fact that it is equally a triumph of the Jamesian viewpoint as extended by Ford Madox Ford. In *The Fathers*, as in Ford's *The Good Soldier*, awareness arises from mysteries. Even to say this obscures the fact that the novel is a triumph of the Fordian viewpoint as extended by Tate. For Ford's mysteries finally make his narrator (like Lacy Buchan, an old man remembering) the perpetrator of an evil which he mistakenly believes is only in the other characters. But Tate's mysteries of evil make of Lacy Buchan a truly innocent hero. One does not mean here the innocence of a child. No, Lacy can claim innocence because he knows evil and is not destroyed by it. This knowledge allows him to act in the world in a way that neither Posey nor Major Buchan can. That is, something of the honor and discipline of his tradition remains alive in him. He will fight in the war which Posey leaves. But Lacy's tutored innocence also means that he can move beyond his tradition. He will stay for the funeral but he will not live with death. Finally, then, if Posey is an apologue of the modern rootless American, Lacy is a token of what Americans might in time become.

Allen Tate has published no more fiction since *The Fathers*. In 1944 Graham Greene, then an editor with Eyre and Spottiswoode which had published *The Fathers* in England, wrote to Tate, mentioning his admiration of *The Fathers* and hoping that Tate would soon have a new novel.[12] Tate replied that in the past three years he had "had two novels in differing stages of completion," one of which he hoped to finish in 1945.[13] One of these projected novels was a sequel to *The Fathers*. Neither was finished. One must regret that fact, but one can hardly be astounded. Into *The Fathers* Tate put as much as he had learned about life, and he packed into it enough intensity for several novels. He might have been able to duplicate the success of *The Fathers* but he has never been content to repeat successes. That is why *The Fathers*, like much else he has written, stands like a dolmen, alone and durable.

CHAPTER SEVEN

🌿 The Season of the Soul 🌿

DURING THE YEARS 1939 TO 1946, ALLEN TATE NOT ONLY BROKE the poetic drought that had plagued him for several years but he also raised his poetry to a new elevation. At the same time the accumulating ripeness and stature of his essays placed him among the English world's leading critics. These attainments naturally gave him power. He used that power wisely and generously. His correspondence from the late 1930s on reveals a staggering number of requests for help in obtaining awards and fellowships. The requests came not only from such friends and acquaintances as Richard Eberhart, Mary McCarthy, and Delmore Schwartz but also from strangers such as George Steiner. That he seldom refused help is characteristic.

If it is true that Tate has always had a profound irritability which has driven him to discover literary and social villains and to chastize them, it is also true that no contemporary writer has assigned more of his energy to the disinterested aid of other artists whether illustrious or unknown. And not only artists; we must include as beneficiaries the ordinary citizens of the literary commonwealth. A pleasant instance of such kindness appears in his tactful concern for some of his students at The Woman's College. In April 1939 Allen and Caroline took part in a writers' conference at Savannah, Georgia. Tate had advised the organizer of the conference on matters of scheduling and participants. He also advised him that some of his students could not be certain about arriving in time to receive the reduced fee offered early registrants. "They are," Tate wrote, "very poor and will probably starve themselves in order to come. Could you let them come in after April 1st at the lower rate? And can you tell me what the YWCA would charge them four in a room, for four nights?"[1]

Tate enjoyed his teaching and his students at The Woman's College, which later on claimed the affection of other important writers such as Randall Jarrell and Peter Taylor. One of his hopes, however, failed of realization. He had entered into a scheme with the University of North Carolina Press, The Woman's College being an affiliate with the larger State University, to publish books of poetry. He thought that a good University press would be able to further the cause of poetry better than commercial publishers which had since the Depression shied away from poetry. By May 1, he had sent out letters inviting submissions to "The Chapel Hill Series" to over fifty poets, including Fugitive friends and John Peale Bishop, Robert Fitzgerald, Ford Madox Ford, and Wallace Stevens. But difficulties developed. The editor of the press, W. T. Couch, suddenly decided he was rather against "modernist" poetry; furthermore, he was against paying royalties, a matter on which Tate was adamant. Because of these disagreements and because subscriptions to the series lagged, the project was abandoned when Tate resigned from The Woman's College in 1939 to take a post as Poet in Residence in the Creative Arts Program at Princeton University.

Prior to receiving the offer from Princeton, Tate had been interested in the possibility of moving to St. John's College, Annapolis, Maryland where he had lectured that spring. But he feared that the Great Books Program there might confine him within a monastic regimen. Unquestionably Tate was pleased to go to Princeton. He had worked hard to obtain the appointment and was elated when Maxwell Perkins asked Charles Scribner to use his influence at Princeton in Tate's behalf.[2] Still, he had some misgivings and wrote to Bishop: "I am depressed because Princeton, pleasant though it may be at 20, seems stuffy to a man of 40." On the other hand, the job was a good one which would relieve Caroline of the need to teach.[3]

After a summer at "Westwood" cottage near Andrew Lytle's

house in Monteagle, Tennessee, the Tates took up residence at 16 Linden Lane in Princeton. It was at the end of this summer that Tate seriously returned to poetry. In some desperation he had sent to Mark Van Doren in June of 1938 a poem which he said was one that had decided him not to attempt any more poetry for a while. It was called "Love Song." And Tate was quite right to see in it symptoms of aridity. In fact it is hard to believe that Tate ever wrote the poem. One quatrain will suffice:

> O Love, have no fear
> Where damned souls leer
> In nice optimism
> Salvation of schism.[4]

But then his gift returned. He wrote of the experience almost as if it were mystical:

> Through the summer all space in a great silence ever flowed. It was a very strange thing, and I am still partly in the flow; and I don't understand it. I didn't write a line, verse or prose until the first week of this month [September, 1939], when I wrote my first serious poem since 1935. (J. C. R. [Ransom] is printing it [in *The Kenyon Review*]; it seemed so remote that I didn't keep a carbon of the final version.)[5]

The luminous vision of space and silence was to be understood and fixed in poetic form some three years later in "Seasons of the Soul." The poem that he wrote in September 1939 had little of the mystical or visionary about it. It is a witty poem done in a metaphysical style, called "The Trout Map." One says that "The Trout Map" is "metaphysical" because it exists entirely within the logic of a presiding metaphor—in this case a map. One remembers Donne's fondness for cartographic metaphors—"through the strait of fever," for example—and one might also remember Marvell's hemispheric geography in "To a Coy Mistress." Tate's map is very special, a map put out by "The Management Area of Cherokee / National Forest" for the use of fishermen. It shows trails, "open streams" and "prohibited streams." Tate extends all the detail to "A fishy map for facile fishing / In Marvell's kind Ocean." Marvell's ocean in his poem

"The Garden" is the mind in which any external object "does straight its own resemblance find." The effect of adducing Marvell's ocean—probably for Marvell a Platonic concept—is that the common, rather ludicrous fishing map turns into an epistemological grid. Other terms, such as "will" and "classic laurel" further extend the map's province, and we begin somewhat wryly to view the poem as involving the "fisher's will" to discover or know through the classic laurel of poetry. The reader is further teased by the introduction of the term "enthymenic." It is a term of the professional logician and refers to a premise that is assumed but not stated. Even more, the radical meaning of the word, "something kept in the mind," returns us in a way to Marvell's ocean, while at the same time it casts doubt on the whole procedure. The doubt is proper, for, alas, the map is false. The fishermen who "had tried to fish the egoed belly's dry cartograph" go astray and are lost. The poem finishes:

> After eighteen miles our feet were clownish,
> Then darkness took us into wheezing straits
> Where coarse Magellan idling with his fates
> Ran with the gulls for map around the Horn,
> Or wheresoever the mind with tidy scorn
> Revisits the world upon a dry sunbeam.
> Now mapless the mountains were a dream.

There is no map, then, of the country in the mind.

"The Trout Map" is the kind of poem that is apt to come after a long vacation from writing. Not that it is rusty. Rather, that it is haughty and very jealous of itself as if the poet were insisting every moment that he will entirely realize an experiment in technique. There is no relaxation. All the breathing comes like Coleridge's anxious fountain "in fast thick pants." No case can be made for this poem's being one of Tate's best. Nevertheless, "The Trout Map" is an important poem because it shifted the direction of his poetry.

In 1937 Tate had written to Maxwell Perkins that one of his reasons for wanting to publish a *Selected Poems* was that he would not again write in the same manner. He could not have meant that he would entirely change. No poet does that. He must have meant that he sensed some fundamental alteration in his views of poetry. One very basic alteration appears in his essay "Tension in Poetry" (1938). The essay possesses subtle complications, but it is not harmed by extracting its simple thesis. We are asked to envision a scale of poetic "strategies." At one extreme stands a poetry of intension; that is, romantic or symbolist poetry. At the other extreme stands a poetry of extension; that is, rationalistic or metaphysical poetry: "and each by strong feat of the imagination tries to push [its] meanings as far as [it] can towards the opposite end, so as to occupy the entire scale." Both strategies Tate believes to be "great" but "incomplete." Hence, he proposes a "poetry of the center: poetry of tension in which the 'strategy' is diffused into the unitary effect." This aesthetic view has something in common with the view Wallace Stevens allegorizes in his poem "Mrs. Alfred Uruguay." Mrs. Uruguay, in rich velvet and mounted on a donkey as she goes from the city toward the mountain, meets a young man in poor clothes and mounted on a horse as he goes down from the mountain toward the city. The moment when they pass is like Tate's center point.

Now the reason that this essay suggests a departure for Tate is that up to his point he had clung to T. E. Hulme's belief that only a classical, finite poetry would do. But the scale in "Tension in Poetry" allows not only for Hulme's preference for determined poetry but also for the sort he abhorred. And the poetry of tension would itself, if it occupies any quantitative part of the scale, have to partake of both intension and extension. For, as a term, "tension" is meaningless without reference to the other terms. But these statements are too mathematical. Enough to say that Tate's scale opens a door to romanticism in his poetry.

We may confirm that the door has been opened by looking again at the last line of "The Trout Map." Those mapless mountains which have become a dream are closer to the intensive or romantic end of the scale than to the extensive. The romantic drift can be confirmed in another way. Although the method of the poem is metaphysical—at least until the very end—the poem does what no metaphysical poem does. It goes on a journey; metaphysical poems occupy a territory within boundaries. "The

Trout Map" is a journey-poem, a poem of search. It moves through symbolic landscape, as does the poetry of Spenser, Rimbaud, Poe, and Shelley. "The Trout Map," then, portends important elements of the poetry Tate was to write a few years later. Finally, in that the poem refracts some doubt about what can be known by the senses, particularly the visual sense, and in that the poet seems at the end to lapse into an ambiguous interior darkness, the poem binds "The Abyss" of *The Fathers* to the late poems to be written in the early 1950s. All of this turbulence of thought and feeling along with this air of auto-prophecy create something of a strain in one poem. Yet the strain was not to be immediately relieved. For war came to the world. The war became an element that at first slightly blurred the focus of Tate's poetry. Then it sharpened the focus.

In the fall of 1939 and the early months of 1940, the Tates were feeling their way in an environment that was quite new to them. Academic life, to be sure, was not new, but Princeton is a very special community. Bemused by it, Tate had wondered in September if Princeton really "existed."[6] He discovered that it did. The academic infighting, the ruthless professionalism were more intense than he had known elsewhere. And though he had felt that he could avoid "battles" at Princeton, he soon found himself chagrined that the "creative" program of the department was segregated from the rest of the department which by and large was devoted to the historical approach to literature. That division seems to inform his essay "Miss Emily and the Bibliographers" (1940), easily Tate's most telling attack on the historical method.

At the same time Tate could not fail to appreciate the civilized charms of Princeton; nor could he ignore its intellectual strengths, even when those strengths seemed allied with the powers of darkness. In the course of time the Tates made many new friends; important among these were Willard Thorp, who eventually produced the first bibliography of Tate's works, and Jacques Maritain. And there were his students at Princeton, too, many of them brilliant. To judge from his correspondence, Tate moved gracefully and happily in this milieu. No more than the average American did he worry about the storm clouds over Europe as the decade moved toward its close.

But after Hitler's armies had crunched through the Ardennes and squeezed the British from the continent at Dunkerque, Tate was not only preoccupied with the war, he became deeply pessimistic about it. He supposed at the end of May 1940 that the Germans would almost certainly win in Europe. Worse than that, he guessed that in order to fight the Nazis, America would have to become as organized as the Nazis.[7] A month later he wrote to Mark Van Doren that no matter what "we do, we're in for it; and I fear our brand will be worse than theirs." However, he added that since he always expected the worst, his words should perhaps be taken as exaggeration.[8] His historical pessimism seems to have surfaced in his next poem "False Nightmare" (1941).

Probably the poem should be read in the usual way as an attack on Walt Whitman's poetry.

> "I give the yawp barbaric
> Of piety and pelf
> (Who now reads Herrick?)
>
> "And contradict myself—
> No matter, the verse is large. . . ."

It does treat Whitman with disrespect, but one may ask if the satiric picture of Whitman does not reflect a repugnance toward the growth of crude patriotism that began even before America entered the war. Not so very much earlier, Tate had written of his fear that all critical sensitivity would be numbed by the war in Europe: "Could the outlook be worse for the future of criticism? In the United States we face the censorship of the pressure group. We have a tradition of irresponsible interpretation of patriotic necessity."[9] "False Nightmare," like "The Trout Map," belongs with Tate's lesser poems. But it is interesting as an example of a modified terza rima with a tetrameter cadence. Tate does not control the form perfectly. The rhymes are too often only forced occurrences without inevitability at the ends of lines. Yet the form, along with his earlier attempt in "Pastoral" (1934), looks forward to his later dazzling success with terza rima. The poem did not please all of Tate's friends, and he wrote teasingly and a little plaintively to Bishop:

Alas, what can we hope for from our friends? Edmund
[Wilson] doesn't like your new poem. You don't like mine.
You think "Herrick" pointless; Edmund thought it a brilliant touch. Whom shall I believe? However, I don't see
how you could have missed the point of Herrick. Isn't it
plain that the barbaric yawp will try to supplant the art of
the Herricks and their kind?[10]

Tate was engaged in confronting the yawp with whatever
resources he could command. Behind the nightmare, false or
true, he tended in the years at Princeton to see the true enemy
as scientism, positivism. In the essays of the period, "Miss Emily
and the Bibliographer" (1940), "The Present Function of Criticism" (1940), and to a lesser degree "Thomas Hardy's Philosophical Metaphors (1940), and "Literature as Knowledge" (1941),
a definable pattern recurs. The difficulty in reading poetry, modern or antique, the difficulties of criticism are laid at the door
of Spencerian positivism. Positivism is envisioned as an abstract-
ing force because it inevitably etherealizes itself by becoming
process rather than object. All along the far-flung lines of the
battlefront Tate observes that there have been historical betray-
als. Matthew Arnold gave poetry over to the scientist. I. A.
Richards in his early career gave poetry over to positivism.
The result, Tate submits, has been a furring of language, and the
reader of poetry has come to think of himself as a passive recipient or respondent. Meanwhile, modern education—professional
educators, professional scholars—seems joyfully to be completing
the vanquishment of the human spirit. Tate's assaults were passionate, and they met with counterattacks. Sidney Hook, for
example, replied in "The Late Mr. Tate," published in *The
Southern Review*, Spring 1941. Robert Penn Warren as one of
the editors of the review was embarrassed by the article, yet felt
it would be better to publish it than to reject it. Ransom wrote
to Tate to say he found the article beyond the pale. Cleanth
Brooks, also an editor of *The Southern Review*, with characteristic calm and sweetness wrote to Tate before Hook's article appeared in order to soften the blow.[11]

In a more subtle way Tate was engaging the enemy. In 1940
he began appearing as a panelist on the program "Invitation to
Learning," a transmission of the Columbia Broadcasting Com-

pany. Each program, for which Huntington Cairns served as moderator, concentrated on a particular literary work—*The Divine Comedy, The Turn of the Screw,* and so forth. The colloquies with participants such as Mark Van Doren, Katherine Anne Porter, John Peale Bishop, and Jacques Barzun were superb. Probably "Invitation to Learning" was the most intellectually mature program ever produced by an American network. Some of the discussions were published in 1941 in *Invitation to Learning* edited by Tate, Huntington Cairns, and Mark Van Doren. In these discussions the reader may observe Tate's agility and tone. Amusing, generous but cunning, he plays those who disagree with him as a good fly fisherman plays a trout he respects. Again and again he agrees with an opponent's words, only to use the agreement to move the argument toward his own view. But far more important than his heuristic skill is the fact that Tate for a time gave to the nation an example of a mind that never descended to jargon and never offered some substitute for intellectual responsibility. Literature, he insisted again and again, was knowledge of life, a supreme knowledge of life to be understood only as the kind of knowledge it is, and not, above all, to be understood only as reason or only as feeling. Unhappily in 1941 bureaucratic disagreements over the direction of the program arose. First Tate was dropped, in August, from the program, then Van Doren.

Although the entrance of America into the Second World War came as no surprise to Tate, it forced a change in his attitudes. He had been able to consider himself isolationist, above the clash of opposed imperialisms. But after Pearl Harber he decided, as indeed did many another critic of American society, that the war must be won. His "patriotism" was, however, circumstantial and empty of illusions. Nevertheless, by February 1942 he was thinking of applying for a commission in the Naval Reserve. John Peale Bishop wrote a recommendation for him to Rear Admiral Jacobs at the Bureau of Navigation.[12] As it turned out Tate did not enter the Navy. Another plan, that of going to South America, to give lectures of a cultural nature under the auspices of the Pan American Union also came to nothing. However, with John Peale Bishop, Tate edited the anthology *American Harvest* whose purpose was similar to the lectures; namely to cement a cultural bond with Latin American countries. The English edition appeared in 1942, and in the same year the Commerce Department approved the project for translation. The book was well-received in Latin America. In the same year Tate also edited two other books, both of them for the Princeton University Press. These were *The Language of Poetry,* a collection of lectures given at Princeton by Philip Wheelwright, Cleanth Brooks, I. A. Richards, and Wallace Stevens; and *Princeton Verse Between Two Wars.*

Old worries dogged Tate. His appointment at Princeton was not permanent, and in 1942 he had to decide what he was going to do for a living in the future. Two possibilities opened to him. Since 1939 Archibald MacLeish, then Librarian of Congress, had been interested in inaugurating a post of "Consultant in Poetry" at the Library and had from the first wanted Tate to fill it. Tate declined the offer in 1940, but it had been left open.[13] At the same time Andrew Lytle, living in Monteagle, Tennessee and connected with the University of the South at Sewanee, had begun urging Tate to come to Sewanee to teach and to edit *The Sewanee Review.*[14] Eventually Tate was to accept both responsibilities, but when he left Princeton in the summer of 1942, he decided only to write. As so often before he found himself drawn back toward the South. On May 20, 1942, he confided to Bishop: "There are two troubles about my living in the East. First, I can't write here. Second, I forget who I am. I had a 'nightmare recently in which I couldn't remember my name." But he had no desire to assume the responsibility of living at Benfolly which the tenant farmer was managing. He decided to take a cottage once again near Andrew Lytle in Monteagle.

Monteagle, lying about five miles north of Sewanee, is an entirely remarkable place. It was established in the last quarter of the nineteenth century as an "Assembly Grounds" where edifying lectures were given along the Chautauqua line. Mark Twain and George Washington Cable both lectured there. The bracing elevation of the plateau, which makes for cooler summers, probably dictated the choice of the spot. Over the years, private cabins and cottages have been built in the hills and coves about the Assembly Grounds. Today one enters the compound through a gateway which if it were not made of rustic

timber would have to be made either of horn or ivory. It is unlikely that edifying lectures are still offered, but the cocktail
parties are famous.

By mid-June the Tates had settled in at Monteagle, and Allen
began his never-to-be-finished sequel to *The Fathers*. He suffered
from war jitters and supposed he would soon be drafted. But an
atmosphere of calamity, as in the past, seemed to stimulate his
writing. By November he was composing poetry again. In early
December he mentions having completed four more "Sonnets at
Christmas" (additions to a sequence he had written in 1934)
three short pieces, and a long ode, not quite finished.[15]

Sometime during the winter Robert Lowell and his first wife,
Jean Stafford, joined the Tates at Monteagle. Here Lowell wrote
a number of the poems which brought him fame. Jean Stafford
worked on her best-selling novel *Boston Adventure*. Caroline
was writing her novel *The Women on the Porch*.

Tate's new poems continued to emerge. By January 20, 1943
he had completed the first draft of a poem he described to
Bishop as a sort of ballad.[16] That was "Jubilo." One week later
he wrote, "I am turning out poems so fast now that you will
soon feel bombarded. Here are two more. *Jubilo* I think, now at
any rate, is my best since The Mediterranean."[17] The poem sent
with "Jubilo" was "Winter Mask," which he revised that February. He referred to it as a "warming up for a poem of 240
lines, 180 of which are written in that stanza, which I think of
as a little canzone."[18] First entitled "Seasonal Confessions" this
long poem was eventually called "Seasons of the Soul," a title
suggested by John Crowe Ransom. Tate also at this time translated the late Latin poem *Pervigilium Veneris*.

"More Sonnets at Christmas" significantly but not altogether
satisfactorily attempts through the four sonnets to unite a personal sense of a loss with the world's loss; a loss of innocence
with the world's loss of peace; a loss of religion with America's
loss of individuality and freedom. Sonnet I envisions Christ as
aging and as a "mummy," therefore inaccessible though still
capable of creating fear. Christ's eyes are "fierce shuttlecocks"
that pierce "the close net of what I failed." The game-metaphor
is most grotesque, though potent in the way of the grotesque
analogies of seventeenth-century religious poetry. What those

shuttlecock eyes see is one whose fear of death has "betrayed" him "dithering in the drift of cordial seas." Here the relationship between the words "dithering" and "cordial" is just right, for "cordial" evokes not only *social formality* but also *heart* and *blood,* so that one sees that the fear has betrayed him into inaction. Nevertheless, the possibility for action in a world at war seems worse than inaction:

> Suppose I take an arrogant bomber, stroke
> By stroke, up to the frazzled sun to hear
> Sun-ghostlings whisper: Yes, the capital yoke—
> Remove it and there's not a ghost to fear
> This crucial day, whose decapitate joke
> Languidly winds into the inner ear.

The sun-ghostlings are more frightening than mummy-Christ. We are told why. The head or reason—the capital yoke—disappears in wartime. Then, we are ironically informed, we have nothing, no ghost at all, to fear. "Capital yoke" puns its way, we note, into "decapitate joke." This temptation to escape from the rule of mind is an old one for Tate. We remember it from "Homily," dating from 1922, in the enjoinder to "tear out the close vermiculate crease" of the brain. We find it later in "The Maimed Man."

Sonnet II sets forth his and his country's loss of innocence. One invites "the ladies toward the mistletoe / With greedy eyes that stare like an old crow." This acrid picture is set against a scene of a now lost faith and beauty, made all the more poignant by the nostalgic greeting card quality, the nursery rhyme naïveté of the verse:

> How pleasantly the holly wreaths did hang
> And how stuffed Santa did his reindeer clang
> Above the golden oaken mantel, years ago!

One is charmed by these lines, for their success is that they are the kind of verse no one in the twentieth century can successfully write. But just as in Sonnet I, the loss in Sonnet II is represented as less bad than the unfeeling tide of the war:

> Then hang this picture for a calendar,
> As sheep for goat, and pray most fixedly
> For the cold martial progress of your star,
> With thoughts of commerce and society,
> Well-milked Chinese, Negroes who cannot sing,
> The Huns gelded and feeding in a ring.

The third sonnet extends the excruciating alternatives between personal inadequacy and public grossness. The irony is doubled and inverted. The sonnet takes note of the earlier "Sonnets at Christmas," referring to the lie that got a black boy whipped and his own failure then and the failure of his world, his father who left him neither "alarmed / Nor even left uneasy by his fall." The sestet wickedly suggests that the easy way out is the way of "violent slumber," untroubled by ghosts of conscience.

The final sonnet gives the screw one final turn. The ghosts to be feared, we are told, are "Plato's Christians in the cave." The irony goes almost too far. For the ineluctable injunction to such Christians must be to leave the church as if it were a cave. This is all negative preaching, of course, for Tate cruelly observes that when the Christian has left the cave he "will be Plato's kept philosopher":

> Albino man bleached from the mortal clay,
> Mild-mannered, gifted in your master's ease
> While the sun squats upon the waveless seas.

The sonnet, thus, inverts Plato's myth of the cave. Tate suggests that the real illusion is contained in seeking the sun, for the sun here is Nietzsche's sun, not Plato's light of truth. And the kept philosopher is the silent conniver in Plato's tyrant state. Even as one must admire the savage involutions of "More Sonnets at Christmas," one must admit that the paradoxes and inversions worse inverted make the poems self-neutralizing. "Ode to Our Young Pro-Consuls of the Air" and "Jubilo" are equally subversive but easier to follow.

"Ode to Our Young Pro-Consuls of the Air" adopts the stanza form of Drayton's "Ode to the Virginian Voyage," as Tate told Bishop in a letter of December 4, 1942, adding in a letter of

December 10 that he had always felt the stanza could be used
for satire. No question about it, Tate does maneuver it smartly
for satiric effects. That is not to suggest that anyone could make
it work that way, for it is an odd form which creates strange
sonics that affect the force of the content. The aural design of
the stanza works toward anticlimax. Here is Tate's first stanza:

> Once more the country calls,
> From sleep, as from his doom,
>   Each citizen to take
>   His modest stake
> Where the sky falls
> With a Pacific boom.

The first line, as do most of the first lines of each stanza
throughout the "Ode," begins with an approximation of a spon-
dee which imparts a slow thrust to the stanza. But then, because
the lines are short, the rest of them thrash. The effect is a little
like a swimmer who pushes into a new lap by thrusting against
the pool side and then begins to sprint. The anticlimax derives
from the rhyme scheme wherein the last two lines seem almost
to lose rhyme, for they are not only separated by three lines
from their comrades in rhyme, but the intervening two lines
form a sputtering couplet that tends to deflect the ear's
memory. While the lines thrash metrically, the rhymes part
from each other to rejoin surprised like dancers in a Virginia
reel. Swift and Pope would have held the form unsuitable for
satire, not triumphant enough for them. Yet it suits Tate's purpose, for he wishes to grieve as much as he wants to satirize. His
orphanic last two lines in most of the stanzas angle away from
wit toward lamentation.

The thesis of the poem is given early:

> Marveling day by day
> Upon the human kind
>   What might I have done
>   (a poet alone)
> To balk or slay
> These enemies of mind?

This, we observe, is the same world as we have in "More Sonnets at Christmas." In the next seven stanzas Tate projects hypertensive slides of history from the American Revolution down to the fall of France and the Japanese attack on Pearl Harbor.

> It was defeat, or near it!
> Yet all that feeble time
>   Brave Brooks and lithe MacLeish
>   Had sworn to thresh
> Our flagging spirit
> With literature made prime!

Here and in the following stanzas Tate refers to MacLeish's view (similar to views of Van Wyck Brooks) which today few remember but which in the early 1940's seemed crucial. This view, proclaimed in MacLeish's essay *The Irresponsibles* (1940), called for a literature responsible to social and political needs rather than to aesthetic ends, subjective and obscure. With something approaching a yawp urbane, Tate announces that now the irresponsibles can be called patriotic: "we follow / *The Irresponsibles!*" At the end the "Ode" addresses the young warriors "with zeal proconsular," whom Tate asks to swear that they will keep "Faith with imperial eye." We are told what this faith entails:

> Take off, O gentle youth,
> And coasting India
>   Scale crusty Everest
>   Whose mythic crest
> Resists your truth;
> And spying far away
>
> Upon the Tibetan plain
> A limping caravan,
>   Dive, and exterminate
>   The Lama, late
> Survival of old pain.
> Go kill the dying swan.

The ending is clear. America will become a world empire, and the world will be completely Americanized. Nothing antique, gentle, or individual will survive. That Tate connected all of this with his quarrel with positivism is suggested by a grim letter he wrote to Van Doren: "How about this little piece of allegory? The lama in my poem is the Liberal Artist. The grammarian will be Charlie [Van Doren's son] a year from now when he drops a bomb on him. It would be just my kind of irony if Charlie accidentally on purpose missed."[19]

"Jubilo" belongs with the "Ode" and "More Sonnets at Christmas." Like them its tone is the harshness which doomed men prefer to solace. The poem seems particularly ferocious for its reference to the old Civil War Song's naïve vision of a world made right. On its own the poem tenders a vision of a world made unendurably sterile by Mars and the positivist's abstractions:

> Then for the Day of Jubilo
> The patient bares his arm at dawn
> To suck the blood's transfusing glow
> And then when all the blood is gone
>   (For the Day of Jubilo)
>
> Salt serum stays his arteries
> Sly tide threading the ribs of sand,
> Till his lost being dries, and cries
> For that unspeakable salt land
>   Beyond the Day of Jubilo.

There exists no need to adduce, as some ingeniously have, The Dead Sea or Lot's wife to account for the "unspeakable salt land." The image derives from the medical metaphor of a salt-water transfusion as a substitute for a blood transfusion, and it requires no complication. The land the patient cries for is death, for in the sterile world the sick man cannot tell the difference between salt water and blood.

On the surface it seems strange that right along with all this *saeva indignatio* Tate was fashioning, with critical advice from Robert Lowell, his masterly translation of the *Pervigilium Veneris*. After all, is not that quaint Bacchic poem quite remote from the war and unspeakable salt lands? Why should the *Pervigilium Veneris* have insinuated itself into Tate's consciousness at this time? He had, he tells us in his "Introductory Note" to the translation, read it first in 1917 and disliked it; had read it again in 1930 and tried without success to translate the famous refrain: *"cras amet qui nunquam amavit quique amavit cras amet."* Then in 1942 the refrain ran unbidden through his mind and suddenly he knew that he had found the right translation: "Tomorrow may loveless, may lover tomorrow make love." Tate says that it was only an "accident" that he made the translation. There are, however, two reasons why the poem may have come back to haunt his ear in 1942. One of these Tate sets forth in his "Introductory Note" where he asks if the poem is "not telling us that the loss of symbolic language may mean the extinction of our humanity?" The answer to that exciting question is flatly *no*. But the important thing is Tate's question, not our answer. His question places the *Pervigilium Veneris* in a relation to the very problems he treats in the poems he was writing at Monteagle, the problems of the future of humanity, the lama, the poet. Perhaps he sees also a possible solution to the problems: if poetry could somehow prevail in its powers of symbolic language and "right imagination," then society itself might be renewed. The other reason lies in the nature of the *Pervigilium Veneris* in relation to the satiric poems written at the same time. The trouble with the satires, which is a fairly common affliction of the genre, is that they lack any form of love. Much of what Tate puts into those poems, except the poor lama, he despises. He must have been aware of this situation himself for he was soon to face that absence of love thematically and to make it the subject of a whole and noble poem "Seasons of the Soul." Meantime, the absence of love was compensated for by the sensual freshets of the *Pervigilium Veneris*. Tate really meant his translation of the refrain; he really wanted the loveless to make love tomorrow.

Reactions to Tate's translation varied. Wallace Stevens felt that Tate should have been writing his own poems rather than making translations. Most felt it was no waste. Edmund Wilson was entranced by it and tried valiantly to get first *The New Yorker*, then *The Atlantic* to publish it. He failed,[20] but it eventually appeared in an elegant limited edition from the Cummington Press.

The translation of the *Pervigilium Veneris* suggests a con-

figuration of sensuousness and conviction which Tate wished to
believe in but could only believe in as a manifestation of the
distant past. Yet it offered the outline of a model. With the
harsh satire of the "Ode to our Young Pro-Consuls of the Air"
and "Jubilo" behind him, he began to turn his poetry in another
direction, even though its elements remained the same. The poem
"Winter Mask" is transitional.

"Winter Mask" sinks down deeper into despair than the other
war poems. But in seeking deeper it touches a nadir at last and
dreams there of ascending. One is conscious of this dream in the
variations of the refrain at the end of each of the "little canzone" stanzas. For that refrain asks again and again if there is
"anything worth living for." There is something worth living
for, and yet it is the very thing that all modern life avoids. In
a devastating analogy Tate tells us that salvation is worth living
for but that man tries to avoid it or seeks it only in death:

> The poisoned rat in the wall
> Cuts through the wall like a knife,
> Then blind, drying, and small
> And driven to cold water,
> Dies of the water of life:
> Both damned in eternal ice,
> The traitor become the boor
> Who had led his friend to slaughter,
> Now bites his head—not nice,
> The food that he lives for.

This analogy between the lost soul and the poisoned rat is one
of the fine moments of modern poetry. It does almost everything
that our poetry has tried to do. In the first place it begins in the
"foul rag and bone shop" where Yeats tells us poetry originates.
We ask if the analogy began with reading the directions on a
package of rat poison. Somewhere down there, we suppose. But
we do not dwell there. We observe the irony: the water that
completes the death of the rat is an innocent compound; it is
the prerequisite of formal salvation. An even graver irony: the
comparison has walked backward in the snow. We are misled by
the footprints; we think they are going in the direction they
actually havē come from. Hence, life is transmuted into death.

Even more, the whole comparison is really an heroic or Homeric simile except that we are not given the whole formula. We are not told, "as a poisoned rat seeks water by which he dies, so man—*etcetera*." Just the one set of equivalents is stated. The effect then is like the metaphysical conceit, yet in reality it goes beyond, becoming a device that binds together the modern sensibility with Homer's or Vergil's. John Donne, somewhere in between, ties the knot. We all suspect that the ordinary street where we walk is an awesome allegory. The poets demonstrate that it is. Tate demonstrates that much and then buttresses the demonstration, the rat analogy, by an allusion to those "damned in eternal ice." The allusion takes us to Cantos XXXII and XXXIII of Dante's *Inferno* in whose Ninth Circle examples of "the treacherous" are given. Among these are Count Ugolino who is frozen together with Archbishop Ruggieri in one cavity in Cocytus where treachery, the sin of cold blood (a deeper sin than violence) is punished. Count Ugolino's story contrasts with Francesca's story in Canto V, for Francesca is bound to another forever through love; Count Ugolino is bound by hate forever to his enemy. The allusion emphasizes, once again, how all the poems of the period are concerned with the absence of love.

It is noteworthy that the original title of "Winter Mask" was "Dejected Stanzas." For, while the poem is dedicated to the memory of W. B. Yeats, the earlier title suggests that Tate might also have been thinking of Coleridge's profound poem "Dejection: an Ode." Though Coleridge's ode is more personal than Tate's poem, it is, like "Winter Mask," a poem of the nadir, of paralysis, of some frozen state in Cocytus, so that Coleridge asks for anything that "might startle this dull pain, and make it move and live!" Tate by implication is asking the same thing. A contrast, however, stands forth. Coleridge, observing a "dead" world bereft of imagination, says "in our life alone does Nature live." Tate also introduces nature into his poem, but his intent is different. In the fourth stanza he advises that "lest the horror" of infernal scenes "freeze / The gentler estimation":

> I go to the sylvan door
> Where nature has been bought

In rational proration
As a thing worth living for.

Nature has been "bought" by positivism and naturalism, or what
Robert Frost deplores as "downward comparisons." Tate is sure
that it is a bad bargain. The proration was never fair. The natural man is the man who dies. He dies like the poisoned rat for
whom innocent water is death.

> I asked the master Yeats
> Whose great style could not tell
> Why it is man hates
> His own salvatiòn,
> Prefers the way to hell,
> And finds his last safety
> In the self-made curse that bore
> Him towards damnatiòn:
> The drowned undrowned by the sea,
> The sea worth living for.

The refusal of salvation, the modern preference for the "natural" over the spiritual, the absence of love in a frozen inscape
—these are the three threads woven together in "Winter Mask."
Because of its themes and its Dantean moments one agrees
with its author that it is a "warming up" for "Seasons of the
Soul." It is also a fine poem in its own right.

"Seasons of the Soul" employs the same canzone stanza, a
form which is Italianate and so rich that one could say "Vene-
tian" of it. But it is also like an elaboration of Drayton's stanza
used in "Ode to Our Young Pro-Consuls of the Air." While it is
a longer (ten-line) stanza, its spacing of rhymes is similar to
Drayton's: A B A C B D E C D E. However, the use of a refrain, varied like the refrain in "Jubilo," pulls in against the
outward drift of the rhymes. Tate's little canzone is a finely
counter-stressed construction. The trimeter cadence is borrowed
from Yeats's poems of civil strife. But the lines do not often
bring Yeats to mind. The spurt and halt, the confluence of sounds
belong only to Allen Tate.

When he began writing "Seasons of the Soul," Tate was
thinking of a poem like James Thomson's *The Seasons*. The seasonal framework is all that remains of that relationship. Each of
the four sections contains six stanzas or sixty lines. And each sec-

tion nods slightly toward one of the four elements of ancient natural philosophy. Summer is linked with air; autumn with earth; winter with water; and spring with fire. One may well say that the use of the elements reminds him of T. S. Eliot's similar arrangement in *Four Quarters*. But one cannot say if the usage shows influence or homage. Similarly, one may say that Tate has followed Eliot by including references to Dante's *Divine Comedy*. Well, no argument on that score. Eliot was there first. Yet the observation dodges the issue, for it assumes that Tate introduces Dante because Eliot had done so. But that would be reason for excluding Dante. The issue is, really, why does either Eliot or Tate find the *Divine Comedy* relevant? The answer is that for both the *Divine Comedy* serves the poem whose field is sin and salvation in the same way as Homeric epic served Vergil—that is, as myth, and as that species of symbolic rhetoric upon which a later rhetoric can be built. At any rate, Tate's poem is no more like Eliot's than it is like Thomson's *The Seasons*.

"Seasons of the Soul," opening with the "Summer" section, returns to Tate's early and pervasive theme of the balance or imbalance between the heart and intellect. Then it moves to a theme emergent in the earlier poems of the same period at Monteagle—that of making "the eye secure," so that the soul may "endure." This can hardly mean anything like "being a better observer." It must mean something like "discovering metaphoric vision." Toward vision the poem proceeds. In the final stanzas of the first section, the lines inch through the atmosphere of war "when, at the June solstice / Green France was overrun / With caterpillar feet." The whole movement reminds one of those pilgrims who on their knees ascend interminable stairs set into mountains—except that Tate is trying to ascend by descending, first to nature, then to the memories of childhood. Neither is of help:

> When was it that the summer
> (Daylong a liquid light)
> And a child, the new-comer,
> Bathed in the same green spray,

> Could neither guess the night?
> The summer had no reason;
> Then, like a primal cause
> It had its timeless day
> Before it kept the season
> Of time's engaging jaws.

Nature and childhood failing, Tate takes us to a lower step, to the inferno of the self, whose quixotic terror he nets with an allusion to a famous passage in the *Inferno:*

> Two men of our summer world
> Descended winding hell
> And when their shadows curled
> They fearfully confounded
> The vast concluding shell:
> Stopping, they saw in the narrow
> Light a centaur pause
> And gaze, then his astounded
> Beard, with a notched arrow,
> Part back upon his jaws.

Down there, where you see the centaur, that blend of human and animal, you may see the way.

The second section, "Autumn," begins where the "Summer" section left us. The scene is "down a well," and specifically that phrase echoes Dante's words for the very depths of hell, *"giu nel pozzo scuro":* "down in the dark well." The scene evokes impressions of waking in a grave, but soon shifts to a scene where the speaker finds himself in an empty hall, staring down bare walls where all the doors are closed. Then he walks "years down / Towards the front door." But he cannot get out the door, and all his running merely brings him, like Donne's gentleman in "Valediction Forbidding Mourning," "back where I began." Here he sees:

> A door open a slit
> And a fat grizzled man
> Come out into the hall:
>
> As in a moonlit street
> Men meeting are too shy

To check their hurried feet
But raise their eyes and squint
As through a needle's eye
Into the faceless gloom,—
My father in a gray shawl
Gave me an unseeing glint
And entered another room!
I stood in the empty hall

And watched them come and go
From one room to another,
Old men, old women—slow,
Familiar; girls, boys;
I saw my downcast mother
Clad in her street-clothes,
Her blue eyes long and small,
Who had no look or voice
For him whose vision froze
Him in the empty hall.

One immediately recognizes the attributes of nightmare—the inability to get to a destination, familiar faces that look upon one without recognition, the devastation of silence and isolation. We enter here the kingdom of the irrational yet nevertheless centauric self. The centaur is of that Nestorian breed which instruct heroes. The lessons, however, are hard to follow. The soul must be given up to desolation. Even the father's squinting "as through a needle's eye," which recalls Dante's meeting his old tutor in the *Inferno,* isolates the soul more poignantly in its own void.

Readers will observe that this section bears a remarkable resemblance to John Peale Bishop's poem "The Dream." Some have wondered if Tate's poem derived from Bishop's. "The Dream" was written at about the same time as Tate's, and, as is well known, these two friends had written companion-pieces before. But the question of Tate's using Bishop's poem as a source for his own is best answered by the fact that both used the same source, a recurring nightmare that Tate had suffered from for years. Under the date of December 22, 1933 Tate wrote to Mark Van Doren:

It is not the ordinary course of life that wears us out; but
the impossible burden of the imponderables is the responsibility that finally defeats us. I have a recurrent dream about
this. It is a large, dark, empty house. Apparently empty, for
the halls are long and wide, and soundless; there are numerous doors that even in the stillness give the sense of tumul-
tuous life; and occasionally a man or a woman, strange to
me but familiar, as if I had known the person in another
life, comes out of a door, and gives me a menacing look.
I have it over and over again, and I think the dream is a
symbol of what I have said, the treachery of the imponderables.

This dream is obviously the basis for the "Autumn" section of
"Seasons of the Soul." Nor is there any deep quarrel between a
motif of "the treachery of the imponderables"—a very Jamesian
phrase—and a motif of being imprisoned in the self.

The third section, "Winter," dominated by images of water,
delineates a different kind of psychic inferno and purgatory,
though it is similar to the previous section in that its infernality
also derives from isolation. As "Winter" opens Venus is called
back to the sea from the burnt land where

> . . . the drying God above,
> Hanged in his windy steeple,
> No longer bears for us
> The living wound of love.

The burned land recalls to the reader the dry summer land of
the first section and therefore recalls the war. Doubtless the
drying God asserts some declination of religion. But why is
Venus called back to the sea in which she was born? The moment is strangely reminiscent of Matthew Arnold's "The For-
saken Merman" who calls for his human wife to leave the
church and come back to him in his oceanic domain. The similarity (we are not talking about "influence") is instructive, for
the sea to which Venus is recalled is a sea of naturalistic sexu-
ality where "a shark swift as your dove / Shall pace our company / All night to nudge and tear / The livid wound of love."
Now, whether or not one takes the word "livid" to mean "black
and blue" or "pale" he notes that "livid wound" has supplanted
"living wound" in the refrain. The "living wound" had been

both humanity's and Christ's. The "livid wound" is a perversion
of that wound, and the sea itself is a perversion of the sea of
love. It is a jungle of passion where

> The pacing animal
> Surveys the jungle cove
> And slicks his slithering wiles
> To turn the venereal awl
> In the livid wound of love.

The melodramatic, almost comic tone of "slicks his slithering
wiles" would be insufferable if we did not see that there is indeed something ridiculous about fanatic seduction. Finally, in
this sea-jungle which becomes "the rigid madrepore," a coral
growth, the speaker seizes

> . . . a branch, which broke;
> I heard the speaking blood
> (From the livid wound of love)
>
> Drip down upon my toe:
> "We are the men who died
> Of self-inflicted woe,
> Lovers whose strategem
> Led to their suicide."
> I touched my sanguine hair
> And felt it drip above
> Their brother who, like them,
> Was maimed and did not bear
> The living wound of love.

The bleeding branch returns us to the epigraph from Dante at
the beginning of "Seasons of the Soul":

> *Allor porsi la mano un poco avante,*
> *e colsi un ramicel da un gran pruno;*
> *e il tronco suo gridò: Perchè mi schiante?*
> (Then I stretched forth my hand a little
> and pulled a twig from a large thorn,
> and the trunk cried: "Why do you tear me?")
>
> (*Inferno,* XIII)

These suicides are "maimed" because they have separated themselves from their bodies in a moment of passion. Still, the pres-

ence of dripping blood moves us toward the haggard renascence
of the final portion. But just before the third section leaves the
mind, the reader feels with a strange suddenness that the sea in
the third section is the blood—but blood made perverse by becoming the tyrant of the self. And then he sees that the concerns
with intellect and heart in the first section have been considered
respectively in the second and third sections. It is the isolated
mind that is "down a well." It is the isolated heart that is
dragged out by the undertow of a suicidal sea. Tate believed,
one suspects, that the war in both the private and social spheres
had widened the fissure between heart and head of which he had
written as a young man.

The final section, "Spring," asks the same question posed in
"More Sonnets at Christmas":

> In time of bloody war
> Who will know the time?
> Is it a new spring star
> Within the timing chill,
> Talking, or just a mime,
> That rises in the blood—
> Thin Jack-and-Jilling seas
> Without the human will?

The final three stanzas do not quite answer the question:

> It burns us each alone
> Whose burning arrogance
> Burns up the rolling stone,
> This earth—Platonic cave
> Of vertiginous chance!
> Come, tired Sisyphus,
> Cover the cave's egress
> Where light reveals the slave,
> Who rests when sleeps with us
> The mother of silences.
>
> Come, old woman, save
> Your sons who have gone down
> Into the burning cave:
> Come, mother, and lean
> At the window with your son

And gaze through its light frame
These fifteen centuries
Upon the shirking scene
Where men, blind, go lame:
Then, mother of silences,

Speak, that we may hear;
Listen, while we confess
That we conceal our fear;
Regard us, while the eye
Discerns by sight or guess
Whether, as sheep foregather
Upon their crooked knees,
We have begun to die;
Whether your kindness, mother,
Is mother of silences.

We are back again with "Plato's Christians." But this time we have help from the mother of silences. This mother is symbolic, but it is well to realize that a stratum of literalness supports the symbolism. We approach that literalness sufficiently if we remember (first) that Tate's mother died in Monteagle in 1929, and (second) Tate's nearly mystical feeling of a flow of time and light during the summer he spent at Monteagle in 1939.

The late Vivienne Koch first pointed out that the old mother in the fourth section of "Seasons of the Soul" is Saint Monica, the mother of Saint Augustine. Once one knows this he can recall the passage toward the end of the *Confessions* where Monica is dying. She goes to the window and looks out. Then she and her son commune *without words*. They participate *wordlessly* in a vision of divine glory. Hence, it is improper to state crudely that the mother of silences is simply death. The silences are divine. The communion between mother and son is vision, vision which makes the eye secure and integrates intellect with feeling. As to whether man trapped in the cave of illusion, his war, his carnality and divisions can approach the vision Tate does not at the end of the poem know. But he knows that it is the only way.

"Seasons of the Soul" is not only a profound and distinguished poem. It is, at a level of formal art, one of the century's most

magnificently sustained poems. And as one considers it in a
progress beginning with "More Sonnets at Christmas," he sees
that Tate upped the technical ante with each poem, as if he
supposed that the confusions of self and of the world could only
be ordered by the most rigorous formality of art. One must be
grateful, but the psychic burden on Tate was heavy. With the
completion of "Seasons of the Soul" exhaustion overtook him,
and his "burst of creative activity came to an end" in an attack
of nervous colitis.[21]

By this time, however, Tate had decided to accept Archibald
MacLeish's offer of the consultant's post at the Library of Congress. He had also decided nearly a year earlier to withdraw his
name from consideration for the editorship of *The Sewanee Review*. But he had withdrawn in such a way as to suggest under
what circumstances he would be willing to serve later. He wrote
to Vice-Chancellor Alexander Guerry:

> I am not a candidate for this position. This sounds abrupt;
> so, with your permission, I should like to be somewhat
> more explicit. I have said consistently to my interested
> friends—whose kindness I shall long appreciate—that I was
> frankly interested in a critical review at the present time,
> when so many journals of that class are suspending publica-
> tion. At the same time I always made it quite plain that
> The Sewanee Review had never been the kind of magazine
> that would interest me as prospective editor. My feeling for
> the profession of letters is so strong that I could not possi-
> bly edit a journal which does not operate on a professional
> basis. I should have to feel that I could command the best
> writing from all over the world. Since the last war the best
> writing in America and Britain has been done not by aca-
> demic men who are willing to give away their work for
> professional advancement, but by professional literary peo-
> ple, who must be paid. This takes money—not much money,
> it is true, but money still. As an editor I could not ask
> these people, many of whom are my friends, to give their
> work away.[22]

The Tates moved to Washington in September 1943. The duties of consultant in poetry were not heavy, but the social life

was demanding. Tate continued to expand his already formid-able list of friends. His greatest interest at the Library centered in expanding its series of recordings of poets reading their own work. The only official document to emerge from Tate's tenure is *Sixty American Poets, 1896–1944, a Checklist,* prepared with the help of Frances Cheney. For each of the poets Tate wrote a brief paragraph of critical impressions, usually generous in tone. These paragraphs do not amount to much as criticism, but they are interesting for the reason that in his essays Tate seldom re-veals what he thinks of most of his contemporaries' work. The *Checklist* is the only public evidence of Tate's sojourn at the Library, but Tate soon found himself involved in a secret ma-neuver to save the life of Ezra Pound.

As is well known, Pound had been foolish enough to make pro-Axis broadcasts in Italy both before and after America's en-trance into the War. If one reads the broadcasts today they seem ridiculous, not dangerous. But today is not 1943, when feeling against the Lord Haw Haws and Tokyo Roses ran high. Archibald MacLeish, who possessed a certain amount of politi-cal influence, was seeking for ways to keep Pound from being shot when American troops entered northern Italy. First he con-tacted Ernest Hemingway in Cuba and shortly afterward Tate. Hemingway and Tate also engaged in correspondence about Pound's case. They concurred that Pound had for many years behaved eccentrically, that much of the *Cantos* was political drivel, and that whether or not Pound was technically guilty of treason, it would be wrong and disastrous for the country to have a poet-martyr. The scheme was to bring pressure to bear in high official places, so that Pound would be arrested rather than shot on sight by the American troops.[23] It is unclear whether or not this humane and rational plan had any practical effect. For when American troops pushed into northern Italy, all was con-fusion, and it is not even certain whether or not Pound was cap-tured or if he voluntarily surrendered in May 1945. But if the official account is correct,[24] it would seem that care was taken to safeguard his legal rights. Whatever the truth of the matter, the affair was the first step in Tate's later involvement in the furor that surrounded Pound after he was returned as a prisoner to America.

In November 1943, Tate arranged for his old friend John Peale Bishop to be brought into a newly-created post at the Library of Congress, that of Resident Fellow in Comparative Literature. Tate had not seen Bishop since June 1942 when Bishop had in ill health resigned his job in the New York Office of the Coordinator of Inter-American Affairs and retired to South Chatham, Massachusetts. Bishop had aged terribly in the meantime and after only two weeks in office he suffered a heart attack, and Tate put him on the train for home, not knowing that Bishop was as seriously ill as he was. His place at the Library was filled by Katherine Anne Porter.

At this time the Tates had to face the serious illness of Caroline's father as well as the ambiguous joy of their only child's engagement to Percy Wood, a student at Vanderbilt. Nancy and Percy were married January 3, 1944. Unhappily, Caroline's father died just before the wedding, and in his wife's absence, Allen had to do the honors as well as all the "work" of the wedding.[25]

In late March, Mrs. John Peale Bishop informed Tate that her husband was dying. Tate asked if she thought that Bishop would like to have him sit with him. But Bishop by that time was beyond recognizing anyone. He died on April 4, 1944. Later in the year Tate began working through Bishop's manuscripts, many of them in his difficult script, in order to gather together a definitive collection of his poems. The collection was finally published in 1948.

In addition to these strains Tate had to consider what he was going to do when his one-year appointment at the Library terminated. In the early autumn of 1943 he supposed he would try to scrape along as best he could without a job. But the conditions he had set on his becoming editor of *The Sewanee Review* were met, and he decided to accept.

In July 1944 Caroline and Allen moved to Sewanee, where they rented a large white frame house. Sewanee, sharing the same elevation as Monteagle, has an excellent climate and great natural beauty. There is no town to speak of, but the campus is extensive and handsome. Most of the buildings are of roseate stone. At this Episcopalian university, where the instructors and senior students wear academic robes in the classrooms, an atmosphere of historical remoteness, of another century, prevails.

Established in 1892 *The Sewanee Review* had remained a rather sleepy academic journal. When Tate took over the editorship there were 397 library subscriptions, 1940 individual subscriptions and 68 free subscriptions.[26] Tate was able to obtain some pledges from private individuals to help pay contributors. He then set about creating a serious but not deadly serious tone for the magazine. He was able to draw contributions from his acquaintanceship with literary people. Within a few issues, *The Sewanee Review* became the leading literary magazine published in English. It became powerful as well; an article or review in *The Sewanee Review* could further or damage literary reputations. It did not become rich, but the subscriptions greatly increased.

Mary McCarthy complained with characteristic charity that under Tate's editorship the magazine tended to feature the same authors over and over again—Robert Penn Warren, Ransom, Tate, and R. P. Blackmur.[27] There was a little truth—no more than that—in her words. But a better way of putting it would be that these writers (with others) gave a critical consistency to the magazine. And that consistency, it is fair to note, was precisely what Tate felt the world needed as an antidote to the divisiveness and raggedness of war. *The Sewanee Review* flourished, and, thanks to Tate, Westerners and Easterners for the first time knew that there existed a University of the South at Sewanee. We may, of course, ask if Tate's editorship of *The Sewanee Review* succeeded so well because it was a time for the "New Criticism" to have its say. Or did that criticism flourish because Tate—and Ransom with *The Kenyon Review*—made it flourish? It must have been something of both, a synergy.

For a while in late 1944 it looked as if Tate might leave Sewanee to take a rather impressive government job. MacLeish had worked behind the scenes to have Tate appointed cultural attaché to the American Embassy in Paris. In January, Tate went to Washington to consult and on January 23, 1945 he wrote to MacLeish that he did not want the appointment. His primary reason for refusing was that the only organization then functioning in France was the Office of War Information. "I am sure," he wrote, "that much of their work is valuable; but it is not in many aspects the kind of thing that I can do or should ever wish to have identified with me." He felt it the better patriotism to refuse a work which he could not do well, thus leaving it open for someone who could.

Tate showed good sense. In any case his work with *The Sewanee Review* was of greater importance than anything he could have done in the fens of bureaucracy. It looked as if he and the *Review* would go on hand in hand forever. Then on October 15, 1945 Tate submitted his resignation to Vice Chancellor Guerry, giving as his reason his impending divorce from Caroline. The divorce was granted in January, and Caroline moved to New York City. In late February or early March, Allen visited her there, and they agreed to remarry. Tate then returned to Sewanee and made his resignation firm. In mid-April, 1946 he drove to New York and then took Caroline to Princeton where they were married. In the meantime, almost as if it were a symbolic gesture, though doubtless there were practical enough reasons, Tate sold Benfolly. They had not lived there for years, and it was a worry and a difficult expense. It is true Tate in later years sometimes congratulated himself on escaping from a white elephant, but as late as 1958 he wrote to Edward Dahlberg that he had never ceased to regret giving up his farm in Tennessee.[28]

Benfolly was gone, but Caroline and Allen were in New York just as they had been when they were first married. The war was over, and they had recently become grandparents.

CHAPTER EIGHT

✕ Ambassador of Culture ✕

IN THE SPRING OF 1946 ALLEN AND CAROLINE MOVED INTO AN apartment at 108 Perry Street in New York City. Allen had become Editor of Belles Lettres for the publishing house of Henry Holt and Company. Smilingly he wrote on April 25, 1946 to T. S. Eliot that he was using Eliot's "example as a precedent" and that he would change his "designation in *Who's Who* from 'poet' to 'publisher.' " Tate indeed had hopes of being able to do something at Holt for the cause of letters. A large commercial publisher, however, as Tate was soon to discover, cherished assumptions rather different from those of *The Sewanee Review*. Besides, the publishing business as a whole fell into difficulties in the years immediately after the war. Costs of production mounted so rapidly that the chances of breaking even with a book of poems or a collection of literary essays were very poor. Unable to help all the writers he wanted to, Tate found himself increasingly frustrated and unhappy. To make matters worse he and Caroline loved New York no more than they had in the 1920s. But they were frequently refreshed by visits to Princeton where they had many friends.

Tate was soon drawn again into the affairs of Ezra Pound who, having been found on February 13, 1946 mentally incompetent to stand trial, languished in St. Elizabeth's Hospital in Washington, D. C. T. S. Eliot wrote from London to Tate, hop-

ing to find some way for Pound to be moved to another hospital
where he would receive better care. Eliot also felt that the
confinement was pointless. Tate agreed but advised Eliot that
with public opinion running as it was this was no time for a
"manifesto."[1] Eliot came to America in May and visited with
the Tates at that time. He also went down to Washington to
visit Pound at St. Elizabeth's. Tate himself visited Pound in the
following year, and Tate's name (along with those of Stephen
Spender, Wyndham Lewis, Robert Graves, Ron Duncan, Robert
Lowell, Randall Jarrell, W. H. Auden, E. E. Cummings, W. C.
Williams, T. S. Eliot, and Marianne Moore) appears in a list
Pound made of the dozen writers with whom he wished to keep
in touch. The presence of Tate's name among Pound's list of
the faithful is something of an absurdity. The two had not been
friends, and Pound had on several occasions expressed contempt
for Tate's work. However, no man of letters could be unaware
of Pound's situation. Tate's relation to the Pound affair did not
depend upon his being drawn in by MacLeish and Hemingway
in 1943, nor recruited by T. S. Eliot in 1946, but upon the nature of the issue, an issue which his own prominence in letters
and his own predilection for literary and moral battle barred
him from dodging. His advice to Eliot to avoid a public manifesto was not a matter of discretion so much as it was an
appreciation of practical strategy.

In the two years Tate spent at Holt he wrote almost nothing:
one essay, "Longinus and the New Criticism" and one poem,
"The Eye." Writing about Longinus worried Tate. He had
agreed to write the essay for a symposium on the New Criticism, yet all along he feared that he lacked the background for
the work. "The subject," he wrote to Herbert Read, "needs a
scholar, and I am the least scholarly member of the symposium."[2] One does not miss the scholar in this essay where Tate
asks to what degree Longinus was able to see beyond a purely
classical theory or descriptive schematic such as Aristotle's *Poet-
ics*. At the beginning he takes up any idiosyncratic phrase and
shakes it hopefully. Then about one third of the way into the
essay he pauses to ask, "whether there is not already, in what I
have said, a certain excess of gloss, commentary cut loose from
the text commented upon, a self-indulgence which seems to at-

tribute to Longinus a comprehension which one is covertly claiming for oneself'" The question *seems* to dare us to agree. What it is really asking is, is it at all possible to bring Longinus into the modern world, is there any point in reading him today? Eventually, Tate does draw Longinus into our world or at least into his view of our world. He quotes Longinus' statement: "Most important of all, we must learn from art the fact that some elements of style depend upon nature alone." His commentary on this statement is indispensable for understanding his own later poems.

> In trying to understand this nice oxymoron, I shall take risks which are perhaps not greater than those taken by most commentators on the *Poetics*. Most important of all, I make Longinus say, we learn from the development of technique that stylistic autonomy is a delusion, because style comes into existence only as it discovers the subject; and conversely the subject exists only after it is formed by the style. No literary work is perfect, no subject perfectly formed. Style reveals that which is not style in the process of forming it. Style does not create the subject, it discovers it. The fusion of art and nature, of technique and subject, can never exceed the approximate; the margin of imperfection, of the unformed, is always there—nature intractable to art, art unequal to nature. The converse of Longinus' aphorism will further elucidate it: we must learn from nature that some elements of subject matter, in a literary work, "depend" upon art alone. There is a reciprocal relation, not an identity—not certainly, the identity of form and content—a dynamic, shifting relation between technique and subject; and they reveal each other. This is my sense of Longinus' primary insight. It is an insight of considerable subtlety that has a special claim to the attention of our generation.

Tate appears to repeat a view which he had held for thirty years; namely, that form and content are inseparable. But he is redirecting that belief here, a redirection predicted by "Seasons of the Soul." Reconsider the sentence: "Style does not create the subject, it discovers it." "Discovery" is the important word here. It suggests one reason why, as Tate moved into his late phase of poetry, his emphasis fell more and more upon vision, and his metaphor, both simple and complex, was the *eye*.

"The Eye," written in 1947, is a poem of agony, for in it the eye can only see what has "happened"; it cannot through a visionary state see beyond the random zigzag of life and cannot therefore transfigure life. Hence the eye accrues adjectives of hardness, scientism and corrosion—"agate," "nuclear," "carbolic." These are inhuman attributions. The failure of the eye, then, is a failure of humanity as well as a failure of vision:

> I see the father and the cooling cup
> Of my childhood in the swallowing sky
> Down, down, until down is up
> And there is nothing in the eye,
>
> Shut shutter of the mineral man
> Who takes the fatherless dark to bed,
> The acid sky to the brain-pan;
> And calls the crows to peck his head.

The last line, with its morbid decision, grants fulfilment to the poem's epigraph from Callimachus: "Sad crow, why does your beak not ache?" Though these two final quatrains are typical of the poem they cannot show that the poem is as elaborately wrought as an illumination in the Book of Kells. There is scarcely a phrase that does not possess a companion phrase, a counterbalance in the poem—"fathered gentleman" and "fatherless dark," for example. And the inhuman adjectives for the eye dictate the inhuman adjective in the last stanza for the man: "mineral." The failure of vision dictates the photographic image of the last stanza: "Shut shutter." A camera, even when the shutter is open, merely reproduces; it does not understand.

"The Eye," along with the superb poems written at Monteagle in 1942 and 1943, enriched his collection *Poems, 1922–1947*, published early in 1948. One detail in an extraordinary way confirms Tate's obsession with a visionary approach. The title page carries four lines from Blake's "London":

> For oft in midnight streets I hear
> How the youthful harlot's curse

> Blasts the newborn infant's ear
> And blights with plagues the marriage hearse.

One's interest does not rest in the misquotation or misprint of "ear" for "tear," though it ruins the poem by making it too logical! The interest is in Tate's having quoted Blake at all. It will be remembered that in an early poem Tate made fun of Blake's mysticism. But he changed his mind, and we can see why.

One of the books Tate had a hand in at Henry Holt and Company was a selection of the poems of Samuel Greenberg whose verses had excited Hart Crane. In his preface to the volume, published in 1947, Tate comments on one of Greenberg's poems as follows: "It is that rare continuation of direct physical sight with imaginative insight which one finds in "Blake's 'London'—a double vision in which what the poem sees beyond the physical world is seen *through* that world." Later Tate would make the same observation about Dante. Here, we become aware that Tate was lamenting in "The Eye" an inability to see beyond the world while at the same time looking at it or through it. Yet he was moving toward the double vision, the coexistence of imagination and observation, which he found in Blake's poem. He would write of the eye's failure in one more poem, then he would seek and find the rare combination of direct physical sight with imaginative insight.

In the same year as the selected *Poems* appeared, Tate's *On the Limits of Poetry, Selected Essays 1928–1948* was published. And in the following year, 1949, the Cummington Press brought out *The Hovering Fly and Other Essays*. These volumes testified to Tate's powers as a literary essayist of the first rank. Yet his best essays were still to be written. These later rich and at times magnificent probings of society, religion, and art begin in 1949 with "Our Cousin, Mr. Poe" and extend to "The Unliteral Imagination: Or I, too, Dislike It" in 1964. They linger near Tate's later poems like anxious lovers.

In the spring of 1948 Tate left Henry Holt and Company to accept a lectureship at New York University. And that summer he became a Fellow of the Kenyon School of English established by John Crowe Ransom. At this first session Yvor Winters was also a Fellow. Winters and Tate had admired each other's work

until about 1937, then there had been a falling out. Here in
Gambier, Ohio, their friendship began again.

The year's summit for Tate was the award of the Nobel Prize
for literature to T. S. Eliot. Under the date of November 5, 1948
he wrote to "Dear Tom":

> Your friends are overwhelming you with messages which,
> because you will acknowledge them, will increase the bur-
> den of your position. I hope that you will not acknowledge
> this note. For I wish less to congratulate you than to take
> the public occasion of the Nobel Prize as the occasion of
> something more private, which I should not otherwise with
> propriety have been able to express. This is the gratitude
> that I feel for what you have done for me in the past
> twenty-five years. You have done it for a whole generation,
> but I speak only for myself. Take your life and your work
> together and we have an *exemplum* of honor and genius in
> rare association, without which I should scarcely have
> known the proper conduct of the profession of letters in a
> difficult age. You will not wonder then that I think of you
> not only with gratitude but with filial affection.

The award of the Nobel Prize to Eliot seemed to Tate comparable to winning the decisive battle in a war. But the battles were
by no means over, and the year 1949 was momentous. It began
quietly enough when he went to the University of Chicago as
Visiting Professor of Humanities. The work was pleasant, the
University interesting, and the pay was good. At the end of the
spring term he wrote to Eliot:

> We leave Chicago next week for a complicated trip to Kan-
> sas and Tennessee before we go on to Kenyon on June 20.
> Which reminds me: we have bought a new car with the
> lush Chicago money, and we hope that when you come
> over next year for your lush Chicago money, you will want
> to go on a trek in the Mississippi valley into the deep
> South. We might manage a little steamboat trip, about
> which Caroline is as enthusiastic as I believe you were
> when it was mentioned in November. Also: we have bought
> a small house in Princeton across the road from the Thorps.
> We've had about as much of New York as we can take.[3]

The house on Nassau Street, which Tate bought from Louis

Coxe, was a bit primitive in its heating arrangements, but pleasant enough in other respects. With characteristic generosity,
Tate's brother Ben paid for it.[4] Remembering Benfolly, Caroline
and Allen called the new house "Benbrackets." Tate wrote
later to Herbert Read:

> We are very snug, if at times a little chilly, in the five
> rooms at Benbrackets, where we hope to live out our natu-
> ral lives, and perhaps to come back to ha'nt it from the
> supernatural state, we like it so well. We had to pass the
> fiftieth year to reach the knowledge that our grandfathers
> had at twenty: how we ought to live. How to make the liv-
> ing remains, of course, always with us.[5]

Caroline helped with the "living" by teaching a workshop in the
writing of fiction at the School of General Studies, Columbia
University. For both, this meant the strain of commuting to
New York, but they were happy with each other and happy to
be living in a community they had grown to love.

Over this felicity a storm gathered and finally broke. In 1948
the Bollingen Foundation established an annual prize of $1000
to be awarded annually to an American poet on the basis of a
book of verse of particular merit. The Foundation designated
the Library of Congress as overseer, and Allen Tate was invited
to serve on the first jury of selection. The other members of the
jury were Léonie Adams, Conrad Aiken, W. H. Auden, Louise
Bogan, Katherine Garrison Chapin, T. S. Eliot, Paul Green,
Robert Lowell, Katherine Anne Porter, Karl Shapiro, Theodore
Spencer, and Willard Thorp. Theodore Spencer died shortly after the jury made its decision, and Archibald MacLeish and William Carlos Williams were added to the panel. The award was
given on February 20, 1949 to Ezra Pound for *Pisan Cantos*.

The announcement of the award from the Library of Congress
took note in a general way of possible objections to awarding
the prize to Pound. In *The Partisan Review* for April, William
Barrett took the jury to task for not having been specific about
what objections might be raised, and he offered a satiric substitute for their statement, in which he emphasized the anti-
Semitic elements in the *Pisan Cantos*. The following issue of
The Partisan Review ran replies from Auden, Shapiro, and

Tate, as well as comments on the case by Robert Gorham Davis, Clement Greenberg, Irving Howe, and George Orwell. Auden's reply was predictably cool and rational. Shapiro observed that he had voted against the *Pisan Cantos* on the grounds that the subject matter "vitiated" the literary qualities of the work. Tate's response did him no credit. He came out swinging, accused Barrett of insinuating that the choice of the jury was motivated by "antisemitic prejudice," and appeared at the end to challenge Barrett to a duel. In the June issue Tate gave what he should have written in the first place, a moderate and reasoned statement of his reasons for voting for Pound. In this statement, later rewritten as his essay "Ezra Pound and the Bollingen Award," he argues that the need to preserve the health of the language is the primary responsibility of the man of letters. His vote, he says, was based on that belief.

Had the matter stopped with an exchange of views in *The Partisan Review*, no great harm would have been done. But the matter did not stop there. Two short articles by Robert Hillyer in *The Saturday Review of Literature*—"Treason's Strange Fruit" (June 11) and "Poetry's New Priesthood" (June 18)—made the issue a national one. Hillyer's invidious articles imputed to modernist poets and publishers in cahoots with the New Criticism a conspiracy to award the Bollingen Prize to a fascist. The assaults were not easy to ignore. In the first place their immediate result was the Library of Congress' decision to discontinue the awards. In the second place, Hillyer's attack appealed all too clearly to anti-intellectualism. That fall Tate and John Berryman counterattacked. They circulated a letter (drafted by Berryman) to about a hundred writers, mostly poets, for signature, with the idea of sending it on later to the editor of *The Saturday Review of Literature*. Hillyer would have been a most vulnerable target, but to the credit of Berryman and Tate the letter was aimed not *ad hominem* but *ad Saturday Review of Literature*. In part the letter stated:

> The literary and political values of the poetry of Ezra Pound offer wide latitudes of support and opposition, as all poetry does in one degree or another. Discussion of the Bollingen award in these terms is to be welcomed.

But the methods employed by Robert Hillyer in the recent attacks published in your pages (June 11 and 18) and supported by your several editorials, are in our opinion reprehensible, in the following terms:

Under the pretense of attacking the award of the Bollingen Prize to Ezra Pound, you sanctioned and guided a prepared attack on modern poetry and criticism, impugning not only the literary reputations but the personal characters of some of its foremost writers. In the blanket attack you included persons not connected with the award in any capacity, as well as its donor. Through the technique of the smear and of "guilt by association" you linked the names of T. S. Eliot, Ezra Pound, Paul Mellon, and Carl Jung, and adumbrated a Fascist conspiracy, for which you did not produce the evidence, and by implication you included in this attack not only certain of the Fellows in American Letters of the Library of Congress, but also a larger group of unnamed writers who were participating in the "conspiracy."

Seventy-three of the writers contacted signed the letter. Among those who refused to sign the letter were John Dos Passos (who pleaded ignorance of the situation), Wallace Stevens, and Archibald MacLeish who at this time was teaching at Harvard University. Stevens assumed a typically Olympian pose: whatever went on in *The Saturday Review of Literature* was, he felt, of no importance. Archibald MacLeish preferred to act in his own way; he deplored Hillyer's articles, but he considered *Pisan Cantos* poor poetry and was, as he studied the book through, more and more astonished by the verdict of the jury.[6] However, he contributed a statement to be included in a pamphlet brought out by Hayden Carruth, then editor of *Poetry*. The pamphlet was called *The Case Against the Saturday Review of Literature*. It reproduced Berryman's letter, the signatures, MacLeish's statement, and others by Malcolm Cowley, Tate, Léonie Adams, Hayden Carruth, and the editors of *The Hudson Review*.

As it happened the letter itself never appeared in *The Saturday Review of Literature*, though it was sent. The magazine demanded to know the names of those who had declined to sign

the letter before it would consider printing it. Finally the letter
was withdrawn and published in *The Nation* on December 17.
That pretty much ended the episode, for while an occasional
article appeared in the next year or two, the excitement subsided. The triumph for Berryman and Tate, however, was that
the Bollingen Foundation decided to continue the prize under
the auspices of Yale University, with the same jury. The cam-
paign had been trying. On January 28, 1950 Tate wrote to Herbert Read:

> Robert Hillyer ought to get some satisfaction out of hav-
> ing taken three months of my rapidly shortening life. It has
> been a rough time; and I think I have been graduated from
> the amateur phase into the professional of literary politics.
> . . .
>
> This whole affair has been very depressing. In spite of
> our "victories" we are still in a bad way. There is a strong
> reaction here against all standards, so pervasive that argu-
> ment can't touch it. We shall have to sit it out, and then
> try to estimate the loss.

If the preceding year had been exhausting, this year was se-
rene. Allen and Caroline worked on their anthology *The House
of Fiction*, published in 1951. One supposes the year was one of
interior richness, contemplation, and study, for at the end of
1950, on December 22, Allen Tate followed Caroline into the
Roman Catholic Church. Although this step came at a time
when a number of other writers were turning to Christianity, for
Tate the step was inevitable rather than modish. A profound
result of his action may be found in his essays and poems which
followed his baptism. Since those poems are part of a longer
work in progress they will be discussed in the final chapter.

There is in Tate's Catholicism no subjugation of mind, will, or
art to religion, for it rests on a basis of intellect and freedom. It
was not the raw fervor of a new convert but the civilized passion for intellectual honor that compelled Tate shortly after his
conversion to write a letter to *The New York Times* (published
February 1, 1951) in which he resisted Cardinal Spellman's
efforts to have the Italian film *The Miracle* suppressed. Tate did
not deny the prelate's right as a Catholic dignitary to prohibit

the movie to the faithful, but he deplored his efforts to have the picture officially suppressed by the state. Tate's basic argument was that censorship is impossible and unnecessary, for bad art will not endure, and good art will prevail whether or not it is censored.

The particular quality of Tate's Catholicism may have owed something to the example of his friend Jacques Maritain. At any rate Tate followed the model of the European intellectual Catholic who demands a rational structure for the house of faith, and excellence in the caretakers. When Thomas Francis Ritt in 1951 sent Tate a copy of the Catholic journal *A. D.* which Father Ritt edited, he responded with a plea for honesty and intellectual rigor:

> I take it that the Kingdom of God will not consent to be served with mediocrity from the republic of letters. I find it hard to say these hard things. They may well strike you as too general to be imputed to any good motive. This I shall have to risk, for it would be invidious to point to examples in this issue of A. D. I shall risk one more general observation. We shall not create a great Catholic literary culture in this country by abusing the great non-Catholic literary culture of our immediate past. It seems to me that our task is to learn from it and at least to equal it. The quasi-Jansenist Know-Nothingism of Catholic "intellectuals" in this country is a disheartening spectacle.[7]

Another significant change soon followed. Though life at Princeton was pleasant and stimulating and though he had recently remodeled their house, Tate decided in 1951 to accept an appointment as Professor of English at the University of Minnesota. One need not seek far for a reason. Tate had reached an age where he could dare to drift no longer like a derelict in an open boat. It is a surprising fact that no university had previously offered Tate an appointment with tenure. Minnesota offered that kind of security, and in the fall of 1951 he and Caroline moved to Minneapolis. They lived at 1409 East River Road.

No reader will fail to agree that an air of restlessness has up to this point characterized Allen Tate's life. Many moves, many engagements, sudden withdrawals. From this point on his activities are even more dizzying. To catalogue all the lectures he gave, all of the readings, all of the writers' conferences where he taught would be pointless. Much, too much, of his energy went to such matters. Yet there was always enough left over for the acts of kindness visible throughout his career. He continued to sponsor the work of writers whom he considered neglected, such able, assured poets as Brewster Ghiselin who directed the annual Utah Writers' Conferences at which Tate served several times as poetry leader. When the black poet Melvin B. Tolson wrote to Tate for help in 1949, the help was forthcoming. Tolson had been appointed poet laureate of Liberia. For the purpose of celebrating that country's centenary, Tolson had written a long, rather fiery and rhetorical poem *Libretto for the Republic of Liberia* and he asked Tate if he would write an introduction to it. Tate not only wrote a very favorable introduction but arranged for the introduction to be published as a kind of advance signal in *Poetry*. Tate also tried without success to get Scribners' to publish the poem as a book. It was eventually published with Tate's introduction by Twayne in 1953.

Though Tate's appointment at Minnesota was the first he had with tenure, one must observe with some amusement that he was away a good deal of the time. In May 1952 Tate was a delegate to the Congress for Cultural Freedom in Paris. Among the addresses he gave to the Congress were versions of his essays "To Whom is the Poet Responsible" and "The Man of Letters in the Modern World." Tate remained in Europe during the summer and in August served as a delegate to the UNESCO Conference in Venice. At this time, with help from Jacques Maritain, Tate was granted an audience by His Holiness Pope Pius XII.[8]

In the following year he and Caroline were again abroad. Under the auspices of the Fulbright Program Tate lectured in the American Studies Program at Oxford in the summer of 1953. Later that year he served as Fulbright Professor at the University of Rome. In the spring, however, Caroline was required by the illness of their daughter to return to America. She and Allen rejoined each other later in Minneapolis where Tate taught for the whole of the school year. He also worked on the American selections for an anthology of modern poetry on which he was collaborating with Lord David Cecil. Unhappily differences had been building again between Caroline and Allen, and in the summer of 1955 they agreed to separate. Caroline moved back to Princeton, and Allen went off to Rome for the summer.

On his return Tate was able to bring into realization a plan which he had been shaping since 1952. T. S. Eliot, who had earlier refused, agreed to deliver a lecture at the University of Minnesota in 1956. The lecture "The Frontiers of Criticism" was given on April 30 in Williams Arena, a "sports palace" for basketball and ice hockey. It was the only building large enough to accommodate the huge audience. The sudoriferous vistas of the gymnasium were disguised by potted palms, gigantic philodendrons and ferns tiered against one end of the arena. Through this tropical flora Tate and Eliot emerged as though they had been swinging cutlasses together in the hot jungle.

Almost as soon as Eliot departed Tate himself left for a reunion of the Fugitives, May 3 to 5. There had been informal meetings and reunions before, but this one was a public occasion underwritten by a grant from the Rockefeller Foundation to the American Studies Association. Donald Davidson, William Y. Elliott, Sidney Hirsch, Andrew Lytle, Merrill Moore, John Crowe Ransom, Alfred Starr, Alec B. Stevenson, Tate, Robert Penn Warren, and Jesse Wills came together and talked much as they had a quarter of a century before. There were public readings and four private sessions. The private sessions were recorded on tape and published by the Vanderbilt University Press in 1959. Tate and Davidson were dubious about the propriety of publishing these conversations. But there is nothing hurtful in the book, and the interflow of voices rewards any reader who wants to know what the tone of a Fugitive meeting was like.

That fall Tate was asked to give several lectures in India under the sponsorship of the American Specialties Program. He had not been very well. Eliot had given him avuncular advice on how to stop smoking cigarettes.[9] Tate did not give up cigarettes, but he made the trip to India. The New Delhi *Times* for October 18, 1956 reported on his "suave, genial personality," as well as on the overwhelming impact of his lecture. His visit was also celebrated in verse by an Indian gentleman who linked Shakespeare, Tagore, and Allen Tate together as the veritable "well-wishers of a state." Despite the strain of the trip, Tate's health improved (to the later amazement of his doctor), and he had the strength on his return trip by way of Europe to give lectures in Turin, Rome, Milan, Florence, Paris, London, and Nottingham. By January 1, 1957 he had again taken up his duties at the University of Minnesota. Two weeks later it was announced that he had been awarded the Bollingen Prize for Poetry for 1956.

The prize was important and gratifying not only to Tate but to his friends as well. However, his friends had begun to worry about the myriad activities that absorbed his strength. John Hall Wheelock as early as 1955 had begged him to stop giving so many lectures and to limit himself to writing poetry. Andrew Lytle advised him that the portions of his unfinished long poem were so good that "you will compound your sorrows if you don't spend all your time finishing it. Your temptation is to assume in your person the paradigm of the fallen state, that is, this wandering of exile . . ."[10] His wandering did not stop. In 1958 he went abroad again as Fulbright Professor for the fall term at the University of Oxford where he was awarded an honorary degree of Master of Arts. In the winter term he moved on to the University of Leeds. With no rest he returned the following summer to teach at the summer school at Harvard University.

During this summer, 1959, Caroline obtained a divorce. And on August 27 at the home of Francis Biddle in Wellfleet, Massachusetts, Allen was married to the poetess Isabella Gardner, the former Mrs. Robert McCormick. She had two children by previous marriages. The marriage, of course, separated Tate from Catholic communion, though he continued to think of himself as Catholic. When Tate had written to Eliot of his intention to remarry, Eliot had replied that he hoped Isabella would stop him from careering about the world lecturing and getting no rest.[11] In truth, with his remarriage, his lecturing became much less frequent.

The next decade brought many public honors to Tate. The Autumn 1959 issue of *The Sewanee Review* was devoted to a celebration of his sixtieth birthday, with tributes from R. P. Blackmur, Malcolm Cowley, Ransom, Davidson, Robert Lowell, Katherine Anne Porter, and Herbert Read, among others. There was also a translation into French of his "Ode to the Confederate Dead" by Jacques and Raïssa Maritain. Brandeis University in the same year awarded him its Medal Award for Poetry. In 1962 he was presented with the *Medaglia d'Oro di Società Ita-*

liana di Dante Alighieri at Florence, Italy. The Academy of American Poets gave him its Fellowship Award of $5,000 in 1963. In 1964 he was elected to the American Academy of Arts and Letters, and in the following year to the American Academy of Arts and Sciences. In 1968 he served as president of the National Institute of Arts and Letters. The decade brought sorrows as well as honors, the deaths of his friends Donald Davidson, T. S. Eliot, and Herbert Read, and of his brother Ben in 1968. There was another sorrow, not new to Tate. He was, one might say, lost in the plaudits of the world. But he missed the region of his being. He had sought the world, but the more he found it and the more it honored him, the more poignant his nostalgia for the South became. His cosmopolitan life with summers in Europe or Cape Cod began to pall. Rather sadly Tate wrote from Sewanee, Tennessee to Herbert Read on October 18, 1965:

> This summer, after Spoleto (an expense of spirit), I couldn't pretend again that I could work in Europe. So I came here, my one remaining spiritual home; Isabella decided to stay on in England and Italy, being somewhat allergic to the South.

That year Isabella and Allen agreed to separate, and she was granted a divorce on March 28, 1966.

Before the divorce Tate had met in one of his classes, Helen Heinz of St. Paul. They were married on July 30, 1966 in Murfreesboro, Tennessee. Helen had been a registered nurse for ten years, and for some time had been head of the nursing staff of a large Minneapolis hospital. Tate took leave from Minnesota to teach at the University of North Carolina in Greensboro in the fall of 1966 and at Vanderbilt in the second term, 1967. Twin sons, John Allen and Michael Paul, were born to the Tates August 30, 1967. The next year was Tate's final year at Minnesota, and upon retirement in June 1968 the Tates moved to a new house Allen had had built in Sewanee. In a tragic nursery accident, one twin, Michael, died in July 1968. A third son, Benjamin Lewis Bogan Tate, was born December 18, 1969. Now near his lifelong friend Andrew Lytle and in surroundings of domestic beauty and love, Tate continues to work on both poetry and prose. It is time to look at his latest work.

CHAPTER NINE

❧ Work in Progress ❧

UNTIL THIS POINT ALLEN TATE'S ESSAYS HAVE BEEN CITED because they illuminated his poetry. Tate encourages us in that practice by remarking of his essays that "the business of the poet-critic" is not with "consistency and system, but merely with as much self-knowledge as he needs to write his own verse."[1] But that does not give us the reason that most people read the essays. They read them for themselves, not as programmatic adjuncts to the poetry. Besides, the essays possess consistency and system.

At the outset it is fair to observe that Tate's essays develop from an acute sense of their historicity. Although he mentions Samuel Johnson with approval, and though he says that he owes "most of all" to Coleridge, still his own essays are addressed to *contemporary* problems invoked by the diffuse social concern of Matthew Arnold and the psychological concern of I. A. Richards. In Tate's mind Arnold's criticism and the earlier criticism of Richards are related. Arnold, Tate believes, seeing the moribundity of religion in nineteenth-century society, placed his hopes on poetry as a substitute for religion. Insofar, however, as the effect of such a step was that of turning poetry over to science, criticism became not the equal of science but the bond slave. At this point the early views of I. A. Richards become relevant. For in *The Principles of Literary Criticism*, Richards,

194

hoping to correct Arnold's hopeful but misty approaches, employed a "laboratory technique" in investigating poetry. Hence both Arnold and Richards take part in a *Zeitgeist* of positivism. And it is to the spirit of positivism, to the faith that something good or true will inevitably come from scientific investigation, that Tate objects.

Positivism for Tate is The Modern Error. It is error because it leans upon only one aspect of man, the mechanical-rational side. A positivist's criticism of poetry must of necessity employ the vocabulary of external investigation—the *partial* jargon of science. The mechanical-rationalistic view destroys the ability to see poetry as a whole object. Tate extends this rejection of positivism as an imbalanced view to the realms of life and society. We suffer, he is sure, from a sensual and a spiritual deprivation. Positivism puts on the mask of Creon and with it the pride of partial knowledge. And so we have in Tate's essays a dramatic situation in which society (and, indeed, the "actual world") must be saved from the *nouveau riche* king who knows only one set of laws, which happen to be the laws of man's mind. In this struggle the duty of poetry is to save the language by keeping it not lexicographically pure but experientially new.

When one observes this dramatic struggle between poet and positivist, agrarian and industrialist, he also sees why Tate's essays have a natural difficulty for the reader. The essays are embroiled in the very battles that his poems are embroiled in. Can the essays dare to be more certain than the poems are? When poems claim victory they cease to be poems because they become static and monumental, entirely finished, and the quiver of muscle freezes in the marble surfaces. Tate claims no more victory in his essays than he does in his poetry. His points are precise, but his procedure is one of a subjective richness, of divagations which do not weary us but exasperate us when we find that we have been led back where we began. Still, that is only to say that we must employ a special skill in reading these essays. We need not "develop a new skill" as educationists are fond of saying, for the skill already exists. We can read the essays as we read poetry. But the reader will complain that essays should be read as essays. Very well, they may be read as prose, and then they are even more demanding.

Tate's essays are punctuated from time to time by self-deprecations and claims of ignorance. Sometimes this self-deprecation becomes a bit maddening, especially when Tate's knowledge seems entirely secure. It may even seem a Ciceronian trick to obtain victory by disclaiming it. But the self-deprecation has a great parallel. It is Socrates, is it not, who continually says that he knows nothing? The reader need not take this comparison very seriously. It is only a way of leading into a comparison that he should take seriously: Tate frequently employs elements of the Socratic dialectic. "The Hovering Fly" offers a good example. At the beginning of the Third section of the essay he writes.

> Suppose we take two terms and relate them. The two terms for this occasion are, first, Poetry, and, second, the Actual World. Do we mean then by the actual world a world distinguished from one which is less actual or not actual at all? I suppose we mean both things; else we should say: Poetry and the World. We might again alter the phrase and get: Poetry and Actuality, which by omitting the world would give us a clue to its bearing in the preceding phrase; that is, world might then mean region, realm, field of observation or experience. . . .
>
> If I seem to be making this matter obscure, let me plead my ignorance, and if you will, add your own ignorance to my plea; or if you like it better, add your skepticism to mine; and we shall examine together our riddle, so far as we can, as if nobody had seen it before: which, I take it, is the *action* of skepticism as distinguished from the mere feeling of the skeptic.

Here is a thoroughly unfashionable patience in dividing the problem into its parts, an unmodern striving for definitions of those parts. Above all, one is cognizant of Tate's compulsion to conduct the investigation dutifully to its end, to *act* within the prescripts of the dialectic. Sometimes it seems, in reading one of the essays, that the method has been arrived at by simply dropping the convention of the question and answer employed by Plato while preserving the ardent chase which the convention paces. Even more extraordinary, at times Tate permits the pursuit to lead to dead places where no answer is forthcoming or where a contradiction appears to impend like a precariously

balanced boulder over the way. These dead places are comparable to the moments of despair that invade, say, the denouements
of the *Parmenides* or the sudden chills of doubt that attack the
Crito. And just as Socrates is never far from denouncing his vil-
lain, the sophist or rhetorician, so Tate is never far from im-
peaching the positivist. Come to think of it, the sophist and positivist share a common belief that they know all there is to know
and can "prove" it!

Just one more extension of the comparison. We shall let it be
outrageous. Both Socrates and Tate shelter a eudemon, and to
both this inner voice speaks not to say what should be done,
only and always to warn against what must not be done. Socrates is very clear about his voice. Tate is not so clear, and we
do not usually find the voice in his essays. But we often find it in
his poetry. The comparison has at this point, of course, become
a metaphor. Tate's warning voice is down a well, the well into
which he descends in "Seasons of the Soul" and revisits in his
latest poems. To these poems we now turn: two written in 1952,
"The Maimed Man" and "The Swimmers," and one written in
1953, "The Buried Lake." They must be approached from several different directions. First, as logical developments in Tate's
poetry as poetry. Second, as logical developments in Tate's
thought. Third, as a logical break on Tate's part with certain
aspects of T. S. Eliot's poetry.

The suggestion behind the phrase "logical development in
Tate's poetry as poetry" is that a writer's poetry possesses a life
of its own. It may be affected by many externalities, yet it possesses a core immune to influences. This is so because poetry
exists in an alliance of rhythmic, imagistic, and linguistic forces.
Any one or all of these powers can be magnetized by event or
another poet's accomplishment, but the alliance will adjust to a
new balance, and the alliance will continue. Another reason that
an individual's poetry has an autonomous existence is that the
compulsive images of a poet come from private experience, and,
even more importantly, these images sometimes beget without
extramural contact further images by parthenogenesis. To observe this process in operation we must go back to Tate's out-
burst of creativity in 1942 and 1943 and ponder once more his
phrase "make the eye secure," that correction of vision entreated

in "Seasons of the Soul." This same fascination with the eye, we remember, continued in a negative way in the poem "The Eye," written in 1947. In 1950 Tate published in pamphlet form from the Cummington Press a poem "Two Conceits for the Eye to Sing, if Possible." The very title of this poem suggests an aesthetic desperation. The poem itself is based on parodic emulations of nursery rhymes—and nursery rhymes often border on hysteria.

> Sing a song of 'sistence
> Pocketfull of Eye

or

> Big, inside the tub,
> Rubbed hey dub-a-dub,

and

> Mary quite contrary
> Light as a green fairy
> Dances, dances. Mary.

No disrespect to Tate is intended in saying that these formulations are "fond and foolish." They are the kind of fatuity that is sometimes necessary to move one's art to another plane. And Tate himself has not thought enough of the poem to preserve it in later collections. The point, however, is this: although the poem takes the image or symbol of the eye, employed suggestively in the poems of 1942–43, austerely in "The Eye," and reduces it momentarily to gibberish, two significant extensions of the image emerge. One, the "eye" obtains a ratiocinative twin (a "conceit") through a pun:

> When the I's were opened
> They saw ne'er a thing

Second, this poem, which is about the triumph of naturalism and science over humanity, terminates with the vision, quoted above, of Mary who is "green." To be brutal in paraphrase: the Mother of Christ is separated from the world of the positivist's

eye and the egoistical "I," and in her greenness, growth, and
life, she dwells only in an infantile world of mysterious dog-
gerel. Now, in the poems of 1952 and 1953, the eye and the pastoral (green) world reassemble, but they do so seriously and
importantly. All this is a way of saying that a poet must sometimes use up his failures before he can find his success. This development, at any rate, lay within the boundaries of the logic of
Tate's poetry.

As to the second direction, the "logical development of Tate's
thought": we must weigh the effect of Jacques Maritain's views
on Tate's own concepts. This is more difficult to do. Tate's ideas
on religion and art were developed and similar to Maritain's
before they met. One needs only to remark how early Tate had
reacted against the secularity of twentieth-century neo-humanism
to see that he and Maritain were intellectual allies. But doubtless
Maritain stood as a confirming hero to Tate, and Maritain's book
The Dream of Descartes (1944) gave support and vocabulary to
him. This book, which was very fashionable reading after World
War II, takes the position that Descartes in giving form and
direction to the rising rationalism, split man in two. He speaks of
Descartes as possessing "two precious truths—one that is old, the
other new." The new is "the living truth of physico-mathematical
science." The old is "that ancient truth, the Socratic and Christian
precept: Go back into thyself and into the spiritual element which
is within thee." Yet, according to Maritain, Descartes' famous
solitude and introspection were not those of a man of prayer;
the solitude and introspection served the creation of a cosmos,
a very abstract one, within Descartes' intellect. It is a mechanical
cosmos free from the senses. It accounts for what Maritain calls
"the three great ruptures" of modern man: "the rupture of
thought with being, of the movement of the soul toward wisdom,
and of the human compound."

Tate incorporated some of this view in his incomparably fine
essays on Edgar Allan Poe, "Our Cousin Mr. Poe" (1949) and
"The Angelic Imagination" (1951). Poe's "angelism" directs the
creation of a world of absolute order, indeed of logic, but one
which yields no true equivalent to the world as revealed by the
senses. Poe's angelism is modern man's:

Poe as God sits silent in darkness. Here the movement of tragedy is reversed: there is no action. Man as angel becomes a demon who cannot initiate the first motion of love, and we can feel only compassion with his suffering, for it is potentially ours.

Against Poe's a-sensuous cosmogony in which Satan has triumphed over God—for it is the sin of intellectual pride Tate is talking about in "The Angelic Imagination"—Tate counterpoises the cosmos of Dante. In his great essay "The Symbolic Imagination," Tate's primary point is that Dante works from the common and sensuous to the extraordinary and the suprasensuous. Tate's word for it is not "suprasensous" but "anagogical," a word that appears frequently in the later essays, just as the word "failure" occured frequently in the earlier essays. Indeed, the anagogical or mystical discovery become Tate's way of surmounting what he once thought to be inevitable failure. In his classes at Minnesota he taught that there were four levels to poetry, the historical, the substantive, the rhetorical, and the anagogical which gives us the spiritual meaning of a poem.[2] The anagogical plane was forbidden to Poe who in order to "discover" God can only become a god. The opposite, Tate came to believe, was true of Dante who employs among his common analogies an analogy of mirrors, which allows him to *partake* of God rather than supplant him.

In these essays Tate is engrossed as always in the pursuit of wholeness, particularly the wholeness of the poet. Yet his concern has shifted from Eliot's "dissociation of sensibility," that split between feeling and intellect, to a dissociation of the self and outer nature. In 1964 Tate put it this way in "The Unliteral Imagination: Or, I, too, Dislike It":

> But if we still find useful the idea of dissociation, I suggest that what was dissociated—whenever it may have been dissociated—was not thought from feeling, nor feeling from thought; what was dissociated was the external world which by analogy could become the interior world of the mind.

The passage makes us think of "The Trout Map." It also contains the third direction, "a logical break on Tate's part with certain aspects of T. S. Eliot's poetry." It was a logical break because it was ordained by Tate's Catholicism.

We may put these directions together by considering his three late poems. "The Maimed Man," "The Swimmers," and "The Buried Lake" are autobiographical poems, constituting but three parts of one long poem. The original, though tentative, scheme, was for nine parts with "The Maimed Man" standing first. Later Tate altered the scheme to include only six poems with "The Maimed Man" standing last. Other sections of the poem exist in various stages of completion, but they have not been published. We deal with the parts, then, not the whole. Just as the poems of 1942–43 materialized through the medium of severe prosodic form, so these poems speak through the form most difficult to employ in English, terza rima. "The Swimmers" retells an experience from childhood; the other two poems also depend upon youthful experiences but they primarily develop from dreams or reveries reminiscent of the nightmare section of "Seasons of the Soul."

At the outset one may well ask why, if Tate wanted to bring into his poetry an external sensuous world after the model of Dante, he should attend to memories of childhood and the inner world of fantasy and dream. The place of childhood is obvious enough. The eye of the child is fierce and fresh. So that we may see here that Tate's desire is like Wordsworth's desire to see in a visionary way. He wishes to recapture the poignancy of "fair seed time" when everything is seen as new, when nothing yet has lapsed into patterns. Hence in "The Swimmers" the voice goes forth crying in the deserts of middle age:

> O fountain, bosom source undying-dead
>   Replenish me the spring of love and fear
>
> And give me back the eye that looked and fled
>   When a thrush idling in the tulip tree
>   Unwound the cold dream of the copperhead.

As to why Tate should have worked into these poems the irrational dream world, the answer must be more complex and less satisfactory. Childhood is held dumb and hidden (dead childhood

is carried like the unborn child in the psyche) beneath adult
consciousness except for times such as dream-states, when the
terrors or fixations of the earlier state break forth. In this way
the dream and the childhood experience are similar. We can
find a stronger reason in a letter Tate wrote to Wallace Stevens
on December 7, 1949:

> I have been reading your ten new poems ["Things of
> August"] in POETRY, and I am very much moved by two
> of them. This is a letter to myself which you have picked
> up from the floor and read because it is about your poems.
> I take these two poems very much to myself as the occasion
> of stating certain differences from the work of an older con-
> temporary which I admire and have learned from. The
> poems are numbers 2 and 3. To attempt to formulate dif-
> ferences is to try to keep on learning.
>
> When I was young I admired "Sunday Morning" more
> than any other poem of our time; and I still do, for what it
> taught me, and for its own magnificence. But I knew then
> that what you were doing was not for me: I could never
> reach it. The *angelisme* of the intelligence which defines
> "horizons that neither love nor hate" I could *believe* in as a
> human possibility but I could not possess it, or live inside it.
> It is perhaps a little presumptuous of me to take these two
> poems of yours as a profound insight, accidentally reached,
> into my own special limitations; if so, you will accept my
> apology. The "air within a grave or down a well" is almost
> the inevitable air for the man of our time who cannot be,
> like the woman in "Sunday Morning," alone in the world
> with the "thought of heaven."
>
> That is my message to myself. The man who breathes the
> air of the well cannot breathe purer air unless it be the air
> of revelation: the angelic intellect is not within his reach.
> What I have learned, then, from these two poems is a new
> way of putting a dilemma of our time—and it may be *the*
> dilemma: either the revealed access to the world or the
> angelic mind looking down upon it.

Quite naturally Tate who in "Seasons of the Soul" had written
"I was down a well" would be arrested by Stevens' phrase.
More significantly, one can see that for Tate the avoidance of
angelisme (in the sense Maritain uses the word, not quite in the

sense Stevens uses it in his essays) derived from his looking out from his "well," his Plato's cave, his mind, rather than gazing gigantically down like Poe's Satan. In other words Tate approaches vision through the self's confined space rather than the universe's isotropic vistas.

"The Maimed Man" is locally confined to the very common space of a street and a vacant lot. Nevertheless, it begins with an invocation to "Didactic laurel" who is asked to "assert your blade / Against the Morning Star, enlightening Thief / Of that first Mother who returned the Maid." The invocation cuts the human universe into three parts, that of the laurel, that of the Morning Star, and that of the myrtle. The laurel, sacred to Apollo, evokes a poetry located in reason; the myrtle, sacred to Aphrodite, evokes Pandemic love. Exactly what association of the Morning Star is intended cannot be so surely asserted since the Morning Star can be a number of planets. But because of the reference to the "enlightening thief," one supposes with R. K. Meiners that the reference is to the planet Mercury, hence to Hermes. It is Hermes who is the son of Maia, which means, "Mother," and he does return Persephone to Demeter. In the Homeric "Hymn to Demeter," the goddesses Demeter and Kore (Persephone) are referred to as the "Mother" and the "Maid." Hence, the beginning of the poem sets Apollonian reason against passion and Hermetic knowledge. The associations of Hermes as the archetypal thief, the god who conducts shades to the underworld as well as the scientist god of alchemy emerge wittily and ultimately associate Hermes through the one word "enlightening" with Cartesian Enlightenment.

> . . . because I am afraid
> Of him who says I have no need to fear,
> Return, Laurel!

The fear is of the scientifically "explained" universe. The poet continues then to sue for the help of Apollonian laurel because the world of sense has failed him and he can no longer feel. His tear is "metal." Hence, his poetry must be realized through form and tradition.

After the invocation the poem veers suddenly to a scene, represented as a memory, where the poet walking in sunlight sees a young man who is headless and whose feet are bluegrass.

The grotesque encounter reminds one of Shelley's encounter with Rousseau, ruined and gnawed like a tree root, in the beginning of "The Triumph of Life"—a poem that like Tate's is also Dantean. One suspects that the headless figure is based, like Part II of "Seasons of the Soul," upon a recurrent dream. There is no evidence for the suspicion, but the suspicion is intensified by a late chapter in Caroline Gordon's novel *The Malefactors.* Here the hero dreams of pursuing two figures who hurl themselves over a precipice. He looks down to see that they are headless. He is prevented from following them by his father who also threatens in the dream to remove his head. A bit later we discover that the abyss is in a cave entered by pushing aside a growth of laurel. It is perhaps of significance also that one of the headless figures in the dream is Horne Watts who is obviously modeled on Hart Crane. Finally, in this context two lines are quoted from Tate's early poem "Homily" (1922):

> Tear out the tight vermiculate crease
> Where death crawls angrily at bay.

All of this may be only coincidence, or if it has any basis in fact, it may have been altered beyond relevance by the exigencies of fiction. In Tate's poem the headless and footless figure is offered as a premonitive symbol of a life without reason and a life—so one takes these bluegrass feet—incapable of movement, hence incapable of moral action. The speaker then observes that he ought to join his own head and feet with the maimed man's body by putting them together in the grave. But he goes on to ask how he could "know this friend without reproach." That very question is the one he says he will be asking "in the poor boy's curse, / Witching for water in a waste of shame." The reference to Shakespeare's sonnet reminds us that one pays for waste of shame by an "expense of spirit." Nevertheless, to these "pastoral terrors of youth, still in the man," Tate promises to devote "emblematic verse / Rattling like dice unless the verse shall scan / All chance away." The rest of the poem will not yield to paraphrase:

> Meanwhile the scarecrow, man all coat and stem,
>   Neither dead nor living, never in this world—
>   In what worlds, or in what has essenced them,
> I did not know until one day I whirled

Towards a suggesting presence in my room
And saw in the waving mirror (glass swirled
By old blowers) a black trunk without bloom—
Body that once had moved my face and feet.
My secret was his father, I his tomb.
(By *I* I mean iambics willed and neat;
I mean by *I* God's image made uncouth;
By eye I mean the busy, lurked, discrete
Mandible world sharp as a broken tooth.)
And then rose in the man a small half-hell
Where love disordered, shade of pompous youth,
Clutched shades forbearing in a family well;
Where the sleek senses of the simple child
Came back to rack spirit that could not tell
Natural time: the eyes, recauled, enisled
In the dreamt cave by shadow womb of beam,
Had played swimmer of night—the moist and mild!
Now take him, Virgin Muse, up the deeper stream:
As a lost bee returning to the hive,
Cell after honeyed cell of sounding dream—
Swimmer of noonday, lean for the perfect dive
To the dead Mother's face, whose subtile down
You had not seen take amber light alive.

This is a parade of earlier poetic materials. The "shades forbearing down a familial well" recalls "Sonnets of the Blood" and,
more obviously, part II of "Seasons of the Soul." The play on
the word "I" recalls "The Eye" and "Two Conceits for the Eye
to Sing, if Possible." But the poem also looks forward to "The
Swimmers" in the icon of the embryo-child whose senses shame
the mature man who has lost the natural world. To this child
beneath the skin the poet at the end turns. And the ending of
"The Maimed Man" is as sublime poetry as the century has
produced. Unfortunately, the rest of the poem does not come up
to it. The puns and colloquialisms are embarrassingly embedded
in the graver matrix of the poem. Some of the passages are incomprehensible; some are clumsy. And the end gives no certi-
tude that the invocation to Apollonian reason at the beginning
squares with the emphasis on "the sleek senses" at the end. It
should square, for Tate had come to believe that true reason

required tutoring by the senses. But the philosophic conviction behind a poem is a different matter from its demonstration. Although "The Maimed Man" was published in *The Partisan Review* in 1952, Tate did not choose to include it in *Poems* (1960). The two poems that followed "The Maimed Man" belong with his best.

"The Swimmers" did exactly what Tate hoped it would. The terza rima worked perfectly. The imagery presented thematic epiphanies. Furthermore, the poem is so lucid that any extended "interpretation" would constitute an insult. "The Swimmers" retells, with only a few facts altered, the experience Tate had of seeing when he was eleven the body of a lynched Negro dragged into the town of Mount Sterling, Kentucky. The lynching was not the standard "rape-case." The Negro had murdered his landlord after an altercation, but Tate does not specify any background to the lynching, for he wants the drama to remain a universal agony upon which he can affix his personal yet conforming specifics. There are visible specifics—even the names of his playmates are given. He goes so far as to make a joke at his own expense. His memory of his parents' apprehension that he suffered from hydrocephalus appears in his reference to "Tate, with water on his brain." A compound joke, philosophical, religious, as well as biographical.

The ending of "The Swimmers" is true to the important fact of the incident—the town never admitted to itself that the lynching had occurred:

> My breath crackled the dead air like a shotgun
>   As, sheriff and the stranger disappearing,
>   The faceless head lay still. I could not run
>
> Or walk, but stood. Alone in the public clearing
>   This private thing was owned by all the town,
>   Though never claimed by us within my hearing.

Unimportant facts were changed for dramatic purposes. Tate did not, as in the poem, follow the sheriff back into town, but cut through the fields and beat him into town. Nor, in the actual incident, did Tate's companions desert him. But the solitariness of the boy who followed the "cloudy hearse" was necessary to the full impact of the Jesus-Christers' ritual sacrifice of the Negro. The town itself had to be rendered as nearly deserted as possible so as to tune to a blinding sharpness the focus upon all humanity's desolation in evil. In that desolation we perceive that the evil must be "owned."

Robert Lowell wrote to Tate to say that "The Swimmers" was the best poem Allen had ever done, the finest terza rima in English. He found it better even than Shelley's use of the form.[3] Yet Lowell was less sanguine about Tate's next poem "The Buried Lake." He found the sound of it like "choking." And he objected to its similarities with "Seasons of the Soul," its "Allenisms," and contorted phrasing.[4] In contrast, W. H. Auden wrote that he thought "The Buried Lake" might well be Tate's best single poem.[5] Let Lowell and Auden both be right: "The Swimmers" is Tate's most nearly perfect poem; "The Buried Lake" is his richest.

It will be remembered that "The Maimed Man" begins with an invocation to the "didactic laurel," while "The Swimmers" begins with an invocation to·the hypersensitivity of childhood. "The Buried Lake" trundles a vulgate epigraph from the Apocrypha: *"Ego mater pulchrae dilectionis, et timoris, et agnitionis, et sanctae spei."* "I, mother of rare beauty, fear, knowledge, and divine hope" (Ecclesiasticus 24). This mother, as versatile as Robert Grave's White Goddess, serves to draw us into the invocation which this time is addressed to the lady of light or Santa Lucia. As others have pointed out, among this Saint's virtues are her power to cure blindness. So that at once we understand her presence. She has been waiting for years for Tate to come to her with his optical problems. These words are not intended to be flippant. The poem, all 120 lines, is about a cure of the vision. The cure requires an approach, a way, to Santa Lucia:

> The Way and the way back are long and rough
> Where Myrtle twines with Laurel . . .

And so the Heraclitean *odos* trod by Eliot in the *Four Quartets*

combines here with the elements of laurel and myrtle kept separate in "The Maimed Man." This twining of love and reason,
which is the cure for the failing vision, takes us for a time down
in a dream trance below the play and terrific babble of childhood toward the buried lake of—shall we say—memory; we
could say "salvation." Finally, he enters a "pinched hotel"
where a dog, like Cerberus, welcomes him with "a sickly cark."
Suddenly it is not really a hotel he has entered. It is a deserted
music room with benches ranged along the walls. We are then
informed that he exults in a secret plan: he has come there to
play his violin.

> I laid my top hat to one side; my chin
>   Was ready, I unsnapped the lyric case;
>   I had come there to play my violin.
>
> Erect and sinuous as Valence lace
>   Old ladies wore, the bow began to fill
>   "The shining box—whence came a dreaming face,
>
> Small dancing girl who gave the smell of dill
>   In pelts of mordents on a minor third
>   From my cadenza for the Devil's Trill.
>
> No, no! her quick hand said in a soft surd.
>   She locked the fiddle up and was not there.
>   I mourned the death of youth without a word.

We can pinpoint one memory to which the poem has returned.
It will be remembered that between October 1916 and April
1917 Tate studied violin at the Cincinnati Conservatory of Music. At a student recital he played for his teacher Eugen Ysayë
Tartini's "Devil's Trill Sonata." Ysayë complimented him on his
left hand but said he had no talent for music. At this time Tate
abandoned aspirations for a musical career. It would seem,
therefore, that the episode records a blighted hope. If this is so,
the dancing girl is not to be taken as a girl Tate knew, but only
as the face that appears in the sheen of the violin. Come to
think of it, the resin applied to violin bows smells, as does this
girl, like dill. With this failure, just as Tate returned to academic studies after giving up music, the poet must seek for

another, more capable existence, asking if "I could go where air was not dead air?" He is met, however, by the enemy:

> And could I go where air was not dead air?
> My friend Jack Locke, scholar and gentleman,
> Gazed down upon me with a friendly glare,
>
> Flicking his nose as if about to scan
> My verse; he plucked from his moustache one hair
> Letting it fall like gravel in a pan . . .

Surely John Locke is really Descartes or Hermes. And how very nicely Tate depicts his own exclusion from the world of "enlightenment" in the ironic picture of the hair falling like gravel into one pan of the scales. And how much this John Locke is like Zeus who is fond of weighing the fates of heroes in the scale pan. The encounter with John Locke dramatizes another failure, not this time a failure of art but of art's antipodes, the positivist's rationalism.

Then the poet sinks deeper into his dream, and a lost love comes to him. She has come back to give him "all," she says. But as he reaches, her head becomes "Another's searching skull whose drying teeth / Crumbled me all night long and I was dead":

> Down, down below the wave that turned me round,
> Head downwards where the Head of God had sped
>
> On the third day; where nature had unwound
> And ravelled her green that she had softly laved—
> The green reviving spray now slowly drowned
> Me,, since the shuttling eye would not be saved.

The conception of the Head of God speeding down is very strange. Literally it refers to the legend of Christ's going down to harrow Hell after his resurrection on the third day. But the image exceeds its literal basis. Perhaps it was originally intended to mate with a line in "The Maimed Man" where we find "I mean by *I* God's image made uncouth." It is also possible that Tate is thinking of one of Thomas Hardy's poems he had admired for a long time, "Nature's Questioning," from which he quotes the following lines with approval:

> Or come we from an Automaton
>   Unconscious of our pains?
>   Or are we live remains
> Of Godhead dying downwards, brain and eye now gone?

In a final estimate, we need neither "The Maimed Man" nor Thomas Hardy. God has disappeared into a pastoral world that has become hidden under a covering of Cartesian science. That insight is William Blake's rather than Hardy's. Indeed, the image of the Head of God speeding down toward hell has much in common with the spatial energies of Blake's graphic art.

In any case the image takes us as deep as we can go into hell. Then from the dark night of the senses the dream begins to rise. And it seems significant that the poet must rehearse his own and history's failures, must go down to the ultimate dark of the self before he can bend his knees and receive the benison of Santa Lucia. He receives this benison or awareness exactly in the way that Tate observes that Dante receives his awareness; that is, through a mirror symbol. In his essay "The Symbolic Imagination" Tate quotes from the beginning of *Paradiso* XXVIII and comments as follows:

> Beatrice's eyes are a mirror in which is reflected that "sharp point," to which Dante, still at a distance from it, now turns his direct gaze. As he looks at it he sees for the first time what its reflection in Beatrice's eyes could not convey: that it is the sensible world turned inside out. For the sensible world as well as her eyes is only a reflection of the light from the sharp point. Now he is looking at the thing-in-itself. *He has at last turned away from the mirror which is the world.*

Tate has further commentary upon the mirror symbol and Be-

atrice's laboratory demonstration of the symbol, but this much is
sufficient to relate the poem with the essay. Once the poet's vision is corrected, "The Buried Lake" moves toward restorations
of the sensuous world, promising that "all the sad eclogue . . .
will soon be merry." The final lines are entirely beautiful:

> [I] knew that nature could not more refine
>   What it had given in a looking-glass
>   And held there, after the living body's line
>
> Has moved wherever it must move—wild grass
>   Inching the earth; and the quicksilver art
>   Throws back the invisible but lightning mass
>
> To inhabit the room; for I have seen it part
>   The palpable air, the air close up above
>   And under you, light Lucy, light of heart—
>
> Light choir upon my shoulder, speaking Dove,
>   The dream is over and the dark expired.
>   I knew that I had known enduring love.

With these confident lines Tate's published poetry ceases.
Looking at the three late poems one sees that they belong to a
pattern repeated throughout Tate's career. It is a pattern in
which we are conscious of a ratio of relative failures to relative
successes. "The Maimed Man," fine as it is in places, fragments,
and the macabre elements will not stay with the rational. "The
Buried Lake" *vibrates* continuously but does not *move* very far.
"The Swimmers," perfectly attuned to Dante's form, moves
through its journey-encounters and stands at last, as all fine poetry does, not as a set of symbols, but as an action which is *in
toto* symbolic. Now, this same ratio may be observed in the
summits of all of Tate's poetry. "Ode to the Confederate Dead"
emerges from a context of several inferior poems that are thematically similar. "The Mediterranean" rises above the lesser
poem "Aeneas at Washington"; "Seasons of the Soul" issues
from the lesser poem "Winter Mask." But that is only part of
the pattern. It remains to be observed that all of these poems
are concerned with integrity or its absence. The visitor to the

Confederate graveyard is locked in his sensibility; the picnicker
at the Mediterranean cove has exchanged the telic search of
Aeneas for a search for those spiritual roots which will give him
a sense of wholeness; the man who looks at World War II and
perceives that the world is a dead land, perceives also that the
world could be restored by love—although he is not sure that
love can be found; the man who sinks into the buried lake of the
self is self-baptized, and his pastoral vision is restored. Tate was
right, then, when he told his friends that he was always writing
only one poem. But there are peaks in the one poem and these
peaks obtained with the most severe effort throughout his career
are the poems which make him one of the masters of a varied
and brilliant epoch. But even if his superior poems had not
come, he would still be an important poet, for we should have
"Death of Little Boys" instead of "Ode to the Confederate
Dead." We should have "The Buried Lake" instead of "The
Swimmers." And we should pay them homage as examples of a
poetry that strained, indeed wrenched, the language with bitter
zeal. We should see, moreover, that that zeal was one that
sprang from a refusal to tolerate falseness either in the self or in
man in general. Tate's language is of that kind which wells forth
when the poet presses with all his force for a victory which he
knows he will not obtain.

Because he has been unable to lie to us about victory, his
poems have never been very popular. For popular poetry is the
kind that encourages people who are not poets to believe that
they are. Tate's poetry cannot have that effect. But the effect it
can and does have is that of reminding us that the heroic, the
saintly act is a subjective—even a hidden—act of such private
intensity that its public implementation is only an inevitable step,
not a greater step. In this way Tate is entirely different from T.
S. Eliot whom he resembles in such obvious but superficial ways
that some critics stopped digging for the treasure when they
found a few coins in the topsoil. Eliot's poetry has no *private*
morality. His figures are either public saints or paralyzed pup-
pets, just as his cats are either practical or dead. But it is by reason of this very difference that Tate in his later poetry could
achieve an optimism that never came to Eliot. One can after all

save what can be saved if he does not try to save what cannot be
saved.

A question remains as to why Tate has not finished or at least
has not published the rest of the long poem of which "The
Maimed Man," "The Swimmers," and "The Buried Lake" are
parts. If the question cannot be answered it can be surrounded.
It is noteworthy that "The Buried Lake" was written just at a
time when the whole life of poetry underwent one of its peri-
odic changes. "The Buried Lake," like Eliot's *Four Quartets* and
Stevens' *Auroras of Autumn,* belongs in a category of poetry
which brings a literary movement to an end. Though they are
not weary poems they are not poems written either with the
bravura of beginnings or the impudence of revolt. "The Buried
Lake" incorporates most of the devices of the great modernist
period, all the effort at "concreteness," which as it becomes
formula threatens to become abstraction; all the subtleties of
symbol which as it becomes decor threatens to become obvious.
These and other devices of Modernism come up like slow, beautiful bubbles in the viscous element of "The Buried Lake." Yet
"The Buried Lake" is a marvelous poem. After all, it takes as
high a talent to finish an age as to begin one. But the phrase "to
finish" applies only to "The Buried Lake." It does not apply to
"The Swimmers" which contains so much organic life that it
could be carbon-dated every day for the next century, and the
reading would always come back: "Born today."

"The Buried Lake" appeared just as a new poetry began to
rise in America. This new poetry's obsessions with oratory, romantic gesture, and exhibitionism have for nearly two decades
altered the way poetry works in the modern world. Even some
of Tate's friends shifted eventually toward the new mode,
among them Robert Penn Warren, Robert Lowell, and John
Berryman. Tate knew that this change had occurred sooner than
the proponents of the new poetry did, for he wrote in 1955 to
Brewster Ghiselin: "The long poem I am doing (at intervals) *is*
difficult, and I fear that even when it's done—if it ever is—it will
make little headway with even the 'literary' people. The drift
today is all against this sort of thing."[6] But would this knowledge keep Tate from completing his poem? Probably not. It is

only part of the picture. In any case Tate has continued to work over other sections of the poem. As late as 1964 with his grandson for company he made an automobile trip through Kentucky, visiting places he had not seen for forty years in order to acquire confidence in what he was writing.[7]

It may be that Tate will publish the rest of the long poem soon and thereby render this chapter obsolete. That is an antiquation devoutly to be wished. For one may be sure that new poems will not be given to the world until Tate is certain that that is where they belong. It is because of this scrupulousness that one can say of Allen Tate, who has not been a prolific poet, what Dryden said of a very prolific poet: "here is God's plenty."

Notes

Note: All unpublished letters cited are housed in the Princeton University Library with the following exceptions:

A. Tate's letters to Mark Van Doren are housed in the Columbia University Library.

B. Tate's letters to Herbert Read are housed in the University of Victoria Library, Victoria, British Columbia.

C. Tate's letters to Brewster Ghiselin are in Mr. Ghiselin's possession.

ONE: *The Early Years*

1 "Several Thousand Books," *The Sewanee Review*, LXXV (Summer 1967), pp. 379–80.

2 Louise Cowan, *The Fugitive Group: A Literary History* (Baton Rouge, 1959), p. 36.

3 *Ibid.*

4 Stanley J. Kunitz and Howard Haycraft, *Twentieth Century Authors* (New York, 1942), pp. 1385–86.

5 Van Doren to Tate, May 11, 1931.

6 Cowan, p. 33.

7 *Fugitives' Reunion*, Rob Roy Purdy, ed. (Nashville, 1959), p. 104.

8 "Gentleman in a Dustcoat," *The Sewanee Review*, LXXVI (Summer 1968), p. 379.

9 *Ibid.*, p. 381.

10 "Several Thousand Books," pp. 380–81.

11 Cowan, p. 38.

TWO: *The Fugitives*

1 Cowan, pp. 17–18.

2 Donald Davidson, *Southern Writers in the Modern World* (Athens, Ga.), pp. 14–15.

[3]Tate, "The Fugitive 1922–1925: a Personal Recollection Twenty Years After," The Princeton University Library Chronicle, III (April 1942), p. 76.

[4] Davidson, p. 12.

[5] Fugitives' Reunion, pp. 166–68.

[6] John M. Bradbury, The Fugitives: A Critical Account (Chapel Hill, 1958), p. 80.

[7] Michael Millgate, "An Interview with Allen Tate," Shenandoah, XII (Spring 1961), p. 34.

[8] "The Fugitive 1922–1925," p. 80.

[9] The Double-Dealer, III (May 1922), p. 262.

[10] "The Fugitive 1922–1925," p. 81.

[11] July 2, 1922.

[12] July 12, 1922. Quoted in Cowan, p. 66.

[13] June 17, 1922. Quoted in Cowan, p. 66.

[14] July 8, 1922. Quoted in Cowan, p. 68.

[15] July 2, 1922.

[16] "The Fugitive 1922–1925," p. 81.

[17] November 5, 1922. Quoted in Cowan, p. 80.

[18] Cowan, p. 81.

[19] Davidson to Tate, June 26, 1923.

[20] "The Fugitive 1922–1925," pp. 81–82.

[21] Ibid., p. 82.

[22] April, 1924. No day given.

[23] "The Fugitive 1922–1925," p. 82.

[24] July 24, 1923. Quoted in Cowan, p. 112.

[25] June 22, 1923. Quoted in Cowan, p. 116.

[26] To Davidson, March 8, 1924. Quoted in Cowan, p. 147.

[27] Dated by Tate as "Early Spring, 1924."

[28] Davidson to Tate, May 21, 1924.

[29] Dated by Tate as "Late Spring, 1924."

[30] Ruth Penn Warren to Tate, June 24, 1924.

[31] June 4, 1924.

[32] To Davidson, June 15, 1924. Quoted in Cowan, p. 170.

[33] June 23, 1924.

[34] July 9, 1924. The Letters of Hart Crane, 1916–1932, Brom Weber, ed. (New York, 1952), p. 185.

[35] Davidson, Southern Writers in the Modern World, p. 30.

THREE: New York

[1] Quoted in Mark Van Doren, The Autobiography of Mark Van Doren (New York, 1958), pp. 156–57.

[2] Davidson to Tate, November 29, 1925.

[3] Harold Loeb, The Way It Was (New York, 1959), pp. 241–42.

[4] "Allen Tate: Upon the Occasion of His Sixtieth Birthday," The Sewanee Review, LXVII (Autumn 1959), pp. 542–43.

[5] Susan Jenkins Brown, "Hart Crane: The End of Harvest," The

Southern Review, IV (October 1968), 956–57.

[6] *Ibid.*, p. 964.

[7] Malcolm Cowley, "Two Winters with Hart Crane," *The Sewanee Review*, LXVII (Autumn 1959), p. 550.

[8] Susan Jenkins Brown, p. 962.

[9] See Matthew Josephson, *Life Among the Surrealists* (New York, 1962), pp. 305–306.

[10] April 11, 1926.

[11] January 16, 1927. Also February 15, 1927.

[12] Cowley, p. 548.

[13] Winters to Tate, February 28, 1927.

FOUR: *Paris*

[1] "Herbert Read," *Essays of Four Decades*, p. 372.

[2] Tate to Van Doren, November 6, 1928.

[3] *Ibid.*

[4] From a broadcast for the British Broadcasting Company, recorded on tape at Wellfleet, Massachusetts, Summer, 1961.

[5] "Random Thoughts on the Twenties," *Minnesota Review*, I (Fall 1960), pp. 53–4.

[6] January 29, 1929.

[7] To Van Doren, March 23, 1929.

[8] Undated letter, probably early 1934.

[9] "Random Thoughts on the Twenties," p. 55.

[10] January 29, 1929.

[11] *The Oxford Anthology of American Literature*, W. R. Benet and N. H. Pearson, eds. (New York, 1938), p. 1516.

[12] *Ibid.*

[13] M. E. Bradford, *Rumors of Mortality* (Dallas, 1969), p. 27.

[14] September 4, 1928.

[15] March 27, 1929.

[16] July 29, 1929.

[17] Tate to R. K. Meiners, March 22, 1960.

[18] R. K. Meiners, *The Last Alternatives: A Study of the Works of Allen Tate* (Denver, 1963), pp. 150–51.

[19] Bradford, p. 40.

FIVE: *The Agrarians*

[1] Van Doren to Tate, February 14, 1931.

[2] Herbert Agar to Seward Collins, December 10, 1934.

[3] *Fugitives Reunion*, p. 203.

[4] See John L. Stewart, *The Burden of Time: The Fugitives and Agrarians* (Princeton, 1965), p. 190.

[5] To Van Doren, June 27, 1936.

[6] *Fugitives' Reunion*, pp. 130–31.

[7] To Bishop, July 7, 1931.

[8] Tate to John L. Stewart, May 28, 1965.

[9] Harriet Monroe to Tate, October 15, 1931.

[10] This account is largely based on a letter from Frank MacShane to Tate, October 7, 1963, which quotes Tate's own account. Also Chapter II of Caroline Gordon's novel *The Strange Children*. Tate gave a slightly different version to John Peale Bishop in a letter dated October 31, 1932.

[11] October 31, 1932.

[12] November 7, 1932.

[13] To Van Doren, September 30, 1935.

[14] To Bishop, November 12, 1932.

[15] To Bishop, April 7, 1933.

[16] October 30, 1933.

[17] December 22, 1933.

[18] Tate to Bishop, October 30, 1933.

[19] To Van Doren, December 22, 1933.

[20] To Bishop, November 7, 1934.

[21] To Bishop, December 18, 1934.

[22] Brewer to Tate, December 19, 1935.

[23] To Van Doren, August 5, 1936.

SIX: *The Fathers*

[1] Frank MacShane, *Ford Madox Ford* (New York, 1965), p. 251.

[2] "Visiting the Tates," *The Sewanee Review*, LXVII (Autumn 1959), pp. 557–59.

[3] To Bishop, December 27, 1937.

[4] To Van Doren, March 6, 1937.

[5] To Van Doren, June 2, 1938.

[6] *Ibid.*

[7] Dated "Autumn, 1932."

[8] To Bishop, February 11, 1932.

[9] To Bishop, October 30, 1933.

[10] October 6, 1932.

[11] Davidson to Tate, October 3, 1938.

[12] August 17, 1944.

[13] January 24, 1945.

SEVEN: *The Season of the Soul*

[1] Ben C. Toledano, "Savannah Writers' Conference—1939," *The Georgia Review*, XII (Summer, 1968), 157.

[2] Perkins to Tate, April 7, 1939.

[3] May 4, 1939.

[4] Copy included in letter to Van Doren, June 2, 1938.

[5] To Van Doren, September 18, 1939.

[6] *Ibid.*

[7] To Bishop, May 30, 1940.

[8] July 3, 1940.

[9] "The Present Function of Criticism," *Essays of Four Decades*, p. 199.

[10] January 12, 1941.

[11] January 30, 1941.

[12] Tate to Bishop, February 17, 1942.

[13] MacLeish to Tate, November 29, 1939 and May 4, 1940.

[14] Lytle to Tate, January 30, 1942 and April 23, 1942.

[15] To Bishop, December 4, 1942.

[16] January 20, 1943.

[17] To Bishop, January 26, 1943.

[18] To Bishop, February 14, 1943.

[19] February 7, 1943.

[20] Wilson to Tate, January 19, 1943 and April 16, 1943.

[21] To Bishop, July 1, 1943.

[22] July 16, 1942.

[23] This account is based on MacLeish to Tate, August 20, 1943; Hemingway to Tate, August 31, 1943; and Tate to Bishop, September 6, 1943.

[24] See Charles Norman, *Ezra Pound* (New York, 1960), p. 395.

[25] To Bishop, January 14, 1944.

[26] Statement sent by Tate to R. P. Blackmur, April 3, 1944.

[27] Mary McCarthy to Tate, April 6, 1945.

[28] July 12, 1958.

EIGHT: *Ambassador of Culture*

[1] Tate to Eliot, April 25, 1946.

[2] February 21, 1948.

[3] May 24, 1949.

[4] Benjamin Tate to Allen Tate, August 9, 1949.

[5] January 28, 1950.

[6] MacLeish to Tate, September 21, 1949 and October 15, 1949.

[7] November 12, 1951.

[8] Lytle to Tate, November 17, 1952.

[9] Eliot to Tate, March 7, 1956.

[10] April, 1957. No day given.

[11] "20.iv.59."

NINE: *Work in Progress*

[1] "Preface," *Essays of Four Decades,* p. xi.

[2] See Warren Kliewer, "Allen Tate as a Teacher," *Descant,* VII (Fall 1962), pp. 44–7.

[3] March 15, 1954.

[4] November 5, 1952.

[5] August 19. No year given.

[6] May 11, 1955.

[7] To Ghiselin, September 5, 1964.

✂ Selected Bibliography ✂

Books by Tate

The Golden Mean and Other Poems. Tate and Ridley Wills. Nashville: Privately printed, 1923.

Stonewall Jackson: The Good Soldier. New York: Minton, Balch and Co., 1928.

Mr. Pope and Other Poems. New York: Minton, Balch and Co., 1928.

Jefferson Davis: His Rise and Fall. New York: Minton Balch and Co., 1929.

Poems: 1928–1931. New York and London: Charles Scribner's Sons, 1932.

Reactionary Essays on Poetry and Ideas. New York: Charles Scribner's Sons, 1936.

The Mediterranean and Other Poems. New York: Alcestis Press, 1936.

Selected Poems. New York and London: Charles Scribner's Sons, 1937.

The Fathers. New York: G. P. Putnam's Sons, 1938.

Reason in Madness, Critical Essays. New York: G. P. Putnam's Sons, 1941.

The Vigil of Venus. Cummington, Massachusetts: Cummington Press, 1943.

The Winter Sea. Cummington, Massachusetts: Cummington Press, 1944.

Poems: 1922–1947. New York: Charles Scribner's Sons, 1948.

On the Limits of Poetry, Selected Essays 1928–1948. New York: The Swallow Press and William Morrow and Co., 1948.

The Hovering Fly and Other Essays. Cummington, Massachusetts: Cummington Press. 1949.

Two Conceits for the Eye to Sing, if Possible. Cummington, Massachusetts: Cummington Press. 1950.

The Forlorn Demon: Didactic and Critical Essays. Chicago: Henry Regnery Co., 1953.

The Man of Letters in the Modern World, Selected Essays: 1928–1955. New York: Meridian Books, 1955. (Paperback.)

Collected Essays. Denver: Alan Swallow, 1959.

Poems. New York: Charles Scribner's Sons, 1960.

Poems. Chicago: Swallow Press, 1961. (Paperback reprint.)

Essays of Four Decades. Chicago: Swallow Press, 1968.

Books Edited by Tate

I'll Take My Stand; The South and the Agrarian Tradition, by Twelve Southerners. New York and London: Harper and Bros., 1930.

Who Owns America? A Declaration of Independence, Herbert Agar and Allen Tate, eds. Boston and New York: Houghton Mifflin Co., 1936.

The Language of Poetry. Princeton: Princeton University Press, London: Oxford University Press, 1942.

Princeton Verse Between Two Wars. Princeton: Princeton University Press, 1942.

American Harvest: Twenty Years of Creative Writing in the United States, Allen Tate and John Peale Bishop, eds. New York: L. B. Fischer, 1942.

A Southern Vanguard. New York: Prentice-Hall, 1947.

The Collected Poems of John Peale Bishop, 1892–1944. New York: Charles Scribner's Sons, 1948.

The House of Fiction: An Anthology of the Short Story, Caroline Gordon and Allen Tate, eds. New York: Charles Scribner's Sons, 1950.

Modern Verse in English, 1900–1950, David Cecil and Allen Tate, eds. New York: The Macmillan Company, 1958.

The Complete Poems and Selected Criticism of Edgar Allan Poe. New York: New American Library, 1968.

Books and Articles about Tate

Amyx, Clifford. "The Aesthetics of Allen Tate," *Western Review,* XIII (Spring 1949) 135–44.

Arnold, Willard B. *The Social Ideas of Allen Tate.* Boston: Bruce Humphries, 1955.

Berland, Alwyn. "Violence in the Poetry of Allen Tate," *Accent,* XI (Summer 1951) 161–71.

Bernetta, Sister Mary. "Allen Tate's Inferno," *Renascence,* III (Spring 1951) 113–19.

Bishop, Ferman. *Allen Tate.* New York: Twayne, 1967.

Blackmur, R. P. "San Giovanni in Venere: Allen Tate as Man of Letters, *Sewanee Review,* LXVII (Autumn 1959) 614–31.

Bradbury, John M. *The Fugitives: A Critical Account.* Chapel Hill: University of North Carolina Press, 1958.

Bradford, M. E. *Rumors of Mortality: An Introduction to Allen Tate.* Dallas: Argus Academic Press. 1969.

Brooks, Cleanth. "Allen Tate," *Poetry,* LXVI (September 1945) 324–29.

Cowan, Louise. *The Fugitive Group: A Literary History.* Baton Rouge: Louisiana State University Press, 1959.

Davidson, Donald. "The Meaning of War: A Note on Allen Tate's 'To the Lacedemonians,'" *Southern Review,* I (Summer 1965) 720–30.

Feder, Lillian. "Allen Tate's Use of Classical Literature," *The Centennial Review,* IV (Winter 1960) 89–114.

Hemphill, George. *Allen Tate.* Minneapolis: University of Minnesota Press, 1964. (University of Minnesota Pamphlets on American Writers, Number 39.)

Johnson, Carol Holmes. "The Heroism of the Rational: The Poetry of Allen Tate," *Renascence,* XVII (Winter 1964) 89–96.

Kermode, Frank. "Contemplation and Method," *Sewanee Review,* LXXII (Winter 1964) 124–31.

Koch, Vivienne. "The Poetry of Allen Tate," *Kenyon Review,* XI (Summer 1949) 355–78.

Meiners, R. K. *The Last Alternatives: A Study of the Works of Allen Tate.* Denver: Alan Swallow, 1963.

Mizener, Arthur. "*The Fathers* and Realistic Fiction," *Accent,* VII (Winter 1947) 101–109.

Nemerov, Howard. "The Current of the Frozen Stream: An Essay on the Poetry of Allen Tate," *Furioso,* III (February 1948) 50–61.

Ransom, John Crowe. *"In Amicitia" Sewanee Review,* LXVII (Autumn 1959) 528–39.

Rubin, Louis D., Jr. "The Serpent in the Mulberry Bush," in *Southern Renascence: The Literature of the Modern South.* Baltimore: The Johns Hopkins Press, 1953, pp. 352–67.

Schwartz, Delmore. "The Poetry of Allen Tate," *Southern Review,* V (Winter 1940) 419–38.

Spears, Monroe K. "The Criticism of Allen Tate," *Sewanee Review,* LVII (Spring 1949) 317–34.

Stewart, John L. *The Burden of Time: The Fugitives and Agrarians.* Princeton: Princeton University Press, 1965.

Vivas, Eliseo. "Allen Tate as Man of Letters," *Sewanee Review,* LXII (Winter 1954) 131–43.

Index